PENGUIN BUSINESS

THE TEN NEW LIFE-CHANGING SKILLS

Rajesh Srivastava graduated from IIT Kanpur and IIM Bangalore. He has over three and a half decades of corporate and academic experience. At United Spirits (now Diageo India), he played a significant role in creating some of India's most recognized, beloved and enduring alcohol brands, including McDowell Signature, Royal Challenge, Bagpiper and Blue Riband Duet. He went on to become the president of JK Helene Curtis, where he re-energized the company and the deodorant category by relaunching Park Avenue deodorant as a 'perfume'. Today, 'perfume' has become a generic benefit for the deodorant category.

Since 2008, he has directed his focus towards teaching and conducting corporate workshops. As an educator, he has taught at IIM Indore and SP Jain School of Global Management. As a corporate trainer, he has worked with prestigious companies like Siemens India, Mercedes-Benz Research Centre and Reliance Industries, among others.

Throughout his career, his columns and writings have appeared in various publications, including *Outlook, Telegraph, Mid-Day, Business Standard* and *Mint*. Penguin Random House published his first book, *The New Rules of Business*, which quickly became a national bestseller. This is his second book. He lives in Mumbai with his wife, Shaily.

ADVANCE PRAISE FOR THE BOOK

'There are two things that every professional brings to the workplace—WILL and SKILL. The will actually depends on the skill. Will gets you accepted, skill gets you admiration plus career progress. If you are skilled, your will be sky high. Rajesh has written a deeply researched book on the skills needed for the future. The first step is to be a lifelong self-learner'—**Shiv Shivakumar, executive president, Aditya Birla Group**

'Rajesh weaves magic while explaining, in his inimitable storytelling style, ten essential skills for the fast-spreading new industrial age where the concept of jobs itself is getting transformed. In times to come, we will need to use technology creatively and imaginatively for earning income and building wealth for our health, happiness and prosperity. The toolkit dished out by Rajesh in this book will enable us to negotiate this new emerging world better. The book is a masterfully told story and is simply unputdownable, though you are not reading a detective novel'—**Subhash Chandra Garg, author of *The $10 Trillion Dream*, and former finance and economic affairs secretary, Government of India**

'How do you prepare yourself for a world which is disrupted by COVID and technology? I would recommend Rajesh Srivastava's book *The Ten New Life-Changing Skills: Get Them and Get Ahead*. It will introduce you to ten 'life-saving' skills which will help you navigate this doubly disrupted world. Each skill is explained through examples drawn from the world of business, sports, lives of people we admire and his own rich experience, spanning over three and a half decades. It is written in an engaging storytelling format and will keep you engaged till you have reached the end'—**Hari T.N., co-founder, Artha School of Entrepreneurship, angel investor, Bigbasket, and author**

'The book is packed with illuminating insights. There's always something new and surprising to learn on every page'—**Sandeep Aggarwal, founder, Droom and ShopClues**

'The book covers ten essential "life-changing" skills, ranging from creativity and critical thinking to storytelling and influencing without authority and more. Many that I thought should have been obvious to me, actually weren't! Rajesh brings these skills to life by illustrating them with memorable examples—drawn from India, across the world and from his own personal experiences—and by narrating them in an engaging storytelling style. The book contains enduring wisdom and crisp insights, which are sure to enlighten and enrich. I think it is a must-read for students of business management, entrepreneurs, start-up founders and professionals. In fact, this book is for anyone who wishes to thrive in Industry 4.0 and beyond'—**Ashutosh Sharma, institute chair professor, IIT Kanpur, and former secretary, Department of Science and Technology, Government of India**

'Rajesh is a thorough professional who has translated his corporate life learnings into small, intriguing snippets into his book. The book is easy to read and contains several takeaways for young business managers, students and avid readers. A must-read'—**Anant Singhania, CEO, JK Enterprises, and director, JK Organisation**

'*The Ten New Life-Changing Skills* is a guide on how to get ahead in business and life. It is well-written and simple to understand, with many practical examples from business and industry. A must-read not only for management students and budding entrepreneurs but also for those who want to get ahead in life'—**Dr Mukesh Batra, founder–chairman, Dr Batra's Healthcare, and Padma Shri awardee**

'Today, when the world is speaking of upskilling being the need at the workplace, this book beautifully captures not just the cognitive, but also the emotive and social skills that are becoming increasingly important in today's work culture. The Fourth Industrial Revolution (4IR), also referred to as Industry 4.0, has commenced. Every person concerned with doing well in Industry 4.0, and it includes most of us, should read this book. It introduces readers to ten "life-changing" skills. Rajesh draws upon cutting-edge insights, research and riveting stories to bring alive these skills. The content is narrated in a style that keeps you totally involved with key insights, seducing you to want more at the end of every chapter and compelling you to immerse yourself till the very end. One of the big takeaways for me from this book was the self-management skill, which is a lifelong learning. This book will leave you armed with skills which will help you navigate Industry 4.0 with ease and dexterity'—**Raj Nayak, founder, House of Cheer, and ex-COO, Viacom18**

'Automation and digitization in the workplace are changing our world at warp speed and may make many professions obsolete very soon. To survive, cope and thrive, we need to understand the new paradigms, and we need to develop or sharpen skill sets that make us uniquely human, creative and innovative. Rajesh Srivastava's easy-to-read yet profound book, with its scores of real-life case studies and exercises, is a must-read for all managers, from junior executive to CEO. This book can change your and your business's fortunes'—**Sandipan Deb, former editor, *Financial Express***

'If you believe, like me, that the speed of technological innovations will make our existing skill sets irrelevant, if not totally redundant, then you must read this book. In it, Rajesh Srivastava, a wise and thoughtful leader, has introduced ten life-changing skills that we should embrace to prepare for meeting the challenges of Industry 4.0. I strongly recommend this book to all those who aspire to shape their future and remain relevant'—**Anil K. Khandelwal, former chairman and managing director, Bank of Baroda**

'The ten critical skills are explained beautifully [in this book] through analogies and illustrations, and in different ways in which they can manifest and be acquired. If I had to pick a favourite chapter, it would be the one on critical thinking. This concept can be so elusive, but Rajesh explains it from different facets, and it becomes so simple to understand and grasp. If his first book, *The New Rules of Business*, was about getting the business future-ready, this one is about getting yourself future-ready'—**Raju Venkataraman, leadership coach, corporate trainer, and former CFO and head of strategy, Walt Disney SEA**

'Another fabulous and captivating book by Rajesh on how to deal with challenges posed by Industry 4.0. In it, he presents ten life-changing skills, in his characteristic style, which is simple and uncomplicated, making it easy to understand them. The book is full of practical insights. A must-read for corporate people around the world'—**Ashok Capoor, former president and managing director, United Spirits Ltd (now Diageo India)**

'*The Ten New Life-Changing Skills* will help you defeat the computers, by becoming sharp, astute and creative'—**Dr Mickey Mehta, global holistic health guru and life coach**

THE 10 NEW LIFE-CHANGING SKILLS

GET THEM & GET AHEAD

RAJESH SRIVASTAVA

BUSINESS
An imprint of Penguin Random House

PENGUIN BUSINESS

USA | Canada | UK | Ireland | Australia
New Zealand | India | South Africa | China | Singapore

Penguin Business is part of the Penguin Random House group of companies whose addresses can be found at global.penguinrandomhouse.com

Published by Penguin Random House India Pvt. Ltd
4th Floor, Capital Tower 1, MG Road,
Gurugram 122 002, Haryana, India

First published in Penguin Business by Penguin Random House India 2022

10 9 8 7

ISBN 9780143451914

Typeset in Sabon LT Std by MAP Systems, Bengaluru, India
Printed at Replika Press Pvt. Ltd, India

www.penguin.co.in

Contents

Why Was This Book Written? xiii

HIGHER-LEVEL COGNITIVE SKILLS 1
Skill 1: Creativity 2
Skill 2: Innovation 33
Skill 3: Critical Thinking 67
Skill 4: Framing the Right Question 103
Skill 5: Smart Problem-Solving 137

SELF-MANAGEMENT SKILL 177
Skill 6: Lifelong Learning 178

SOCIAL SKILLS 211
Skill 7: Storytelling 212
Skill 8: Influence Without Authority 241

EMOTIONAL SKILLS 267
Skill 9: Humanness 268
Skill 10: Entrepreneurial Spirit 297

Notes 331

I dedicate this book to:

My late father, who believed that I had the talent to be a writer. I am happy to have lived up to his expectations.

My mother, who believes that I can achieve anything I put my heart into. I am happy I have proved her right yet again.

My wife, Shaily, who happily reviewed multiple drafts and played the role of a professional dissenter to perfection.

My son, Kautuk, a published author, who made me a better writer by insisting I write every word, instead of getting it ghost-written for me.

My friends and well-wishers, who invested their valuable time to review and make valuable suggestions. It has made the book practical and interesting.

'The future depends on what you do in the present.'

—Mahatma Gandhi

Why Was This Book Written?

Automation is eating up blue-collar jobs, while smart automation, powered by algorithms and Artificial Intelligence (AI), is chipping away at white-collar jobs.

Is there an independent validation of this trend?

McKinsey & Company says that in an era marked by rapid advances in automation and AI, some jobs will be lost and many others created; almost all will change.[1]

The World Economic Forum has also predicted that the rise of automation and digitization in the workplace will displace millions of jobs.[2]

These tectonic disruptions can be attributed primarily to computers powered by smart software. Here's why.

Blue-collar work entails doing repetitive jobs. For example, cashiers in banks handing out cash, typists typing letters and other documents, security guards guarding assets or people working in warehousing moving and stacking goods. Computers powered by appropriate software have the unparalleled ability to do repetitive jobs with unrelenting accuracy. This is resulting in large-scale automation of blue-collar jobs. As a result, cashiers' jobs are being taken over by ATMs, typists' jobs by computers, security guards' jobs by surveillance cameras and warehousing jobs by robots.

White-collar jobs require decision-making. Computers, powered by

- AI, which enables machines to mimic human actions and decision-making processes
- Robotics, which can replicate human efforts and provide better outcomes
- Machine learning, which enables machines to learn from past data, identify patterns, detect anomalies and make decisions with minimal human intervention

can do many jobs, which require the basic cognitive skills involved in decision-making, much better than humans.

The Future of Jobs

The earlier 3 Industrial Revolutions (3IR) created blue-collar and white-collar jobs. Now, the era of the Fourth Industrial Revolution (4IR), also referred to as Industry 4.0, has commenced. It is characterized by a fusion of technologies that is blurring the lines between the physical, digital and biological spheres.[3]

The nature of jobs in Industry 4.0 is still not fully formed. It is still not entirely clear what shape and form they will take. Then how shall we prepare for jobs that are not entirely formed and are still evolving?

A consensus is emerging that Industry 4.0 is creating 'thinking and reflective' jobs which can be labelled 'green-collar' jobs, because the colour signifies growth and renewal, sustainability and moving ahead.

Green-collar jobs would require people to possess higher levels of cognitive skills, self-management skills, social skills and emotional skills. Let us dive deep into them to gain a cogent understanding of them.

- Higher-level cognitive skills
    - Skill 1: Creativity. It requires the use of imagination to combine and connect different ideas in new and imaginative ways to come up with big ideas.
    - Skill 2: Innovation. It requires the discovery of opportunities and implementing ideas to achieve profitable results.[4]
    - Skill 3: Critical thinking. It requires challenging traditions, questioning assumptions and defying norms that have outlived their utility, and installing new ones in their place.
    - Skill 4: Framing the right question. It will lead to the right answer, which will open up a treasure trove of new business opportunities that would have remained undiscovered but for the right question.

    - Skill 5: Smart problem-solving. It requires leveraging creativity, innovation, critical thinking and similar skills to come up with smart solutions.
- Self-management skill
    - Skill 6: Lifelong learning. It increases employability, accelerates career advancement, enhances self-confidence, helps one remain relevant and face the unexpected with aplomb. In brief, it is a passport to being a lifelong winner.
- Social Skills:
    - Skill 7: Storytelling. It is the most powerful way to put ideas into the world.[5]
    - Skill 8: Influence without authority. It helps to get people to see your way of thinking, motivate them to support your initiatives and adopt your idea of their own free will.
- Emotional skills
    - Skill 9: Humanness. In the earlier 3IRs, people did what they were told to do. Therefore, they bought their bodies to work, leaving their minds and hearts behind.

      Industry 4.0 is giving birth to green-collar jobs which entail 'thinking and reflection'. Therefore, people must bring their minds, hearts and bodies to work. It has the potential to unlock people's unlimited potential.
    - Skill 10: Entrepreneurial spirit. It is an intangible energy that inspires people to harbour aspirations greater than the resources

at their command. When this spirit is alive, businesses keep their mojo and maintain their edge.

These skills will help you adapt to yet unborn jobs, no matter what shape and form they shall take.

A word of caution: These skills are not substitutes for hard skills, i.e., technical knowledge or training. Those you must acquire. But the combination of hard skills coupled with these skills will help you thrive in the workplaces of Industry 4.0.

Can Computers Powered by Smart Software Not Eat into Green-Collar Jobs?

An eagle does not fight the snake on the ground. Instead, it picks it up in its beak, soars up to the sky and drops it from there. The fall proves fatal and the snake dies. Height is the eagle's area of strength and the snake's area of weakness.

The skills mentioned above are those that will provide us with strength because we have the ability to master them, and computers don't. Like the eagle, we can fight them by drawing them to our areas of strength and checkmating them.

Let us unpack each of these skills to understand how they fall into the computer's areas of weakness.

- Computers can merely compute. Creativity is non-computable. Therefore, computers cannot be creative.[6]

- Computers find it challenging to discover opportunities and implement ideas profitably.
- Computers cannot think critically because they are programmed to be slaves to traditions, assumptions and norms.
- Pablo Picasso said that computers are useless because they can only give answers. They find it challenging to frame the right question.
- Computers solve problems by following a set of conditions, constraints and rules, which are programmed into them. This enables them to throw up 'predictable' solutions, not necessarily smart solutions.
- Computers can learn what they are programmed to learn and from other computers, too.
- Computers lack the skill of narrating compelling stories that are emotionally arousing.
- Computers excel in using data and logic to influence people. They touch the minds, not the hearts, of people. Hence, computers are less effective in influencing.
- Computers are bereft of hearts. They can be programmed to think, but cannot be made to feel.
- Computers lack imagination, power to dream, resilience and grittiness.

Are These Skills Newly Minted?

Since the 1st IR, captains of industry had mastery over these skills. They leveraged them to think and come up with visions and strategies, to build businesses that captured the world's attention. Here are a few examples:

- Henry Ford revolutionized car production.
- Thomas Alva Edison invented the incandescent bulb and lit up the world.
- Tom Watson gave birth to IBM.
- Walt Disney revolutionized the animation industry and conceptualized entertainment parks.
- Steve Jobs co-founded Apple.

Even though the captains of the industry possessed these skills, they did not encourage their employees to acquire them. They wanted them to merely execute their vision and strategy. As a result, employees bought their bodies to work, leaving their brains and hearts behind.

However, we are now in Industry 4.0, which is leading to proliferation in thinking and reflective jobs. This requires leaders at all levels, not just at the top. Therefore, it is imperative that every person should gain proficiency in these skills which, during the earlier 3IRs, only the captains of the industry possessed.

You too should gain proficiency in them. Bereft of them, you will be at a disadvantage.

I Know Many, if Not All These Skills

I was travelling in a taxi. It started to rain. I asked the driver, 'What is happening?'

'Raining,' he replied.

'Why does it rain?' I asked.

'I don't know,' he replied.

The taxi driver knew it was raining but did not understand why it rains.

The same is true for us also. We may 'know' these skills. But we may not understand them.

Knowing is about awareness and is more superficial, while understanding is deeper, and it takes a conscious effort and longer time to acquire.

This book will help you understand these skills. Armed with them, you will not fall victim to false knowledge, which, as George Bernard Shaw said, is more dangerous than ignorance.

Overlapping Traits

To gain proficiency in a skill requires gaining mastery over traits associated with it. But many traits are not exclusive to one skill. They will form an integral part of other skills too. An example is 'learn from your own mistakes and from those of others'.

Can I Gain Proficiency in These Skills?

A young man approached Socrates to learn the secret of success. Socrates told the young man to meet him near the river. They met. Socrates asked the young man to walk with him into the river. When they were neck-deep in the water, Socrates grabbed the neck of the young man and dunked it into the water. The man was struggling. But Socrates was a strong man. He kept the man's head under water till he started to turn blue. Then Socrates pulled his head out of water and asked him, 'What do you want the most?'

'Air,' said the young man.

'That is the secret of success. When you want success as badly as you wanted the air, then you will get it,' replied Socrates.

The same is true for you. You will gain proficiency in these skills when you have a burning desire to acquire them. Otherwise a day will come when circumstances will grab you by your neck, metaphorically push your head 'under water' and keep it there, till you decide to acquire mastery in these skills.

How Will I Gain Mastery in These Skills?

By following the strategy adopted by elite sportspeople, like Cristiano Ronaldo and Virat Kohli, to gain mastery. They consistently practise honing their football and cricketing skills, respectively, till they become a part of their muscle memory.

On the playing field, they do not have to think. The muscle memory takes over and they end up scoring breathtaking goals, or hitting the right shots, which leaves us awestruck.

You too can amaze your network by practising these skills till they become a part of your muscle memory. Then you can effortlessly come up with big ideas and smart solutions, and leave you peers awestruck.

Will I Make a Mistake by Not Acquiring These Skills?

Warren Buffet's biggest mistakes in investments are not the ones that he made and lost, but the investment decisions he could have made but did not. Take technology stocks.

He did not invest in them till he took a decision to invest in Apple and hit a gold mine.

The same is true for you. The worst decisions are not the ones you make and lose, but those which you should have made and did not. For example, not acquiring proficiency in these skills. In such an eventuality, you may find yourself standing on a proverbial 'burning platform'.

Burning Platform

> A man working on an oil platform in the North Sea woke up one night from a loud explosion, which suddenly set his entire oil platform on fire. In mere moments, he was surrounded by flames. Through the smoke and the heat, he barely made his way out of the chaos to the platform's edge. When he looked down over the edge, all he could see were the dark, cold, foreboding Atlantic waters.
>
> As the fire approached him, the man had mere seconds to react. He could stand on the platform, and inevitably be consumed by the burning flames. Or, he could plunge 30 metres into the freezing waters.
>
> In ordinary circumstances, the man would never consider diving into icy waters. But these were not ordinary times—his platform was on fire—and he decided to jump. The man survived the fall and the waters.[7]

If you are unskilled in these essential skills, then you too are standing on a proverbial burning platform and you must decide what to do: stay put on the burning platform, jump into the water or get skilled.

If you do get skilled, then it will amount to coming aboard the Noah's Ark.

Noah's Ark[8]

God told Noah to build an ark—a big boat. Noah's neighbours laughed at him because there wasn't any water in the desert where they lived. But God told Noah that a great flood was coming.

God also asked Noah to collect two of all the creatures on the earth and bring them into the ark. Pairs of each kind of animal were put safely inside the ark. When everyone was aboard, God shut the door.

Noah and his family and the animals lived in the ark for seven days before the first raindrops fell. Then it rained for days on end. Soon, the earth was covered with water. Even after it stopped raining, Noah and the others had to stay in the ark for several more months while the earth slowly dried out. Then everybody moved off the ark to start life all over again.

This book will introduce you to ten life-changing skills, which will help you get a seat on the mystical Noah's Ark and flourish in the workplace of Industry 4.0, or 4IR.

How to Get the Most Out of This Book

This book cannot teach you these skills. For that, you will have to assign the responsibility of learning them to yourself. Then only will you be able to internalize and benefit from them.

Here are a few pointers for getting the best out of this book:

- When you are reading this book, look upon it as having a discussion with me. It will put you in a relaxed state of mind and you will be more receptive to the learnings.
- Pose questions to me and keep on reading to see if I have answered them. If not, then pause and make a conscious effort to discover the answers to your questions. In this way, your knowledge base will keep increasing and you will gain a deeper understanding, too.
- While reading this book, keep making notes about ideas, concepts, frameworks, tools and techniques that appeal to you. If possible, make an independent summary of key takeaways for each skill.
- A summary is also given at the end of each chapter for each skill. Compare it with what you have made. Now make your own, unduplicated summary. This exercise will help you review, think, challenge and revise the concepts and in the process, you will gain a deeper understanding of them. The unduplicated summary you make will help you revise and refresh each skill presented in the book, whenever you desire.
- Practise these skills at every opportunity. The more you practise, the stronger your muscle memory will become. When the day comes when you must apply these skills, then you will not be found wanting.

- Teach others these skills because to teach is to learn. Every teaching opportunity will help you gain a deeper understanding of them.

Time for Action

The time is always right to do what is right. Let us begin to acquire these skills now. Otherwise, a year from now, you may wish you had started today.[9]

Higher-Level Cognitive Skills

Skill 1

Creativity

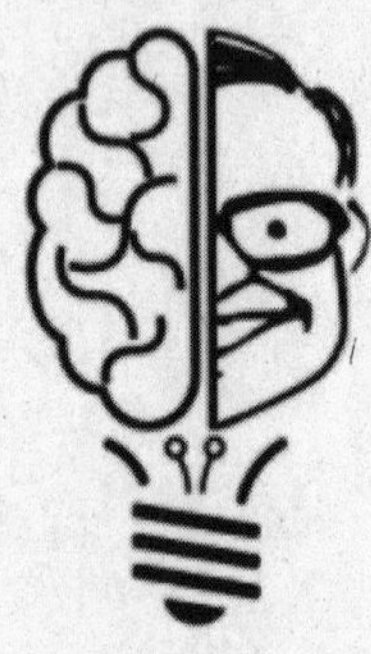

Creativity is a learnt skill, which is activated when traditional thinking is bypassed and the imagination is allowed to wander freely to import, combine and connect ideas in new and imaginative ways to come up with big ideas.

In the early 1990s, I took charge as head of marketing at McDowell & Company (now Diageo India). Soon, I was summoned by the company's president.

'We have decided to launch a premium whisky and named it McDowell "oldé". In this, the "e" is silent. This is how "oldé" was spelt during the olden times. The name has been selected to indicate that the blend is "old", therefore it is good!' he informed me.

I was taken aback. Noticing this, he asked, 'You did not like the name?'

'Yes, sir. I did not like it because when the brand reaches the market, many people may call it "olde", because they may not know that the "e" is silent. This will corrupt the brand name. Once that happens, the chance of the success of the new brand will be adversely impacted,' I argued.

He saw merit in my argument and said, 'Meet me in a week's time with an alternate brand name.'

Post-haste, I assigned this task to my subconscious mind by self-talking and telling myself, *come up with a name for a premium whisky!*

Self-talk is like submitting a problem to a junior (read: subconscious mind) who can tap into your private treasure trove of experiences and learnings and strive to make connections between unrelated and independent ideas in new and unexpected ways. This process happens unconsciously.

Till a day before the scheduled meeting, no solution was in sight. But I did not let that worry me. On the other hand, I became more playful and relaxed. I loitered aimlessly around my home. Unknown to me, I was putting into practice Adam Grant's observation,[10] 'You're most creative at the times you are least alert. It is important to give your brain time to rest.'

In this mood, I was flipping through a magazine when I noticed an advertisement for Signature Bindi. That got me thinking: Signature Bindi feels so incongruous, because 'bindi' is vernacular while 'Signature' is western. But McDowell Signature sounds so cool! My subconscious mind had miraculously made a connection between two dissimilar ideas, bindi and whisky, in a new and meaningful way. With every passing minute, I was falling in love with the name.

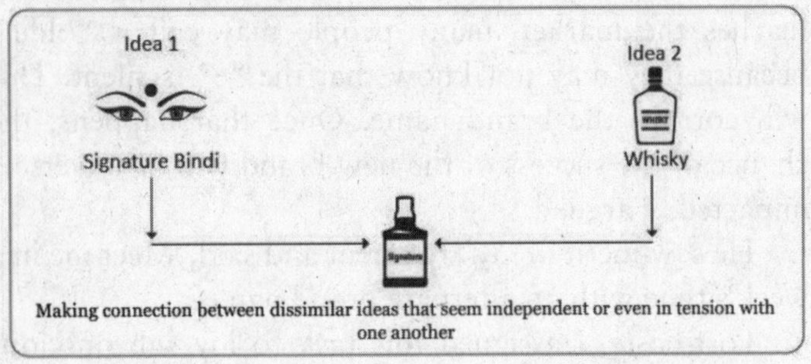

Making connection between dissimilar ideas that seem independent or even in tension with one another

This was my eureka moment. A burst of adrenaline flooded me.

The following day, I walked into my president's office and shared the name.

He liked it and asked, 'How did you get this name?'

'From seeing an advertisement of Signature Bindi,' I candidly confessed.

'Why do you think this name will work?' he asked.

'Paintings become valuable when painters put their signatures on them,' I said and paused before continuing, 'Similarly, the name McDowell Signature will inspire confidence among connoisseurs. They will conclude that since McDowell has put its "signature" on the whisky, it must be good.'

Thus, McDowell Signature got its name. The 'naming' exercise is an excellent example of creativity.

What Is Creativity?

Creativity is a learnt skill, which is activated when traditional thinking is bypassed and imagination is allowed to wander freely to come up with big ideas. It happens by:

1. **Importing** ideas from one industry and intelligently adapting them to another industry.
2. **Combining** dissimilar products to give birth to a new product category.
3. Forming new **connections** between dissimilar ideas that seem independent or even in tension with one another.[11]
4. Discovering '**commonality**' between unrelated events.
5. Uncovering new **patterns**.
6. Seizing **serendipity**.

Applying Creativity

Sir Isaac Newton, Henry Ford, Steve Jobs, Jeff Bezos, Elon Musk and others have harnessed the power of creativity to come up with big ideas to solve some of the world's wicked problems. You can also harness the power of creativity to come up with big ideas to slay the wicked problems facing you.

Presented below are case studies to educate you about how creativity has been applied to come up with big ideas.

1. Importing Ideas from One Industry and Intelligently Adapting Them to Another Industry

Henry Ford was visiting a meat packing factory. He noticed that the carcass of the animal was hung from the ceiling and moved through the plant to the various workstations where it was processed. By the time it reached the end, the bare skeleton of the animal remained.[12]

It was a eureka moment for Henry Ford. He 'imported' this idea and intelligently adapted it to car production. There was 'disassembly' being performed in the former and, in the latter, he visualized an 'assembly' happening.

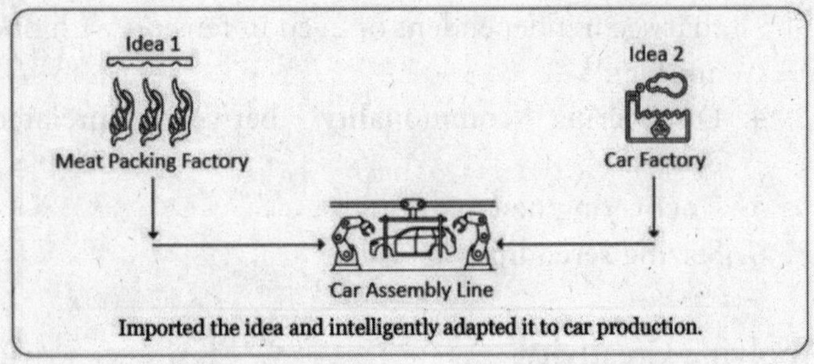

Imported the idea and intelligently adapted it to car production.

He started with the bare skeleton of the vehicle, which was pulled along the assembly by a rope tied to the chassis. Workers were stationed at workstations to carry out the jobs assigned to them. By the time the chassis reached the end of the assembly line, the car was assembled.

The adoption of the moving assembly line for the production of cars dramatically reduced the time of production from twelve hours to approximately ninety minutes. This revolutionized car manufacturing and resulted in the price of Ford Model T dropping from \$850 to \$300, which led Ford to capture a sizeable share of the automobile market.[13]

Apple Store

Apple Store houses a 'Genius Bar'. It comprises a long counter, the kind found in bars, complete with bar stools. Like the bartender, who has extensive knowledge of pouring and serving liquor, wines, beers and other beverages, the 'geniuses' manning the bar have extensive technical know-how to troubleshoot most problems which Apple products are likely to encounter during usage.

A customer visiting a Genius Bar is made to sit on the bar stool, which has no back rest. Hence, they must lean forward while speaking to the genius. The genius who is standing behind the bar counter too must lean forward to listen to the customer. As a result, the distance between the customer and the 'genius' decreases, which helps in building intimacy between them.

Similar to a bartender who serves the customers after greeting them, taking their drink orders, mixing their drinks and serving them, the geniuses also follow an APPLE routine to serve the customers: '**A**pproach customers with a personalized warm welcome, **P**robe to understand the problem, **P**resent a solution, **L**isten for issues and **E**nd with an invitation to return.'[14]

The idea of the Apple Store appears to have been imported from a bar and intelligently adapted to suit Apple's requirements of building and deepening relationships with customers and repairing broken relationships.

Red Bull

Dietrich Mateschitz was visiting Thailand. He was tired and jet-lagged. In this state, he drank the popular local drink Krating Daeng and felt an instant rush. He decided to 'import' this drink and introduce it to the western audience after making suitable modifications to appeal to them.

He named it Red Bull, because Krating Daeng in Thai means Red Gaur, and 'gaur' is an Indian bison.[15]

Red Bull heralded the launch of the energy drink, which boosts energy, alertness and overall performance. Since its launch, Red Bull has dominated the energy drinks market. In 2021, the brand value of Red Bull was estimated to be 15.99 billion euros.[16]

Ahimsa

Mohandas Karamchand Gandhi was heavily influenced by Jainism in his youth.[17] The heart of Jain teaching is 'ahimsa', which means non-violence. Gandhiji adapted ahimsa into a movement to defy the British empire in the period leading up to Indian independence.[18]

2. Combining Dissimilar Products to Give Birth to a New Category

Steve Jobs connected two dissimilar products—computers and cell phones—to give birth to the smartphone, which is easy to carry, makes calls and has the computing power of a computer.

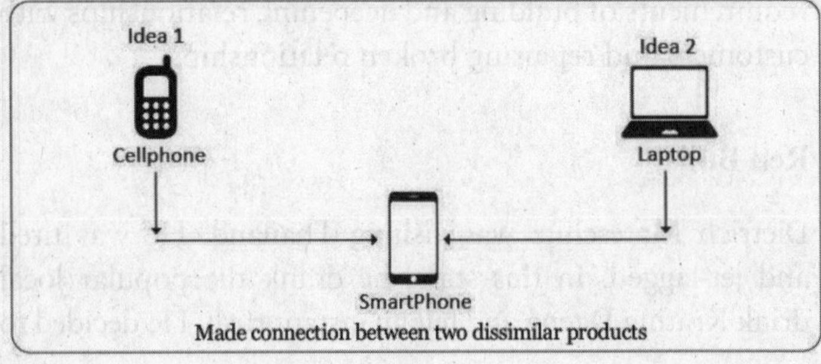

Made connection between two dissimilar products

The smartphone (read: iPhone) has enriched our lives and put Apple on the road to becoming one of the world's most valuable companies.

Barbie Doll[19]

Ruth Handler, co-founder of Mattel, watched her pre-teen daughter act out stories with her paper dolls. This made Ruth wonder: why were there no grown-up dolls for kids who had outgrown baby dolls?

Meanwhile in Germany, there was an adult doll named Lilli, who was flirtatious, racy and a sex symbol. It was handed out to men at bachelor parties.

Ruth Handler[20] imaginatively combined two dissimilar products that seemed at an arm's length from each other—traditional dolls and the adult doll Lillie—to create a new product category, a fashion doll, which was busty, thin-waisted and had several features of a fashion model. She called it Barbie.

Barbie became a hit and is now sold in over 150 countries. Its brand recognition is almost at par with that of Mickey Mouse.

3. Forming New Connections between Dissimilar Ideas That Seem Independent or Even in Tension with One Another[21]

In times gone by, hard liquor (read: whisky) was patronized by the 'masses' with the intent of getting high (read: a kick). Beer, on the other hand, was patronized by the 'classes' while socializing.

The 'masses' loved the sophisticated imagery associated with beer because it was patronized by the upper class. But on the few occasions they consumed it, they were disappointed. It did not give them even a semblance of a 'kick', a benefit they expected from alcoholic beverages. That was to be expected, since mild beer has a low alcoholic content (less than 5 per cent).

This insight must have inspired the denizens of the beer industry to form new connections between two dissimilar ideas that seemed independent or even in tenson with one another—'image' and 'kick'—in an imaginative and unexpected way to give birth to a new segment—strong beer. It has the 'image' of beer and delivers the 'kick' expected from alcoholic beverages. Today, strong beer (alcoholic content of 6–8 per cent) market commands a dominant share of the beer market in India.[22]

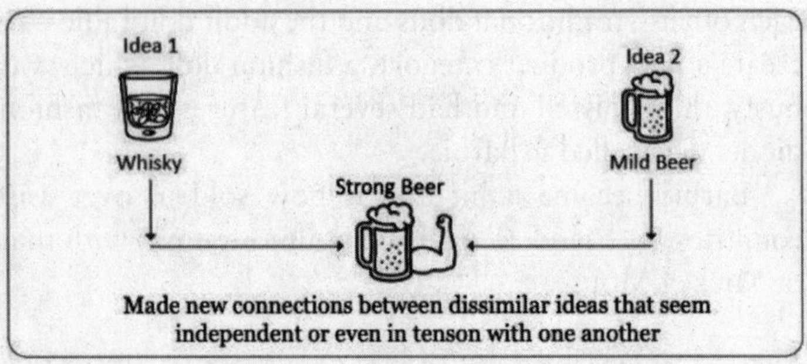

Spider-Man[23]

Stan Lee was asked to create a superhero. He wanted to endow it with a unique superpower. As luck would have it, he saw a fly crawling on the wall, and he thought to himself, 'Wow, suppose a person had the power to stick to a wall like an insect.'

Stan Lee had fortuitously formed a connection between two dissimilar ideas—a lowly fly and the superhero—to conceptualize Spider-Man. A legend was born and, over time, acquired a universal appeal that few characters can match.

Alexa

As a child, Jeff Bezos loved Star Trek, the science fiction show set 250 years in the future. It had talking computers that accepted voice commands and executed them. This inspired Jeff Bezos to visualize Alexa, as a virtual assistant who accepts voice commands to perform a range of tasks: play music, tell the weather, place orders for products on Amazon and many more tasks, thereby enhancing the user experience.[24]

4. Discover 'Commonality' between Unrelated Events

Sir Isaac Newton witnessed the event of an apple falling straight down to the ground. He noticed that the apple had not moved upwards, neither had it fallen sideways. In a flash, he discovered commonality with another event which he would witness every day: how we are held to the ground. He concluded that the force that makes the apple fall and the force which also holds us to the ground are the same. He called it the gravitational force, which led to the formulation of the law of gravitation.[25]

The laws of gravity helped engineers and scientists work out how much energy was needed to break the gravitational bonds of the earth and put satellites into space. These satellites, as we know, significantly benefit us: they are used for facilitating communication, observing the earth and other planets in our solar system, navigating information (global positioning information [GPS]) and sourcing data for climate research, among others things.[26]

Microwave

Percy Spencer[27], a self-taught engineer, noticed that the high-powered microwave beam from an active radar set melted a chocolate bar he had in his pocket. This made him realize the 'commonality' between two unrelated events, microwave beams and cooking, and resulted in the birth of the microwave oven.

Today, the microwave oven has become an integral part of a kitchen and is employed for cooking, reheating food and many more jobs.

5. Uncovering New Patterns

Jack Dorsey,[28] the co-founder of Twitter, grew up in St Louis, USA. As a kid, he was shy and reserved. He spent a lot of his time at home, playing with computers. He was fascinated with how things worked in the real world and wanted to bring them into the virtual world. Using his hacking skills, he gained access to the police scanner and the messages coming out of the St Louis Emergency Dispatch Centre. They were engaged in saving and protecting lives and they communicated in short busts by broadcasting where they currently were, where they were going and what were they doing.

Intuitively, Dorsey understood that emergency services communicated among themselves in short bursts and shared only critical information. This is in sharp contrast to how the rest of us communicate: we tend to be verbose, long-drawn and, on many occasions, ineffective.

It made him wonder why communication among people could not also be short, precise and in short bursts.

Thus was born Twitter, where people were constrained to communicate in short burst of 140 characters. Recently, it has been increased to 280 characters. By 2021, it had 73 million users. Among them are heads of state, celebrities and most of us.

6. Seizing Serendipity

Horace Walpole, an English historian, politician, and writer, is credited with coining the term 'serendipity'. He was inspired by the protagonists of the story *The Three Princes of Serendip*, who made discoveries, by accident and sagacity, of things they were not in quest of. Many scientific discoveries owe their birth to serendipity.

Law of Buoyancy

A goldsmith was assigned the task of making a pure gold crown for Hieron, the king of Syracuse, a historic city on the island of Sicily in Italy. When the crown was ready, doubts were expressed that it was not made entirely of pure gold. Archimedes,[29] a leading scientist of the era, was hired by the royal court to resolve this conundrum.

While lying in a bathtub, he was thinking about how to solve this intractable problem. In a moment of serendipity, it dawned on him that the buoyant force of a submerged object is equal to the weight of the fluid displayed by it.

This discovery excited him so much that he jumped out of his bath and ran naked thorough the streets of Syracuse, screaming 'Eureka!'—I have found it!

The law of buoyancy is named in his honour as the Archimedes Principle. It can explain how ships float, submarines remain underwater, hot-air balloons fly and many more such occurrences.

Birth of Amazon

In 1994, Jeff Bezos was working at D.E. Shaw, a hedge fund based in New York. His job was to identify possible business opportunities that would involve the then brand-new Internet landscape. That's when Bezos found that the Internet was growing at 2,300 per cent per year. In a moment of serendipity, he realized that 'anything growing that fast, even if its baseline usage was small, it's going to be big'.[30] He decided to come up with a business idea linked to the Internet and grow with it.

He started Amazon as an online bookstore selling books over the Internet. Since then, Amazon has grown into a trillion-dollar company and Jeff Bezos, the founder, finds a place among the richest people on the planet.

Invoking Serendipity[31]

To invoke serendipity, permit yourself to be surprised. Trust that randomness might lead to positive outcomes or unexpected strokes of luck. Here are two strategies to help you invoke serendipity.

- Cultivate an open mind. You can discover opportunities in the most unlikely places: while commuting to work, from your peers and friends. For this to happen, practise 'serendipitous networking', or connecting with others for the sake of getting to know them, their perspectives and their stories. The goal is to not focus too much on a clear objective but merely to have a conversation for the joy that it brings you. These interactions are meant to keep you curious, teach you new things and push you to imagine different ways of thinking.

- Approach change—career-related or otherwise—from a place of possibility rather than fear. Of course, change is going to feel uncomfortable and difficult at times, but it can open up new possibilities.

Why Is Creativity Rare?

The brain is designed to be non-creative. If it were creative, life would be impossible. Take clothing. If you have eleven pieces of clothing, then there are 39,916,800 ways of getting dressed. If you tried one every minute, you would need to live to be seventy-six years old and use your entire waking life trying ways of getting dressed.[32]

Also, the education system does not encourage questioning because it would mean challenging authority and tradition. Instead, it rewards conformity, obedience and convergent thinking, which sound the death knell for creativity.

The workplace, too, is a graveyard for creativity. Managers shoot down 'out-of-the-box' ideas presented to them. Constant exposure to this brutality results in a feeling of 'learnt helplessness' among employees, who start to feel that no matter how good an idea they present, it will always be shot down, so why even try? This leads to stifling of creativity. Therefore, 'sameness' prevails and ideas that have outlived their utility continue to rule the roost.

Here are more factors that stifle creativity:

- **Free Association**

I play a game with my students. I say a word and ask them to say aloud the first word that comes to their mind.

Me: Tandoori!

Students: Chicken!

My students have fallen victim to free association. In their minds, association between objects are already formed, which they blurt out. This proves to be an antidote for creativity. After all, creativity requires new associations to be formed between and among ideas and objects.

- **Efficient Market Theory**

I was taking a session on entrepreneurship at a business school located in Academic City, Dubai. Adjacent to it was a food court.

The class was divided into five groups and an assignment was given to them—to identify a 'themed' food outlet which could be opened in the food court.

A week later, the groups made their presentation. The first group, using the framework, tools and techniques that I had introduced to them, concluded that they would open a tandoori chicken outlet. Their recommendation seemed brilliant, since the majority of students in the Academic City are from the Indian subcontinent. They would make a beeline for tandoori chicken, which was conspicuously absent in the food court.

But imagine my surprise when the next three groups also arrived at the same conclusion: of opening a tandoori chicken-themed outlet. Only one group recommended opening a Kerala-themed outlet.

How did four out of five groups arrive at the same conclusion?

The culprit is the 'efficient market theory'. It states that if the same information is available and the same framework, tools and techniques are used to analyse it, then people are likely to arrive at the same conclusion. If that happens, then the unique solution (read: creative solution) becomes a commodity solution which does not offer competitive advantage and hence is of little value.

Creativity Enablers:

There are innumerable techniques to enable creativity.

Enabler 1: Unbounded Curiosity

During our childhood we are at our creative best, because we are curious. Nothing is too small to escape our curiosity. As we grow up, the child inside us starts to die and along with it, our curiosity. We can be creative again by reawakening the child inside us and becoming curious. This enabled George de Mestral, a Swiss electrical engineer, to discover Velcro. While hunting in the Jura mountains in Switzerland, he realized that the tiny hooks of the cockleburs were stuck to his pants and to his dog. He got curious and wondered how they attached themselves. Under the scrutiny of the microscope, he observed the hooks engaging the loops in the fabric of his pants. He duplicated Mother Nature's hook and fastener and branded it Velcro.[33] Today, Velcro fasteners are used in clothing to replace buttons, in shoes to replace laces, and even in medical bandages.

To reawaken the child in you, renew friendships with five childhood friends: Why? Where? When? What? How? Let them be your constant companions and use them ceaselessly.

If this sounds complicated, then follow the advice of Albert Einstein: question everything!

Enabler 2: Keen Observation

Robert Taylor had a keen sense of observation. This made him observe how soap appeared while it was used in bathrooms. Zooming in on the soap dish, he noticed an unpleasant puddle of ooze in an otherwise spotless setting. It was an appalling sight. He felt that the answer was liquid soap dispensed from a beautiful pump dispenser. That is how SoftSoap was born. [34]

You may be tempted to certify yourself as having keen observation skills and claiming that nothing escapes your observation. I thought so too till I administered a drawing test to myself. I challenged myself to draw the face of the watch that I see every day. I drew it, but missed many details that make it distinctive. Then it dawned on me that what I thought was keen observation was merely seeing!

Sherlock Holmes had it right when he told Watson, 'You see, but do not observe.' Practise the art of observing that which is for all to see, but few observe it.

To sharpen your sense of observation, learn to:

- Slow down.
- Refrain from multitasking.
- Observe everyday things with a fresh pair of eyes.

- Be mindful about what you are doing. This will help you be present in the moment.

These simple strategies will help set your mind free to form associations and be creative.[35]

Enabler 3: No Time[36]

Most people's daily routine keeps them busy. This stifles creativity.

Creative people, like Steve Jobs and Albert Einstein, overcome this issue by committing a part of their time to 'no time'. For Tim Cook, it is 4 a.m., when he gets up. He says that the early morning is free of distractions and it is his.[37]

'No time' is the quiet moment in which a person can isolate themselves from the noise and distractions of the world. During this time, they can take a walk or spend some quiet time on their own. These moments relax them and are ripe for creative thoughts to take birth.

Enabler 4: Positive Environment

A positive and nurturing environment helps us think more clearly and more creatively. In this environment our brain accesses learning, wisdom and experience, and can combine them in new and unexpected ways. It results in free-flowing creativity.[38]

Negative environments and thoughts derail our normal brain functioning. In extreme cases, our brain shuts down. In such environments, we seek information that will help us survive. This sounds the death knell for creativity.

Enabler 5: Broaden Your Experience

'Bombard your mind with new experiences which are completely outside of your chosen field.'[39] You can do this by:

- Seeking out 'new' people, places, experiences.
- Increasing the diversity of your acquaintances. In their presence you are exposed to different viewpoints and perspectives.
- Cultivating varied interests.

Enabler 6: Modest Constraint

Elon Musk faced a constraint. If he sold Tesla Electric Vehicle (EV) through a traditional multi-car dealership network, then it would receive stepmotherly treatment. If he decided to set up a dealership network from the grassroots up, it would require humongous capital and would also prove to be time-consuming.

Hemmed in by these constraints, he came up with a 'creative' solution to sell Tesla online, i.e., directly to customers, and support it with flagship stores akin to Apple Store. The flagship stores would be staffed with company employees with the aim of educating potential buyers about owning EVs and allaying their fears. This creative solution also ensured that the malice of price fluctuation caused due to various car dealers offering varying discounts was eliminated.

Constraint enhances creativity. It forces us to think in ways we may skip in prosperous times. But there is a caveat: constraint should adhere to the Goldilocks'

Principle, which is that too much constraint will choke creativity and too little will give it free reign. When it is just right, it spurs creativity.

If the constraint is self-imposed, then it spurs even greater creativity. In the 2000s, the Audi racing team desired to win Le Mans under a self-imposed constraint: it could not go faster than its competitors.

Working with this self-imposed constraint, it developed diesel-powered cars, which required fewer fuel stops than gasoline-powered cars. The result: Audi went on to win Le Mans three years in succession.[40]

Enabler 7: Freedom to Experiment and Fail

New ideas are born through experimentation. Experimentation by nature is prone to failure. Permit yourself to experiment and fail. But learn from each failure. In fact, you should double the number of experiments that you do in a year. In this way, you will double your inventiveness, says Jeff Bezos.[41]

Apart from learning from your own failures, learn from other people's failures as well. After all, you can't live long enough to make them all yourself.

Enabler 8: Healthy Body

Focus on getting sufficient sleep, nutrition and exercise.

- Sleep offers the body and brain time to restore and recover.
- Regular exercise reduces anxiety and improves quality of sleep.

- Nutrition leads to a healthy body and a healthy mind.

These three are the basics for brain functioning and they ignite our creative side.[42]

Techniques to Improve Creativity

- **Technique 1: Defamiliarization aka 'Vuja De'**

When the brain works, it consumes a high amount of energy. This drains us. To conserve energy, nature has ensured that when we are in familiar surroundings, or when we feel comfortable, our brain goes to sleep—it shuts down. It is akin to what happens to our computer when we do not work on it for some time. It automatically goes into sleep mode to save battery power.

This is referred to as Troxler Fading, named after a nineteenth-century Swiss physician who discovered the effect. In neuroscience, it is termed habituation: neurons stop firing once we are in familiar surroundings or in unchanging situations.

This syndrome is a death knell for creativity. To guard against this pitfall, Victor Shklovsky, a Russian literary theorist, offered a way of 'making strange' (defamiliarizing) the otherwise familiar.[43]

It can be achieved by vuja de, the opposite of déjà vu, which occurs when we experience something new but it feels like we have seen it before. Vuja de is the opposite. We encounter something familiar but view it with a fresh pair of eyes, which inspires us to extract new insights from the familiar.

Warby Parker[44]

Warby Parker, widely believed to be the Netflix of eyewear, owes its birth to vuja de.

The founders were familiar with the eyewear industry. Among themselves, they had spent over sixty years wearing glasses. Inspired by vuja de, they started to evaluate this industry with a fresh pair of eyes to extract new insights from the familiar.

It struck them that eyewear had been around for a long time, but it had hardly witnessed any major changes. Still, it commanded a hefty price tag. The question they posed to themselves: why does it cost so much?

The answer led them to Luxottica, a European company, which dominates the eyewear industry. It either owns or has licences to the most aspirational brand names, like Chanel, Bulgari, Burberry, Emporio Armani and more. It enjoys a monopoly and has been taking advantage of it to price its products exorbitantly. The high price was not a default—it was due to the monopoly status that Luxottica enjoyed. This insight gave the founders hope that the prices could be reduced.

Traditionally, glasses were being sold through brick-and-mortar stores.

Could the selling practice be challenged, they asked themselves.

An analysis of shoppers indicated that they were comfortable buying online from Amazon. Even shoes, from Zappos. So why could glasses not be bought online? Warby Parker stared selling glasses online at attractive prices. In 2020, it was valued at $3 billion.[45]

Kaun Banega Crorepati

Star Plus, now Star India, originally conceived *Kaun Banega Crorepati* (KBC), the official Hindi adaptation of *Who Wants To Be a Millionaire?*, a British television game show, as *Kaun Banega Lakhpati*, with a prize money of Rs 1 lakh.[46]

During this time, Rupert Murdoch, the bossman at StarPlus, happened to be in India and asked how much Rs 1 lakh was in dollars. He was told it would be approximately $2200. He felt that the prize money was too little to trigger any interest from viewers. He increased it to Rs 1 crore, resulting in *Kaun Banega Lakhpati* becoming *Kaun Banega Crorepati*.

'Had Rupert not been in town that week and turned *KBL* into *KBC*, I doubt if Star TV would have been able to make a go of it in India,' reminisces Peter Mukerjea, former head of Star TV.

- **Technique 2: Step into the (Big) Shoes**

When I am stuck for big ideas or need a second opinion, I ask myself a simple question: what would Steve Jobs do? To get more options, I pose the same challenge to Jeff Bezos and Elon Musk.

Here is an example. I wanted to get a second opinion on whether I had reimagined the deodorant market correctly. I crafted the following question: how can the deo category be reimagined to reignite the market? Thus, I posed it to the three stalwarts. I wrote down their likely responses:

- Jeff Bezos: Identify the pain points customers face with the existing best-selling deo. Then design a deo that reduces or eliminates them.

- Steve Jobs: Create a better product which gives a pleasurable customer experience.
- Elon Musk: Challenge the tradition of the industry.

Based on the directions given by these giants, I arrived at the following decisions:

- Young people of opposite genders want to come closer, but body odour (BO) drives them apart. I needed to reduce or eliminate this pain point.
- Create a better product by formulating a recipe which had 2x more authentic French perfume. It enhanced the mood of the users and gave them a pleasurable experience.
- Challenge the tradition of the industry by marketing deodorant as 'perfume'.

I amalgamated their thoughts into a cohesive strategy and arrived at a conclusion that the deodorant should be sold as perfume.

- **Technique 3: Let Hundreds of Ideas Bloom**

We were visiting a safari park in Africa. As luck would have it, we witnessed a lion chasing an antelope.

'The antelope is dead meat,' my colleague predicted.

But reality turned out to be different. The antelope outran the lion.

Our guide, who overheard the conversation, said, 'It is the law of nature that most of the efforts go waste and only a few succeed. Fish lay hundreds of eggs. The majority of them are eaten by predators and only a few survive. In the forest, hundreds of seeds are strewn around, but only a few grow into trees. The rest wither away.' He paused for a moment and then continued, 'This does not cause the animals or nature any despair. They keep trying. This is second nature to them.'

Pablo Picasso produced an estimated 50,000 artworks, which included 885 paintings, 1228 sculptures, 2880 ceramics and 12,000 drawings.[47] Only a few hundred of these are remembered.

Creative people let hundreds of ideas bloom. It increases their chances of stumbling upon a good one.[48]

- **Technique 4: Improvisation Technique (IT)**

A study of ideas reveals that they never come fully formed. At birth, they are deformed, ugly and fragile. At this stage, if they are subjected to unbridled criticism and scrutiny, they die a premature death. But if they are nurtured and polished, they start to sparkle.

Improv Technique (IT) polishes a fragile and ugly idea to a sparkle.

In this technique, one person comes up with an idea. The next person says 'yes' and builds upon it. This cycle continues till the idea starts to shine.

The strategy of building upon each other's ideas instead of being critical and judgemental ensures that good ideas survive their birth. If we focus only on their weakness, good ideas die at birth. Also, the absence of criticism ensures the unbridled flow of creative ideas in the group.

But this system has a drawback. Merely highlighting the good aspect of an idea may result in the mushrooming of crummy ideas. But positive and well-intentioned criticism can transform ideas into prodigiously good ideas.

To overcome this problem, Roberto Verganti and Don Norman suggested that people should build upon the previous person's idea by prefixing their response with, 'Yes, but, and . . .'

Let me hand over the stage to them to explain their idea: 'When you propose Idea A, a colleague first addresses what he perceives to be a flaw in it, provides constructive feedback (this is the 'but'), and then suggests a possible way to overcome or avoid the flaw, yielding Idea B (this is the 'and'). Then you do the same: You acknowledge Idea B, provide a constructive critique and develop a new, even more improved result. Others can jump in with their critiques and proposals during the process. This kind of constructive interaction encourages a deep cycle of critical dialogues that can lead to a coherent, breakthrough idea.'[49]

Bagpiper Gold

In the 1980s, Herbertsons Ltd, a group company of United Spirits (now Diageo India) had Bagpiper whisky, a mass brand, in its portfolio. When its loyal customers rose in their career, they 'graduated' to a more premium whisky, thereby leaving the Bagpiper brand. My boss decided to address this problem.

'Let us extend the Bagpiper trademark to a premium whisky. In this way, we will be able to keep Bagpiper loyalists in our fold. We will call this new brand Bagpiper Premium,' he said.

At the time, Aristocrat Premium was a popular premium whisky brand.

I followed the 'Yes, but, and . . .' technique to build upon his idea.

'*Yes*, sir, your idea is good. *But* the brand name you have proposed should be revaluated. Since Aristocrat Premium whisky is available in the market, people will think that we have "copied" them. *And* therefore, I recommend that we call it Bagpiper Gold. In India, gold is aspirational and therefore, Bagpiper Gold will also become aspirational.'

My boss reflected on my recommendation and green-lit it. Thus, Bagpiper Gold got its name!

Blue Riband Duet

A few years later, I applied the same strategy to propose a brand name for a new category of gin we were launching, in which lime had been pre-added. The story about how this new category of gin was born is discussed later.

The task for coming up with a brand name for it was given to our advertising agency. A few days later, they came to our office to present their recommendations.

'In the new brand, two things, gin and lime, are mellifluously blended together, just like a "couplet" which has two lines of rhyming verses. Therefore, the brand name should be "Blue Riband Couplet",' recommended our agency.

I built upon their suggestion, saying, '*Yes*, you are right. *But* customers may corrupt the name "couplet" and call it "cup and plate". If the brand name gets corrupted, then new brand's chances of success decrease dramatically. *And* therefore, I propose that we call it

"Blue Riband Duet", which will indicate to consumers that it is a perfect "duet" between gin and lime.'

This is how Blue Riband Duet got its name.

Advantage of Being Creative

Being creative will help you come up with a big idea to overcome the problems plaguing you. Here is the proof:

- Henry Ford 'creatively' imported the idea of the assembly line to car production. This revolutionized car manufacturing.[50]
- Steve Jobs 'creatively' combined two dissimilar products—computers and cell phones—to give birth to the smartphone, which has enriched our lives.
- Beer industry professionals 'creatively' connected dissimilar ideas—the 'image' of beer and the 'kick' of alcohol—to give birth to a new segment, strong beer.
- Sir Isaac Newton 'creatively' discovered a commonality between unrelated events—an apple falling straight down and how we are held to the ground—which led to the discovery of gravitational forces. This paved the path for space exploration later on.
- Jack Dorsey 'creatively' uncovered new patterns which gave birth to Twitter.

Now it is your turn to be creative and come up with big ideas to change your industry, if not the whole world.

Postscript[51]

The world wants you to be typical and normal. It is much easier. It takes less effort. But don't let it happen.

Instead, choose to be creative!

It will make you distinctive, original and valuable. Do not expect it to be easy or free. But, in the end, it will be worth the effort.

Creativity in a Nutshell

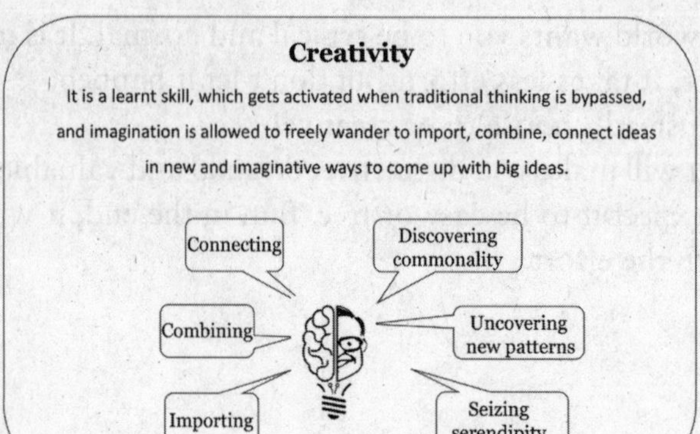

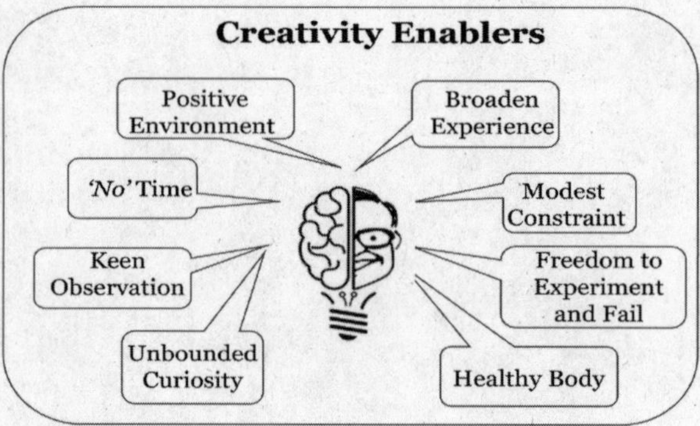

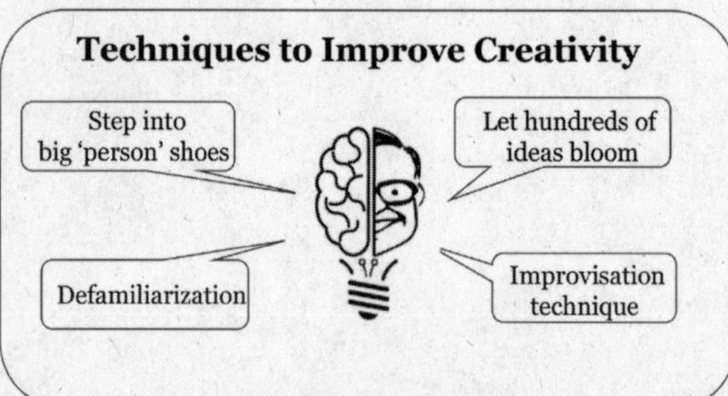

Skill 2

Innovation

*Innovation = Creativity * Execution * Profit*

In 1997, Steve Jobs rejoined Apple after having been forced out of the company he had co-founded in 1985. The company was months away from bankruptcy. When asked about his strategy to revive the company, he said, 'Not through cost-cutting, but by innovating our way out through the current predicament.'[52]

What Is Innovation?

'We like to think of an organization's capacity for innovation as creativity multiplied by execution. We use "multiplication" rather than "sum" because if either creativity or execution has a score of zero, then the capacity for innovation is zero,'[53] says eminent academician Vijay Govindarajan.

3M, awarded the US government's highest award for innovation,[54] believes that innovation is '. . . new ideas, plus action or implementation, which result in an improvement, a gain, or a profit'.[55]

The essence of innovation can be captured in an equation:

Innovation = Creativity * Execution * Profit

If any of the components is zero, then innovation too will be zero.

Is Profit the Sole Objective of Innovation?

Profit does enter the equation when it comes to business innovation, which can also be called practical innovation.

When innovation generates a profit, then it pays for itself and also creates a surplus for investment into future innovation.

Social innovation, which is done for the good of society, is not burdened with this responsibility.

We will restrict our discussion to business or practical innovations.

Are Innovation and Creativity Not Synonymous?

'Usually, managers equate innovation with creativity. But innovation is not creativity. Creativity is about coming up with the big idea. Innovation is about executing the idea—converting the idea into a successful business,' says Vijay Govindarajan.[56]

Is there an independent validation of his perspective?

'Innovation involves two stages—the generation of new ideas and the implementation of the ideas. Creativity is the first stage of innovation,' says Roger Schwarz .[57]

Types of Innovation

There are as many ways to innovate as there are business challenges. Here is a curated list for you to devour.

1. Incremental Innovation

Heinz noticed that customers had to turn the bottle upside down to pour the ketchup. It decided to introduce a new packaging, where the bottle was stored upside down to aid easy pouring. This incremental improvement, aimed at solving a consumer problem, led to sales and profit improvement.

Incremental innovation involves making small and marginal improvements aimed at solving real customer problems, for which customers are willing to pay a little more. With each incremental improvement, sales and profits grow. It gets quick wins in the market and helps a company stay ahead of competition, at negligible investment.

Once incremental innovation is launched in the market, and it wins customer approval, competition attempts to quickly follow (read: copy) by launching a 'me too' version at a lower price.

Companies like Gillette blunt such moves by the competition by adding more blades at regular intervals. Everything—well, almost everything—remains the same, but the new version is nicer. Pursuing incremental innovation ensures that Gillette continues to maintain a strong hold over the men's shaving market.

Incremental innovation is also referred to as Lorenzian strategy (or the 'butterfly effect'), named after Edward Lorenz, an MIT mathematician. He described how a small action, such as a butterfly flapping its wings, can lead to an improbably large event (such as a tornado).[58]

2. Improver Innovation

Question: Name the first person to set foot on the moon.

Answer: Neil Armstrong.

Question: Name the second person to set foot on the moon.

Most of us may find it difficult to name him.

This may make us surmise that it pays to be the first mover in every walk of life, including innovation. After all, the first mover captures the market and establishes an invincible lead. Unfortunately, when it comes to business innovation, the reality is different.

'First movers had a 47% failure rate. While companies that follow the first movers, had only an 8% failure rate,' says Shane Snow, entrepreneur, journalist and author.[59]

The first movers take on the role of pioneers. They move in and clear the path of the innumerable hurdles, risks and dangers. Then the 'followers' move in and take on the role of an 'improver'. This involves studying the first movers, learning from their mistakes, offering solutions superior to those of the first movers and usurping the market from them.

Market data supports this inference.

- Search engines: WebCrawler (1994), Lycos (1994), AltaVista (1995), Yahoo (1995) and Ask Jeeves (1996) were the first movers in the search market. Google made its entry in 1998. Today, it dominates the search market.[60]
- Social Networking:[61] Friendster (2002), Myspace (2003), Second Life (2003) and Orkut (January 2004) were the early entrants. Facebook made its entry in February 2004. In 2020, it has over 2.8 billion active users and dominates the market.
- Email: Hotmail and Yahoo pioneered email service. Gmail followed and has established a dominant hold over the market.

Not surprisingly, best beats first![62]

3. Reverse Innovation

General Electric (GE) had developed an ECG machine for its home market, the USA. In India, it was priced at a premium and hence catered to the high-end market segment. To expand in India (read: local market), GE needed to innovate.

Its team in Bengaluru assessed that the 'local' market[63] required an ultra-low cost, durable, easy-to-use and portable ECG machine. They also concluded that the existing GE ECG machine could not be stripped down to meet these requirements.

This motivated the team to develop from scratch a portable low-cost ECG machine. The market gave it a positive response. In due course, this product was introduced in the home market, the USA, making it a lighthouse example of reverse innovation.

Historically, innovation flowed from first-world to third-world countries. But the tide is turning. Now, innovation from third-world countries is finding its way into first-world countries. This is because ideas and products in an emerging market are so compelling that they flow uphill to western markets.[64] This phenomenon is labelled 'reverse innovation'.

Even technology companies have embraced reverse innovation.

Offline Viewing

India's Google team noticed that people residing in areas where Internet was unreliable would download the content when it was working and view it offline.

This innovation winged its way back to the USA—Googlers at the head office realized that there were many areas in first-world countries where Internet reach was poor or there were frequent outages. Offline offered an excellent solution to address this challenge.

Could Googlers sitting in the USA not have conceptualized this innovation? The chances are low—they cannot imagine a world where Internet does not exist 24/7 or there are areas plagued with Internet outages!

Cash Payment

In its home market (the USA), Uber accepted payment through cards. But in third-world countries, the penetration of cards—credit and debit—is low. This acted as a barrier for many people from availing the services.

Uber innovated and introduced cash payment. This innovation boosted the adoption of Uber. It became so popular that Uber has introduced it in many markets across the world.

Reverse innovation is preferred by companies who are headquartered in the first world and are looking to capture markets in third world countries. By following this strategy, they kill two birds with one stone: not only do they score wins in third world countries, but also open up new segments in the home market.

4. Open Innovation

Many companies are infected with a 'Not Invented Here' (NIH) virus. Such companies restrict their innovation to what can be accomplished inside their four walls.

This strategy has several drawbacks. For starters, the best talent and cutting-edge knowledge may not reside within the company. Therefore, the innovations that may emerge from within may not be the best!

To overcome this drawback, companies are embracing 'open' innovation. They seek to attract outside talent, ideas, resources and expertise to address the daunting business challenges they face. Boeing and Wikipedia are two companies that have experimented with it.

Boeing embraced open innovation when the Dreamliner was being designed. It opened the development of aircraft design to engineers from 100 different companies and got suppliers to design more than 35 per cent of the Dreamliner. The development process was a year shorter than what it would have been if Boeing were working on it alone.[65]

Wikipedia, too, disrupted the 'encyclopaedia' by embracing open innovation. It encouraged large-scale, highly diverse collaboration among strangers.

Open innovation offers a slew of advantages:

- It supplements the in-house team by tapping into talent residing outside the company.
- The company does not have to start from scratch and so the time to market is shortened.
- It reduces cost since the wheel does not have to be reinvented.
- It is voluntary. Therefore, people who are intrinsically motivated will throw their hat in the ring. This can result in the creation of elegant solutions.
- It opens doors to new partnerships and collaborations.
- Usually, payouts are linked to success. If solutions do not emerge, then the company is not expected to pay. In short, the company does not have to fund failure.

If all these reasons do not make sense, then just remember that by embracing open innovation, a company can get more from less

5. Frugal Innovation

A city had been attacked by terrorists. Citizens were feeling insecure. The police commissioner faced the mammoth task of restoring confidence among them.

Brainstorming revealed that the visibility of a large number of policemen moving briskly around the city would restore confidence.

Analysis revealed that police personnel, upon completing their daily duty, would change into civil dress and take the public transport to their homes. The same was true of police personnel coming from home to join their duty. They would be in civilian dress and, upon reaching the police station, would change into police uniform.

In a moment of serendipity, it struck him to instruct police personnel going home to keep wearing their police uniform while commuting, and those coming to join duty to wear their uniforms at home, before their commute.

By implementing this strategy, a large number of police personnel were seen criss-crossing the city. This restored confidence among the city residents.

This is an example of frugal innovation. It is a flexible approach to problem-solving that uses limited resources in an innovative way. It is not just about doing more with less but about doing '*better* with less'.

Yoga T-Shirt

As a part of my job, I had to frequently travel overseas. This meant being away from family. It made me feel guilty. To reduce this feeling of guilt, I made it a point to buy gifts each time I returned home.

This time, I was returning from Dubai. The previous evening, I had visited Dubai Mall to buy a gift for my wife. She is a yoga enthusiast and I decided to surprise her with a yoga T-shirt. I entered a store dealing exclusively in yoga accessories. After going through myriad options, I decided to buy a T-shirt. The one I choose was prohibitively priced.

'Why is this priced so high?' I asked the storekeeper. 'After all, it is just a T-shirt.'

The shopkeeper took the T-shirt from my hand and started to educate me about its finer points. 'It has a mild elastic band on the stomach area so that it "sticks" there. This is to ensure that no matter what pose is taken, the T-shirt does not flip over and cause embarrassment.'

Happily, I paid for it and upon reaching home, gifted it to my wife. Unfortunately, the price tag had not been removed. Noticing it, she exclaimed in horror, 'Why did you buy such an expensive T-shirt?'

I educated her about the special feature it had. She went to her wardrobe and returned with a T-shirt and said, 'This is for only Rs 300.'

'But it will flip over and embarrass you,' I protested.

'Yes, it will. Therefore, our teacher has instructed us to tuck it into our tights!' she educated me.

I wanted the floor to open up and swallow me.

Tucking the T-shirt in was a frugal solution to the problem.

The Immunity Charm Project[66]

Vaccination is critical to develop the immune system in children. But in Afghanistan, many infants were not vaccinated because of a lack of their immunization history, since parents did not maintain their vaccination records. Even worse, they sometimes lost them. Making the situation worse was a prevalent bias against vaccination in remote areas, which was further aggravated due to illiteracy. As a result, doctors faced the nightmarish challenge of having to vaccinate infants without having access to a proper immunization history.

The solution came from identifying a prevalent tradition in Afghanistan of making infants wear a bracelet to protect them against evil spirits.

Health-care workers provided mothers with a bracelet containing colour-coded beads. It was like those worn by infants to protect them against evil spirits. Each time the infant received a vaccine against a disease, such as measles, polio or diphtheria, a coloured bead corresponding to it was added to the bracelet. Doctors would be able to tell the status of the infant's vaccination from the bracelet.

The Immunity Charm Project is a lighthouse example of frugal solution, where more was achieved by spending less. It boosted the vaccination rate among infants and saved many lives.

Bring Down Wastage

In a student mess, food wastage was not showing any signs of abating. A review of the process followed in the dining hall indicated that a student picked up a plate and bowls and moved down the table, filling them with whatever food they liked. Since the plate and the bowls were quite large, the normal serving each student took appeared less. This made them take larger helpings which they could not finish, and it ended up as waste.

A decision was taken to reduce the size of the plates and bowls. A single helping appeared to fill the smaller plates and bowls. Now, students were able to consume what they had in their plates and bowls. This led to a dramatic reduction in wastage.

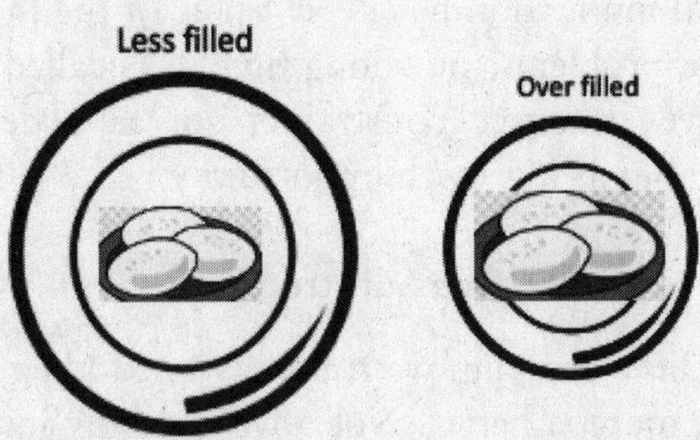

By merely changing the size of the utensils (read: adopting frugal innovation), food wastage was reduced.

The reverse can also happen. To increase sales, retailers increase the size of the shopping trolley. A shopper, while shopping with a larger shopping trolley, feels like they have not shopped enough. So they continue to shop till the trolley looks filled, which results in a larger bill.

Divine Intervention

While studying in school, I visited Delhi. I was advised that the most cost-effective way of exploring the city was by travelling in Delhi Transport Corporation (DTC) buses. They came packed, but I had no difficulty boarding them because I had years of experience of getting into the crowded local trains of Mumbai. As my destination neared, I made my way to the front of the bus to await my stop. Invariably, I would find many people had put their feet on the bonnet, while a few of them were sitting on it. This was distracting the driver, who kept requesting the passengers to keep away from the bonnet, but to no avail. But in some buses, I found people reverently standing away from the bonnet. This made me curious. These bonnets were adorned with colourful pictures of gods and goddess. It restrained people from putting their feet or sitting on the bonnet.

Frugal innovation has been a part of the Indian way of solving problems for a long time. It is called 'jugaad'. It perceives resource constraints not as a debilitating challenge but as a growth opportunity.[67]

6. Innovation through Substruction

Many believe that innovation calls for adding features. After all, more is better. Not always. Many innovations have happened by removing features or components to create something new.[68]

Low-Cost Carrier (LCC)

LCCs have 'subtracted' several features from a full-service airline and created a new market by attracting non-fliers.

- Ticketing agents are 'subtracted' and fliers are directed to book tickets over the Internet.
- Printed tickets have been 'subtracted'. Instead, a soft copy of the ticket is sent to the email address. This eliminates the cost of paper, which was incurred when issuing paper tickets.
- Many airline staff have been 'subtracted' because the flyers are asked to check themselves in.
- Seat allocations have been 'subtracted'. In its place, 'free seating' is permitted. A flier can choose from any of the available empty seats.
- Flight attendants have been 'subtracted' and just enough retained as mandated for the safety of passengers.

Subtraction innovation enabled LCCs to offer brilliant value to fliers at attractive prices, the saving of time, less fatigue at the end of the journey, the prestige associated with flying and more. As a result, they converted non-fliers, and those who used rail and road transport, into flyers.

Apple

Steve Jobs peeled (read: subtracted) away features from the product which he deemed to be either distracting, superfluous or ornamental.[69]

- The CD drive and a range of ports from the MacBook Air.
- The keyboard from mobile phones.
- Unnecessary steps and functions from iPod, iPhone and iPad so that a function could be accessed in no more than three clicks.[70]

Steve Jobs stopped only when there was nothing left to 'peel' away. Now what remained was the essence of the product in its simplest form. At this point, he must have intuitively deduced that the product had attained sophistication. After all, Leonardo da Vinci has described simplicity as the ultimate sophistication.

If 'substruction' innovation is so powerful, then why is 'addition' preferred?

'Simple can be harder than complex,' said Steve Jobs. 'But it's worth it in the end because once you get there, you can move mountains.'[71]

Also, the human brain loves to add. It helped us survive by adding people to the tribe or adding food (read: hoarding) when available.

Professionals resist subtraction innovation because by engaging in it, they are deliberately eliminating their contributions. There will be nothing for them to show for their effort.

7. Invisible Innovation

Netflix can be credited with introducing the world to 'binge watching'. The credit, or the blame, rests at the door of Cinematch, its proprietary recommendation software, which predicts the content viewers are likely to watch and proactively recommends it. When the accuracy of Cinematch is high, then the viewers spend more time (read: binge watch) on Netflix. This increases stickiness and has resulted in the soaring valuation of Netflix.

Cinematch is an apt example of invisible innovation. It is invisible to customers but creates value for them and for Netflix.

iPhone has its proprietary iOS operating system. Uber too has its propriety algorithm, which helps it to match riders with drivers. These proprietary software (read: algorithms) are invisible to users but are at the heart of providing them with delightful experiences. They create value for users and provide competitive advantage to companies owning them.

Invisible innovation involves the creation of operating systems, process simplification, automation or propriety algorithms. It is usually unseen by users and hence is called 'invisible' innovation. It also acts a business moat and hence is a source of competitive advantage for the company.

8. Accidental Innovation

A pharmaceutical company was developing a drug to treat cardiovascular diseases. It contained sildenafil, an active ingredient which dilates the heart's blood vessels. During human trials, a peculiar thing was noticed. When the nurse came to examine the men enrolled in the study, they would find them lying on their stomachs because they were embarrassed by the erection caused by the dilation of blood vessels in the penis. The sildenafil was working—but not in the intended part of the body. Thus was born Viagra, the potency pill,[72] due to accidental innovation.[73]

Chanel No. 5

Madam Coco Chanel commissioned a perfumer, Ernest Beaux, to create a perfume like no other. It took him several months to come up with ten samples. They were numbered one to five and twenty to twenty-four and were presented to Madam Chanel for selection. She selected number five, exclaiming that it was a woman's perfume with 'the scent of a woman'.

The number five sample was the result of a laboratory accident. Beaux's assistant had accidently added a dose of aldehyde in a quantity never used before.

Coco Chanel called her choice Chanel No. 5. Although it owes its birth to an accident, its popularity since its birth has remained undimmed.

Post-It Notes

In 1968, a 3M scientist, Spencer Silver, was striving to develop a super strong adhesive. Accidently, he created a weak adhesive that stuck to surfaces without bonding strongly. He did not see any immediate use for his invention, and nor did 3M, since the adhesive was seen as too weak to be useful. This, despite the wonderful features of this adhesive: it could be stuck on a surface and peeled away without leaving any residue.

It took years of persistence for Post-Its to be accepted as a standard stationery for offices. They are now available in many shapes, sizes and colours in more than 150 countries.

Innovation can't always be planned, but neither can it be termed 'accidental', even though it involves accident. The key is to be prepared for the unexpected.[74]

We can become proficient in accidental innovation by following French chemist and microbiologist Louis Pasteur's advice of being prepared, because chance favours the prepared mind!

9. Disruptive Innovation

Airbnb started by serving an underserved segment, budget travellers, who travelled on a shoestring budget. It offered them a platform to take on rent residences at pocket-friendly prices. In the process, they created a market where none existed and converted non-customers into customers. Established hospitality players did not cater to this segment because they were deemed to be unprofitable to serve. After establishing themselves in this niche market, Airbnb started to move to adjacent markets and up the value chain.

Now Airbnb offers vacation homes and uber luxury offerings with the highest standard of service.[75] Airbnb's market capitalization, which measures the worth of a company in the market and what the investors are willing to pay for it, is more than the combined market capitalization of the three large hotel chains combined—Marriott International, Hilton Worldwide and Hyatt Hotels.[76] On this critical financial parameter, it has dethroned and decimated the well-entrenched top dogs of the hospitality industry.

Netflix

Netflix entered the unprofitable mail-order movie rental business. Blockbuster, the reigning king, did not feel threatened. This enabled Netflix to get a toehold. Only when technology had sufficiently advanced to enable streaming over the Internet did Netflix started to move up the value chain by offering on-demand streaming of content, particularly movies. This model appealed to Blockbuster customers, who deserted it in favour of Netflix. Eventually, Netflix dethroned Blockbuster. In 2010, Blockbuster went bankrupt.[77]

Airbnb and Netflix are prime examples of disruptive innovators who first gain acceptance in the low end of the market (read: lower profit), the segment ignored by dominant market players who are focused on serving the more profitable high-end customers. Once they establish themselves at the lower end of the market, they slowly and covertly move up the value chain, eventually upending the industry leader.

10. Radical (Transformational) Innovation[78]

Oil Lamps and Candles

For centuries, oil lamps and candles provided lighting. Over time, they kept on getting better and brighter. But they could not be improved beyond a point. For that, radical innovation was needed, which meant leaving behind oil lamps and introducing light bulbs.

Transportation

For centuries, horses were the preferred means of transportation. Over time, their speed and stamina improved. As a result, they were able to travel longer distances in less time. But they could not be 'improved' to become as fast as automobiles. For that, radical innovation was needed, which involved jumping the curve. The introduction of automobiles heralded jumping the curve, which resulted in leaving horses behind.

Smartphone

Nokia dominated the handset market. It kept improving its offerings. Each version was marginally better than the previous one. But it could not be improved beyond a point. For that, radical innovation was needed, which involved jumping the curve. Apple jumped the curve by launching iPhone. It created a new product category, smartphones, which changed the world.

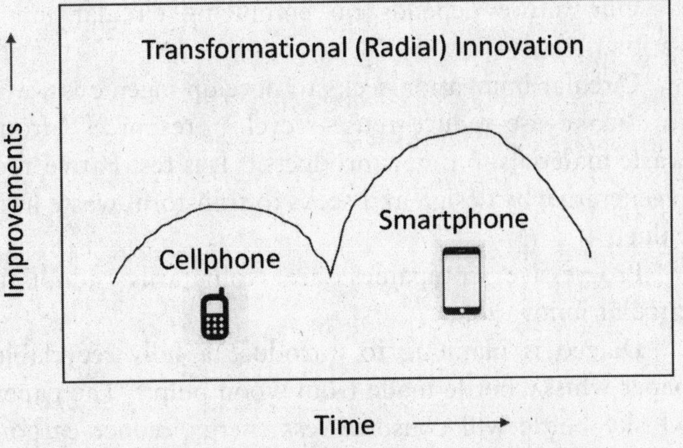

Transformational innovation occurs when the existing product cannot be significantly improved. Or when there is a desire to introduce a radically different product or change the existing rules of the industry. Such cases require jumping the existing curve and starting a new curve, which gives birth to a completely new product category that displaces or makes the existing product obsolete.

11. Circular Innovation

We consume 1.7 times what the earth can produce. This rate of consumption is unsustainable.[79] This situation has arisen due to the widely adopted linear business model which involves 'mining–manufacturing–selling–using–discarding' strategy. This strategy is leading to the dwindling of natural resources at an alarming rate and has resulted in the creation of large number of landfills, which is harmful for the environment.

Our future depends on embracing circular innovation.

Circular innovation seeks to develop ingenious ways to 'make–use–reduce–reuse–recycle' resources from waste materials into new products.[80] It is restorative and regenerative by design and seeks to transform waste into value.

Progressive companies are voluntarily adopting circular innovation.

Diageo is planning to introduce a fully recyclable paper whisky bottle made from wood pulp.[81] The paper whisky bottle will consume less energy, reduce carbon emissions and be more eco-friendly.

The Signal Switch toothbrush is designed with sustainability at its heart. It has interchangeable brush heads coupled with the durable metal handle, which will reduce their virgin plastic use by 95 per cent.

12. Business Model Innovation[82]

A business model defines the way a firm creates, delivers and captures value.[83]

Amazon and Uber adopted innovative business models to dethrone traditional retailers and taxi businesses, respectively. You too can deploy innovative business models to upend competition and give your business a competitive advantage. Here is a partial list of popular business models that have gained wide acceptance.

- Advertising-led business model: The revenue comes not from charging users who are on the platform, but by charging the advertisers who wish to advertise to the users on the platform.
- Pay-per-use business model: The users pay only for the service they use. This makes the service attractive to potential users.
- Freemium business model: The basic features are free. It motivates potential users to sample the product. If they are satisfied, then they must pay to access premium features.
- Subscription business model: Users subscribe to services. The company receives recurring payments at regular intervals while subscribers gain access to a large body of content, at attractive prices.
- Pay-as-you-earn business model: This business model proves to be irresistible to users since they must pay only from the earnings made from using the product or services they have purchased. It eliminates the risk associated with purchasing.
- Outsource business model: Companies can outsource business activities barring those that

are core to their business. This frees up the management's time to focus on the most essential part of the business, which provides them with a competitive advantage.

- Outcome-based business model: Users get billed only when the promised outcome is delivered. This caveat melts away almost all objections that users may have against buying the product.
- High-touch business model: It is adopted to pamper users with high quality services and experiences. It enables brands to command premium pricing.

How Many Types of Innovation Should Be Used?

Apple has concurrently deployed multiple types of innovation, which have turbocharged its business and catapulted it to the league of the world's most valuable companies.

- **Improver Innovation**

In 1964, IBM designed and distributed Simon, a handheld touch screen PDA.[84] The Nokia team developed a phone with a colour touch screen set above a single button. The device could locate a restaurant, play a racing game and order lipstick. Fearing cannibalization, Nokia did not launch it into the market.[85] Simon and the Nokia colour touchscreen phone preceded the launch of the iPhone.

Based on these facts, Apple cannot be labelled as the first mover, but a follower who pursued the improver innovation strategy to take the market by storm by launching the touchscreen-based smartphone.

- **Radical (Transformational) Innovation**

Nokia was the market leader in the handset market. But Nokia's cell phone could not be improved to transform into a smartphone. Apple jumped the cell phone curve and introduced a new curve, the smartphone curve, by launching the iPhone. The world was never the same again.

- **Incremental Innovation**

Since the launch of the iPhone, Apple has been pursuing incremental innovation by launching newer versions at regular intervals and branding them as iPhone 2, 3, etc. In 2021, the iPhone 13 was launched. Each version is marginally better than the previous one and their introduction boosts sales and results in profit improvement. Incremental innovation helps Apple lead the field.

- **Invisible Innovation**

Its propriety iOS, which is invisible to its users, is the reason they are able to deliver a pleasurable experience. It also provided a business moat to Apple.

- **Open Innovation**

Apple provides app developers with resources to develop apps. These apps, available on its iOS platform, make iPhone more useful, versatile and an indispensable part of our life.

- **Circular Innovation**

When users are done with Apple devices, the company is willing to accept them back with the promise of recycling so that precious materials can be saved, and less is extracted from the planet for making new Apple products.[86]

- **Business Model Innovation**
  - High-touch business model: Apple Store pampers its customer with high-quality experiences and seeks to mend strained relationships caused due to the malfunctioning of an Apple device.
  - Subscription business model: Apple Music, Apple TV+ have embraced this business model.
  - Direct-to-customer business model: Apple also makes it products available on its e-commerce site, Apple Store Online, so that its customers can directly order them.

Amazon

Amazon is concurrently powered by multiple types of innovation, which have propelled it into the league of the world's most valuable companies:

- **Radical (Transformational) Innovation**
  - One-click ordering is an easy and fast way to order, and it saves time.
  - The Amazon Dash button lets customers reorder household items by the simple process of pressing a button.
  - Amazon Echo allows customers to place an order on Amazon using voice commands.

- The Amazon Go retail store has no salespeople and no checkout counters. Shoppers must help themselves, pay and go!
- Amazon Air aims to deliver by drone in 20 minutes.

- **Open Innovation**

Amazon Studio is engaged in producing original content. It relies on open (crowdsourcing) innovation to increase its success rate. It encourages people to submit stories. It also crowdsources feedback from customers on stories that have been selected.[87]

- **Circular Innovation**

Amazon is committed to reducing its environmental footprint by recycling initiatives in their own operations and for their customers.[88]

- **Business Model**
  - Razor blade business model: Amazon sells Kindle (read: razor) at attractive prices. But it makes money when people buy books (read: blade) on their Kindle.
  - Advertising-based business model: Amazon charges advertisers to display advertisements to its users.
  - Subscription-based business model: Amazon Prime offers subscription plans to its users.

- Pay-as-you-go: Amazon Web (AWS) expects to be paid only for services used by users.

You too should put into play multiple types of innovation to turbocharge your business.

Innovation Enablers—for Individuals

Here is a curated list of pointers which will enable you to become proficient in innovation:

- Shoot the breeze: 'Be willing to take time to float, be curious and do not be afraid to experiment.'[89]
- Block distractions: Do not spend an inordinately large amount of time on emails, answering messages or succumbing to digital distractions. For that:
  - Turn off notifications.
  - Keep your devices away from you. In fact, in another room.
  - Unsubscribe from all text alerts and newsletters except the most critical ones.
  - Put your phone on airplane mode.
  - Say no to unimportant meetings, learn the art of delegating and do not allow yourself to be interrupted.
- Block time to think and reflect.
- Be mindful of your environment.
- Strive to be proactive, persistent, gritty and resilient.
- Display boundless enthusiasm.
- Do not be harsh on yourself. Avoid being conscious about your own assessment of your shortcoming and failures.

- Entertain positive thoughts. It spurs your innovative juices. Do not entertain negative and debilitating thoughts. Otherwise, your mind will be filled with fear and anxiety, which in turn will cripple the brain and impede its ability to think freely and make connections.
- Take calculated risks, not reckless risks. Seek feedback. Make midway corrections based on it.
- Always be ready to pivot.
- Subscribe to the mantra 'fail early, fail fast'.

Innovation Enablers—for Organizations

Innovative organizations exhibit five key behaviour traits:[90]

- 'They always assume there's a better way to do things.
- They focus on deeply understanding the customer's stated and unstated needs and desires.
- They collaborate across and beyond the organization, actively cross-pollinating ideas.
- They recognize that success requires experimentation, rapid iteration and frequent failure.
- They empower people to take considered risks, voice dissenting opinions and seek needed resources.'

Diversity Matters

Let me invite John Stuart Mill, philosopher and economist, to convince you: It is hardly possible to overrate the value of placing human beings in contact with persons dissimilar to themselves, and with modes of thought and action unlike those with which they are familiar. In the present age, it is one of the primary sources of progress.[91]

Countless Experiments

Experimentation is the first step towards being innovative. Says Jeff Bezos, 'If you double the number of experiments you do per year, you're going to double your inventiveness.'

Reward Failures

'We reward failure,' said Jack Welch, former head of GE, 'because doing otherwise would only squelch daring.' General Motor's Charles Kettering, regarded as second only to Thomas Edison as America's leading inventor mogul, liked to say that a good research man failed each time but the last one. 'He treats his failures as practice shots,' he said. Kettering noted that he himself had been wrong 99.9 per cent of the time. What every educated person needed to learn, he felt, was 'that it's not a disgrace to fail, and that you must analyse each failure to find its cause. You must learn how to fail intelligently. Failing is one of the greatest arts in the world. One fails forward toward success.'[92]

To encourage intelligent failure, don't judge people strictly by results but by the quality of their efforts. This will encourage people to take intelligent business risks without also risking their compensation or their careers.[93]

If you are still not convinced, then let me invite Thomas Watson to convenience you. He believed that 'The fastest way to succeed is to double your failure rate.'

You too can reward failure by instituting a monthly award which is given to a team or a person who has failed while pursuing innovation. The 'winner', in their acceptance speech, must narrate the lessons they have learnt from the failure.

Slack Time

Google grants 20 per cent percent of time to Googlers to 'engage in exploring or working on projects that show no promise of paying immediate dividends but might reveal big opportunities down the road'.[94] The has resulted in blockbuster innovations like Gmail and Google Maps.[95] You too should grant your employees time to pursue things about which they are passionate. This time can also be devoted by employees to discussions with colleagues. This ensure that there is cross-pollination of ideas across the company.

Encourage People to Voice Their Opinions

You can do this by posing open-ended questions like:

- What do you think?
- How can we solve this problem?
- Can you tell us a better way of solving this problem?

Seek Actionable Feedback

Elon Musk tries to seek actional feedback: 'I ask specifically what I am doing wrong. And if I've asked that a few times of people, then they will start automatically telling me without me having to always ask the question. So, like for the Model S, I said I don't really want to know what's right about the car. I want to know what's wrong with the car.'[96]

Harper Lee had hit the nail on the head when she said that many receive advice and feedback, only the wise profit from it. Be wise and actively seek advice and feedback from your well-wishers on what is wrong. Listen to it with an open mind. Also, seek their suggestions for correcting what's wrong. It can help you in making your product better.

Innovation Derailers[97]

Here are a few things that can derail innovation. Guard against these:

- Intolerance towards failure. Innovation requires experimentation, which often results in failure. If an organization frowns upon failures, then people will refrain from engaging in experimentation (read: innovation).
- The incorrect belief that innovation is the responsibility of R&D or the marketing department. Maybe it was true earlier. Not now. Innovation is the responsibility of everyone in the company. It can originate from any person. In the case of Walmart, an innovative idea, greeters, originated from a humble store worker.

Walmart wanted to be perceived as a friendly store while curbing shrinkage (read: shoplifting). A store employee suggested having greeters at the entrance. They would greet the shoppers and their presence would deter shoplifting. Since the 1980s, greeters have been a part of Walmart culture.[98]

- Silo thinking and protecting the turf: People protect their turf and engage in silo thinking. They are like a frog in a well. Smash the silos to smithereens and lay the foundation of a borderless organization. Let ideas flow and discussions happen unhindered across the organization!
- Innovation is an event: Not true. It is a continuous process. Every idea, no matter how ingenious or successful, will eventually need to be replaced with a new one. The world's most innovative companies, like Apple, do not rest on their laurels. Therefore, iPhone, since its launch in 2017, has been continuously improved by launching a new version at regular intervals.
- Competitor obsession: It is erroneous to believe that competitors should be crushed. It is flawed thinking. A company is not in the business of crushing its competitors but of serving its customers. Moreover, competitor-obsessed companies tend to be followers, not leaders.
- Wedded to 'Not Invented Here' (NIH) syndrome. Such companies are obsessed with fiercely protecting their IPs. They pursue innovation within the four walls of the company. Most of the time, it results in lacklustre innovation. After all, the best talent may not be residing within the company!

Benefits of Innovation

There are many. Here are but a few of them.

- Aids in commanding price premium.
- Turbocharges growth.
- Results in margin expansion.
- Creates lust for brand.
- Blindsides competition.
- Lowers cost without compromising on quality.
- Throws up new and imaginative business models.
- Keeps business in robust health.
- Offers sustainable way of doing business.
- Keeps existing customers and attracts new ones.
- Re-energizes business.
- Re-imagines business.

Postscript

During British colonial rule, parts of India were infested with cobras. To eradicate this menace, an innovative scheme was announced. People were offered a reward for producing a dead cobra. This motivated the people to kill cobras and claim the rewards.

The population of cobras started to shrink and, with it, the opportunity for making money. This made enterprising people breed cobras.

When the authorities became aware of it, they scrapped the reward. Now, people were left with worthless cobras. They let them loose. This resulted in an even larger numbers of cobras. This phenomenon came to be referred to as the 'cobra effect'. It serves as a warning to not come up with an innovative solution that leads to the creation of a bigger problem than the one it sought to solve.[99]

Innovation in a Nutshell

Innovation = Creativity X Execution X Profit

Types of Innovation

1. Incremental Innovation
2. Improver Innovation
3. Reverse Innovation
4. Open Innovation
5. Frugal Innovation
6. Subtraction Innovation
7. Invisible (Process) Innovation
8. Accidental Innovation
9. Disruptive Innovation
10. Radical (Transformational) Innovation
11. Circular Innovation
12. Business Model Innovation

Innovation Enablers

Individual

1. Block distraction.
2. Be mindful of your environment.
3. Be proactive, persistent, gritty.
4. Display boundless enthusiasm.
5. Do not be harsh on yourself.
6. Endeavour to be happy.
7. Entertain positive thoughts.
8. Take calculated, not reckless risk .
9. Be curious. Block time to think and reflect.

Organization

- Assume there is a better way to do things.
- Understand customer's needs & desires.
- Collaborate & cross-pollinate ideas.
- Empower people.
- Seek dissenting opinions.
- Celebrate failures.
- Offer slack time to people.
- Encourage people to voice their opinion.
- Do countless experimentation.
- Tolerate failures.

Innovation Derailers

1. Intolerance towards failures.
2. Incorrect belief that innovation is the responsibility of R&D/ marketing.
3. Silo thinking and turf protection.
4. Innovation is an event.
5. Competitor obsessed.
5. Wedded to 'Not Invented Here' (NIH) syndrome.

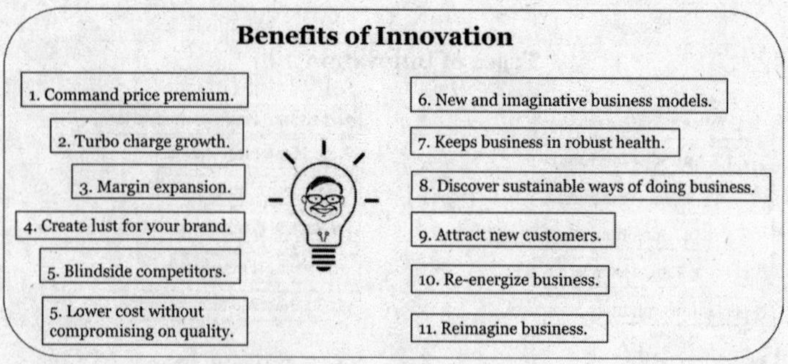

Skill 3

Critical Thinking

Critical thinkers challenge traditions, question assumptions and defy norms. They reason through logic, filter out biases, possess diversity of thoughts and do not fall victim to heuristics. This enables them to arrive at better judgements, think deeply and become skilled problem solvers.

In 1983, Steve Jobs told his team, 'It's better to be a pirate than join the navy.'[100] He did not want his team to wear an eye patch and come to the office. Instead, he wanted them to acquire the mindset of a pirate and defy norms, challenge tradition and question assumptions. By following his own advice, he upended many industries.

1. Music: If we liked a song from an album, the complete album had to be bought. Jobs challenged this 'norm' and made it possible for us to buy just a song on iTunes. The music industry was never the same again.
2. Retailing: Historically, retail stores sold products. Apple Stores challenged this tradition by re-imagining it as a place not for selling Apple products, but for building and repairing broken relationships with its customers and trying to make people's lives better.[101] As a result, Apple Retail garnered the highest revenue per square foot in the world.
3. Smartphone: The iPhone challenged tradition, norms and inviolable assumptions of industries and in due course, upended them.[102]

    - Personal computers (PCs) sat on our desks and provided us access to the Internet. iPhones put the Internet into our hands and reduced our dependence on PCs.
    - Telecom businesses were built around voice. The iPhone compelled telecom providers to transform into data communication companies. They added features like information and entertainment services and become conduits for multiple types of data services for their customers.
    - Movies were watched in theatres, and TV was viewed by sitting in front of it. The iPhone made watching movies and viewing content possible anytime, anywhere and even while

on the move. This compelled major movie and TV studios to expand their distribution methods to include download and streaming services to mobile devices.

- Games were either delivered by way of game consoles, a PC or a dedicated handheld device. iPhones expanded the market for mobile games by creating an entirely new category of touch-based gameplay.

Arguably, Steve Jobs passed on the 'pirate' way of thinking to Elon Musk. He and his team challenged the norm that online money transfer was safe between institutions, not individuals.[103] PayPal, a digital payment platform, enabled individuals to safely transfer money among themselves.[104] In February 2021, it was valued at over $300 billion.[105]

Next, he challenged the assumption that automobiles pollute by launching Tesla, an EV that offers clean transportation. In July 2020, Tesla became the most valuable car company on the planet.[106]

In recent times, he has turned his attention to space and is challenging traditions, assumptions and norms again:

- Why can't humans be a multi-planetary species?
- Why can't humans aspire to colonize Mars?
- Why must space travel occur on a fixed schedule and be paid for by the public? Why can it not be privately funded? Why can't rockets be reusable?

This led him to establish SpaceX. In July 2020, Morgan Stanley valued SpaceX at over $100 billion, describing it as best poised to be a leading player in the emerging space economy.[107]

How can Steve Jobs and Elon Musk be best described? As critical thinkers par excellence!

What is Critical Thinking?

There is little agreement on what critical thinking is.[108] But there is a consensus that it involves:

- Challenging tradition, which is the way of doing things and is passed on from person to person or generation to generation.
- Questioning assumptions, which are accepted as true or as certain to happen, without proof.
- Defying norms, which are regarded as normal or typical.
- Reasoning through logic.
- Questioning data, information and knowledge.
- Analysing issues objectively by asking probing questions.
- Filtering out biases.
- Not falling victim to heuristics.
- Possessing diversity of thoughts.

Critical thinking helps people become better thinkers, arrive at better judgements, make logical and superior quality decisions, and become skilled in problem-solving, because they are not encumbered by cognitive biases, crippling emotions, the excuse of 'too little time', unhealthy ego and prejudices and ceding control to the reptilian brain.

Are Critical Thinking and Intelligence Quotient (IQ) the Same?

IQ refers to higher-level abilities such as abstract reasoning and mental representation: word fluency, verbal comprehension, numerical ability.

Here is the dampener: you can have high IQ but still make poor judgements. It 'consists not only of applying evidence and rationality to decisions, but also the ability to recognize when they are insufficient for the problem at hand'.[109] People with a high IQ have a good brain but may not make good judgements.

Why Is It Difficult to Be a Critical Thinker?

We like normalcy, sameness, predictability and familiarity. But critical thinkers challenge sameness, predictability and familiarity. These traits do not come naturally to us. The good news is that critical thinking is a learnt skill and can be improved through training and practice.

Strategies for Becoming Proficient in Critical Thinking

It entails becoming proficient at challenging timeless traditions, questioning written-in-stone assumptions and defying established norms. Let us unpack each one:

1. Challenge Tradition

Scoring a triple century, 300 or more runs, in Test cricket, is difficult. More so if it must be scored in a day.

Indian Test cricketer Virender Sehwag decided to challenge this 'traditional' thinking, a belief that had been passed from one generation of cricketers to the next. He reasoned: in a Test match, the opposition must bowl a minimum of ninety overs in a day. Let me assume that ten overs will be good, and they will be maiden (overs where no runs are scored). That leaves me with eighty overs. If I can hit a four in each of the eighty overs, then in a day, I can score a triple century.

He is the only Indian cricketer to have scored a triple century twice: 309 against Pakistan in Multan and 319 against South Africa in Chennai. The latter was the fastest triple century in Test cricket, with 300 off just 278 balls.

What did Virender Sehwag intuitively do? He challenged tradition through simple reasoning and in the process, transformed into one of the most destructive batsmen that the game of cricket has seen.

- **Wrestling**

Wrestler Mahavir Singh Phogat's dream of winning a medal for India remained unfulfilled. Instead of abandoning it, he decided to fulfil it through his yet unborn son. But this dream was also shattered when he was blessed with two daughters.

One day, luck smiled on him when he received a complaint from parents that his daughters had thrashed their boys.

It was a moment of serendipity for Phogat. He realized that he had fallen victim to a long-standing tradition—that only men could wrestle! He challenged this tradition and began training his daughters to become wrestlers. Results followed and at the 2009 Commonwealth Championships, both his daughters won gold medals for India.[110]

When traditions are challenged, only then can the mental barriers that prevent us from progressing be breached.

Have I Challenged Tradition?

I began my career in the alcoholic beverages industry. The hallowed tradition of the industry dictated that brand equity was built through lifestyle advertising evoking glamour, recreation, vitality, risk or daring.

We challenged this traditional thinking by posing a question to ourselves: why can alcoholic beverage brands not be marketed as a solution to people's problems? The 'problem-solution' strategy is widely adopted by FMCG companies to sell their brands. A detergent bar promises to work on dirty clothes (the problem) and make them sparkle (the solution).

We uncovered a problem faced by connoisseurs. While they were having a 'good evening', their concern for the next morning was 'How will I attend office the next day?' Or, 'How will I make the presentation the next day?'

We addressed this problem by launching a whisky with the promise of 'Good Mornings After Great Evenings'. It struck a chord with the connoisseurs, and they gave the brand a thumbs up.

2. Question Assumptions

Till 1954, it was assumed to be true, although there was no proof, that running a mile under four minutes was impossible. Roger Bannister did not allow this written-in-stone assumption to act as a mental barrier. He demonstrated that when assumptions are put to the test, they can fall like nine pins. On 6 May 1954, he busted the four-mile barrier on a cold day, on a wet track, before a crowd of just a few thousand people at a small meet in Oxford, England.

Human evolution did not gather pace after Bannister broke the barrier. But his performance told other runners that this feat was doable. With that confidence, when this barrier was approached then, it was conquered again and again.[111]

Just forty-six days later, John Landy, an Australian runner, not only broke the barrier again, but bettered Bannister's record. Then 'a year later, three runners broke the four-minute barrier in a single race. Over the last century, more than thousands of runners have conquered a barrier that had once been hopelessly out of reach.'[112]

- **Light bulb**

'The development of the earliest lanterns and light bulbs was based on the assumption that "light is created by burning something." Once this box was established, engineers innovated by trying different materials, such as various wicks or oils, to improve the quality and duration of the light. Only when Thomas Edison shifted his, and the world's, perception to embrace a new box — that light is created by *preventing* something (the filament) from burning — could he then create the first incandescent light bulb,' say Alan Iny and Luc de Brabandere.[113]

3. Defying Norms

High jumper Dick Fosbury did not perform well during high-school competitions when he jumped using the straddle-roll jumping style. This style of jumping was the prevailing norm and was regarded as the normal or typical way of jumping. In this technique, the jumper, while crossing the bar, had their face down and their legs straddling the bar.

Fosbury decided to defy this norm and jumped with his back facing the bar. By going over the bar backwards, raising his hips and then kicking his legs up and over it, he cleared the bar. This technique came to be known as the Fosbury Flop.

In the 1968 Summer Olympics, held in Mexico City, Fosbury used his new and innovative technique of jumping, the Fosbury Flop, to take the gold medal and changed the way high jumpers jumped.[114]

The Fosbury Flop was dubbed an aberration because it defied the norm. But soon, criticisms faded away as the world embraced the Fosbury Flop.

How to Challenge Hallowed Traditions, Inscribed-in-Stone Assumptions and Prevailing Norms

Here are a few pointers:

- Frame questions which challenge traditions, assumptions and norms:
    - What are the long-held traditions?
    - What are the assumptions?
    - What are the prevailing norms?
    - Are they valid under the present conditions?
- Pose a 'challenging' question:
    - Why should it be so?
- Seek the opinion of others by posing open-ended questions:
    - What do you think?
    - Can you add to my thinking?

    - What have we overlooked?
- Seek additional information:
    - Can you tell me something that I do not know?
    - Can you tell me something new?
- Being open to suggestions, new ideas and information which may be at variance with what you expect.
- Engage in self-reflection:
    - Is there another way of doing it?
    - After completing a task, pose a question to yourself: If I had to do it all over again, how would I approach it? What improvements would I make?
- Think for yourself. Do not let others guide you. Question their assumptions and conclusions.
- Engage in deliberate (conscious) thinking instead of making snap judgements. This habit will help you to be alert.

Barriers in the Path of Becoming Proficient in Critical Thinking

Forewarned is forearmed!

Below is a list of barriers which can trip you as you embark on the journey of becoming proficient in critical thinking.

- Cognitive biases
- Crippling emotions
- Too little time
- Allowing the reptilian (lizard) brain to seize control
- Permitting unhealthy ego to have a free run

- Allowing prejudice to colour your decision-making
- Making unethical decisions

To gain a deeper understanding of them, let us unpack each one.

1. Cognitive Biases

I had an enviable track record of successfully launching new products. Later, when I joined a start-up and launched a brand, it failed. I could not stomach the failure.

Unknown to me, I had fallen victim to cognitive bias. It occurs due to our brain's attempt to simplify information processing.[115] It can also be looked upon as a simple procedure that helps us find adequate, though often imperfect, answers to difficult questions.[116] It helped us survive when we were hunter-gathers. But not anymore. Most such biases are now ineffective, bordering on harmful. Coming back to me, here are a few cognitive biases to which I had inadvertently fallen victim.

- Overconfidence bias:[117] I had overestimated my ability, talent and intellect.
- Dunning-Kruger effect:[118] My past success had made me believe that I was smarter and more capable than I was.
- Confirmation bias: I looked for data and evidence which confirmed my beliefs that products launched under my watch had succeeded because of me. Indeed, there were many data points to support this belief. But had I looked deeper, I would have found many more data points, facts and evidence to indicate otherwise. Here are a few of them:

- Presence of in-house R&D and manufacturing facilities, which facilitated development and manufacturing of products.
- Presence of an elaborate distribution system which ensured that the new product was extensively distributed and occupied prime position, at eye level, in retail stores.
- Presence of a well-trained and disciplined sales team who educated the channel partners about the product's unique selling proposition.
- Financial appetite to support the new products with handsome advertising and sales promotion budgets to create awareness, interest and desire among customers.

I realized then that my past successes could not be attributed entirely to me. There were many factors that contributed to the success. Finally, luck, too, played a critical role in my success.

By being wilfully blind to these cognitive biases, I ensured that I had egg on my face.

The hallmark of cognitive bias is that we are blind to our own biases, while believing that everybody else suffers from them. It prevents us from becoming proficient at critical thinking.

How Can We Outsmart Our Own Biases?[119]

- Acknowledge it and refrain from self-certifying that you are not biased. It would be wise to remember that everyone is biased.
- Be open to being challenged.

  - Begin with challenging your thinking by puncturing holes in your arguments. In short, play your own devil's advocate.
  - Invite professional dissenters to critique your thinking and decisions. This will help you discover flaws in your arguments which escaped your attention.
  - Invite external viewpoints. They are likely to offer a balanced perspective.
- Look at things from opposing viewpoints.
- When faced with a problem, make a rule that you will have at least three solutions to choose from before finalizing one. This will help you arrive at a better decision.
- After a solution has been chosen, put a hypothetical condition on it—that it is not available. This will force you to think for one more solution.
- Refrain from falling in love with your idea or getting emotionally attached to it. Then you will have a pathological desire to make it win at all costs.
- Encourage your team members to freely express their opinion. You should actively listen to them with the intent of understanding what is being communicated. Do not interrupt them when they are speaking. If you must speak, then be the last speaker. In this way, you will get many different perspectives.

If all this appears convoluted, then compile a list of past decisions that you have made where you were a victim of cognitive bias and the impact it had on your career. In my case, the list is long and the consequences on my career were adverse. Constantly referring to it tempered my proclivity to falling victim yet another time to cognitive biases.

If this too seems arduous, then try to be in the company of critical thinkers and be open to being challenged by them.

2. Crippling Emotions

When we attempt a new task, the spectre of failure gives rise to crippling emotion. It gets aggravated by two self-defeating questions which we pose to ourselves.

a. What will people think if I fail?
b. Failure will irreparably smear my reputation.

The answers we give ourselves give rise to crippling emotions and paralyse us into inaction. This prevents us from becoming good critical thinkers.

How I Overcame Crippling Emotions

As president of J.K. Helene Curtis, I wanted to reimagine the deodorant segment. This involved challenging the prevailing tradition, assumptions and norms of the deodorant segment. This thought filled me with fear, dread and anxiety. This category was dominated by MNCs and I thought to myself: if it could be reimagined, then by now the MNCs would have done it.

To reign in the crippling emotions, I decided to work concurrently on three fronts:

- **Draw upon my experience:** In the 1990s, while working in the alcoholic beverages industry, we discovered that connoisseurs enjoyed their drink. On reaching home, when they got close to their lady love, they faced rejection. Their mouth odour put off their companion. The rejection greatly upset our connoisseurs. Based on this insight, we re-launched a vodka with the promise 'It Leaves No Trace' and therefore, you can come a little closer! Sales of the vodka brand headed north.

This experience gave me confidence that when odour is reduced or eliminated, then customers vote for the product with their wallet.

My belief was further strengthened when my research indicated that a famous brand of toothpaste had carved out a dominant market share by promising customers freedom from bad breath.

- **Data and statistics:** 65 per cent of Indians are below the age of twenty-five. Young people of opposite genders want to come closer and body odour (BO) drives them apart. This made me frame a hypothesis: Why not launch a mood-enhancing perfume at pocket-friendly prices? The mood-enhancing perfume would boost the mood of young people and enable them to come closer.
- **Crowdsourcing for validation of the idea:** I tested the hypothesis among young people by posing a question: Do you want your companion to come closer? The answer, almost always, was a resounding yes!

The insights gave me the confidence to reimagine the 'deodorant' as 'perfume'!

Now fear, dread and anxiety were replaced with self-belief, courage and confidence.

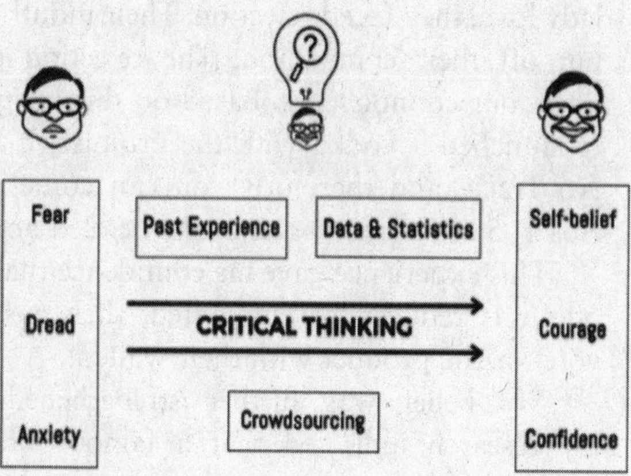

Armed with these positive feelings, Park Avenue deodorant was re-launched as 'perfume'. The sales skyrocketed. The industry took notice and fast-followed (read: imitated) us. Today, 'perfume' has become a generic category benefit.

3. Too Little Time

Confucius had advised an aeon ago: Do not be desirous of having things done quickly. Do not look at small advantages. The desire to have things done quickly prevents their being done thoroughly. Looking at small advantages prevents great affairs from being accomplished and also acts a barrier for critical thinking because under the guise of too little time, sameness prevails, tradition continues and assumptions go unchallenged.

But our sales team decided to turn a blind eye towards this sagacious advice.

Too Little Time to Achieve Sales Target

During the last week of every month, we heard a constant refrain coming from the sales team: Sir, there is too little left to achieve the sales target. We need a scheme!

We fell for these cleverly camouflaged blackmail tactics. After all, we also wanted to achieve 100 per cent of our monthly sales target.

'Too little time' acts as a barrier to critical thinking because when accosted with it, we tend to succumb to it and come up with a 'band-aid' solution. As a result, the problem remains unresolved, and it continues to raise its ugly head time and again.

Steps Taken to Overcome the Excuse of 'Too Little Time'

We decided to tackle this barrier to critical thinking by building redundancy in the system and putting in place a process which eliminated it from the root.

- The company Annual Plan was drawn up based on a sales 'budget'. But we gave our sales team a sales 'target'. It was 10 per cent more than the sales budget. In this way, we built a 10 per cent redundancy into the sales budget. Even if there was a minor slippage in the sales target, we were still able to achieve our annual sales budget.
- Earlier, the sales target would be divided into twelve months (read: twelve sales cycles of roughly thirty days) and the sales team was expected to achieve the sales target each month. We marginally

shortened each sales cycle from thirty days to twenty-seven days. Now, instead of twelve sales cycles of thirty days each, we had thirteen sales cycles, each of approximately twenty-seven days, to achieve the annual sales 'target'.

We added one additional sales cycle to make good any sales shortfall. The extra sales cycle gave us confidence that we would achieve our annual sales 'budget'.

- Earlier, during the monthly sales review, we did the post-mortem of the month that had just ended. Now, we moved to a weekly review process and shifted our focus from reviewing 'sales' numbers to focusing on 'quality of sales'. This made the sales team focus on the process of getting sales and this, in turn, made them proactive, not reactive.

These steps ensured that we did not succumb to the blackmail threat of 'too little time'. Nor did the sales team use this excuse to extract schemes from us.

Aircraft Cockpit and Checklist

The aviation industry must have must have realized that the safety of aircraft could be jeopardized if the pre-flight checks were not earnestly conducted due to the banal excuse of 'too little time'.

Therefore, the cockpit is designed to be operated by two pilots who must go through the checklist. One reads from the checklist, while the other confirms. The aircraft cannot take off unless this process is completed.

This design of the cockpit and the process put in place eliminates the excuse of too little time and makes flying the safest way of travelling.

4. Allowing the Reptilian (Lizard) Brain to Seize Control

The reptilian brain, also called the lizard brain, is the oldest and most primitive part of our brain. When faced with a threat, it is instinctively activated and provokes the 'fight or flight' response. Both these responses are anathema for critical thinking. The reptilian brain must therefore be kept on a tight leash.

During my career, I tried to keep my reptilian brain on a tight leash. It prevented me from wading into needless controversy.

Blue Riband Duet

In the 1990s, Blue Riband Gin was under my charge. A decision was taken to extend the brand name to the premix gin category by launching Blue Riband Duet (BRD), with the promise of 'Gin and Lime Pre-Mixed to Perfection'.

To piggyback on the lineage of the mother brand, Blue Riband, we decided to use the same clear bottle. It offered another advantage: the clear bottle would enable people to notice the mildly yellowish colour of the BRD blend and give them the confidence that 'lime' had indeed been added.

A meeting was scheduled to present the strategy of BRD to the CEO. I made a compelling case that BRD would take the market by storm and presented a fully dressed bottle of BRD, filled with the actual blend, for his approval. I was awaiting an avalanche of accolades.

My CEO surveyed the bottle and said in a matter-of-fact voice that the colour of the blend reminded him of urine.

It was as if Mike Tyson had punched my face. I could sense a feeling of anger, pain and hurt rising in me. It was an advance sign that my reptilian brain[120] was all set to take control of me. It is activated when we are attacked or sense a threat. When it is in control, our power of rational thinking is impaired. I was heading in that direction and wanted to tell my CEO, in no uncertain terms, that he did not know even the 'm' of marketing. Had I done that, I would have given free rein to my reptilian brain. It would have led to a full-blown conflict, and I would have found myself in hot water.

I took a sip of water and a few deep breaths. It had a calming effect on the fight or flight response and on my brain. When the brain is calm, it takes control back from the reptilian brain and hands it over to our rational and thinking faculties. My rational brain was gradually taking back control.

I critically thought about his comment and reviewed the colour of the blend, considering his comment. Now, it reminded me of urine too. If customers got a similar feeling, the brand would die a premature death. I decided to take a poll among the people in the room. They too held the same view as the CEO.

On impulse, I suggested that the Blue Riband bottle be frosted. That would make the bottle translucent, and would effectively camouflage the yellow tinge of the blend. This solution proved to be cost-effective and eco-friendly.

Bottle suppliers of Blue Riband gin charged us a price premium to supply a clear bottle, devoid of any visible defect on the bottle. This entailed a high rejection rate. We called the bottle suppliers and told them, 'Take the rejected Blue Riband bottles and frost them. Then supply them to us for bottling BRD.' The cost of the bottles for both Blue Riband gin and Blue Riband Duet came down—without in any way compromising on the quality.

BRD received a rousing response in the market. The frosted look of BRD also came in for praise. It happened because I was able to keep my reptilian brain on a tight leash and was able think critically to make a better judgement and solve a problem.

Advice for Keeping Reptilian (Lizard) Brain in Check

- Take deep breaths and sip water. It will calm your brain. When the brain is calm, it takes back control from the reptilian brain and hands it over to our rational and thinking faculties.
- Do not allow System 1 thinking, which is automatic, intuitive and requires no effort, to take control of your responses. If it does, then make a conscious effort to hand over control to System 2 thinking, which is deliberate and effortful.

Should Control Ever Be Handed Over to the Reptilian Brain?

Only when faced with life-threating situations. When the threat recedes, let the rational mind take back control, so that you can think critically to arrive at a better judgement or solve a problem better.

5. Permitting Unhealthy Ego to Have a Free Run

A new brand was launched. The boss had taken a vow to make it a success. An attractive scheme was offered to the distributors. This encouraged them to place orders. In the inaugural month, the company recorded good sales. A wave of happiness swept through the company.

As the month ended, grim news started to trickle in. Distributors refused to place new orders, saying that retailers were not placing repeat orders.

The boss analysed the situation and announced a scheme for retailers, with a caveat that only the stocks that moved from distributor to retailer would be eligible for the scheme. The strategy ensured that even in the second month, we recorded good sales. In the company, a belief started to gain ground that the new brand was making a place for itself in the market.

The third month brought more distressing news. Now, both channel partners, the distributors and the retailers, were not buying stock because customers were not buying.

When this news reached the boss, his ego would not allow him to admit that the brand was showing signs of failure. He decided to prop up the brand with an attractive consumer offer.

This made the distributors and retailers buy the 'consumer offer' stock.

As a result, the company recorded good sales even in the third month. The feeling in the company was jubilant.

The fourth month bought bad tidings: sales continued to be weak. If earlier it was the boss's ego at stake, now it was his ego and his pride. This made the boss dig in his heels and resolve to make the brand a success. Result: good money was poured into propping up a 'failed' brand.

It is only when there was a change of leadership, and unhealthy ego and false pride were taken out of decision-making, that the truth emerged: the brand had failed. It was withdrawn and the company had to take a huge write-off.

What Traits Did the Boss Display?

He allowed his unhealthy ego to be in control, which is tantamount to allowing a bad dictator to take decisions on his behalf. During his reign, critical thinking is given a pass. Finally, when the reign of the bad dictator ended, it made the boss appear in a poor light and left him professionally bruised.

How to Rein In Unhealthy Ego?

Here are a few tips that that can help you rein in your unhealthy ego:

- Unhealthy ego gives birth to false pride, which prevents us from accepting our mistakes. In fact, we continue to defend a bad decision (read: mistake). Accept your mistakes, learn from them and take a pledge not to repeat them.
- We do not have a monopoly over good ideas. But our unhealthy ego insists on making our ideas

win. It is good for our ego but bad for our learning and growth.

I checked my proclivity for falling victim to this malice by posing a question to my team after arriving at a decision or solving a problem: Does anyone have a better idea for arriving at a better decision or solving the problem? Most of the time, they did. When we implemented their ideas, the results were better. Since it was their idea, therefore they put their best foot forward to make it a success. I appeared taller in the eyes of the world.

- Have diversity of opinions. Expand your horizon by expanding your circle of friends and acquaintances. Do not restrict your engagement only to people who think like you.
- Learn to give credit to your team and refrain from gobbling it up yourself.
- Empower your team to make decisions.

If all this sounds abstruse, then follow the solution proposed by Albert Einstein: more knowledge, less ego and less knowledge, more ego. Become knowledgeable!

6. Allowing Prejudice to Colour Your Decision-Making

Joanne Rowling was newly divorced and was struggling to make ends meet. Although besieged by misfortunes, she decided to start work on a novel that she had been outlining for five years. This resulted in the manuscript of *Harry Potter and the Sorcerer's Stone*. Twelve different publishing houses rejected it before Bloomsbury accepted it. But they were apprehensive about whether a women writer would appeal to young boys. They recommended she use a gender-neutral name. She chose to add her middle name, Kathleen, and the book was released under the name J.K. Rowling.[121] Since its publication, *Harry Potter* has won the hearts of young boys and girls alike.

Were the publishers prejudiced against women writers appealing to young boys? The truthful answer would be yes!

Prejudice is bad. It influences people to behave in a discriminatory manner and prevents them from becoming dexterous in critical thinking.

Critical thinkers control their prejudice and arrive at better judgements by boldly facing this inconvenient truth.

Selection of Musicians

A symphony wanted to select the best musicians. But they accepted an inconvenient truth: that there was prejudice against women musicians. This ensured that only male musicians made the cut, not necessarily the best musicians. To overcome this 'prejudice', they decided to hold the audition 'behind the curtain'.

An eclectic selection panel was assembled in an auditorium, where the aspiring candidates were invited to display their musical talent. The panel members were given details about each candidate—except that the name and gender were replaced with alphabets. Each alphabet was invited to showcase their talent. But there was another twist—the candidates performed behind the curtain and the panel members gave marks based purely on the musical talent, unbiased by gender. When the result was declared, women musicians too found a place in the final list.

When prejudice is curbed, if not eliminated, from decision-making, then it activates critical thinking, which results in better judgements and sound decision-making.

7. Making Unethical Decisions

The financial year was ending. As a team, we wanted to end the year with 100 per cent achievement of our sales budget.

As if on cue, the sales head walked into my room: 'Sir, Canteen Stores Department (CSD) have issued a large purchase order (PO).' With this, we were sure to surpass our annual sales budget.

Disappointment awaited us when we physically received the PO. The order had to be dispatched after 15 April. This put us in a bind: our financial year (FY) closed on 31 March and as per existing norms; we only recognized sales when the goods physically left our godowns. If CSD had specifically instructed us in writing to dispatch the order after 15 April, and our FY ended in March, we could not record the sale in the current FY. The CSD order was of no use.

Seeing the disappointment writ large on my face, my sales head said, 'Sir, we can invoice the CSD order on 31 March, but keep the invoiced stock aside and dispatch it in fifteen days.'

I reflected on his suggestion and after deliberation among a wider circle of people, took a decision that if, on 31 March, we were still falling short of the sales budget, we would take this risk and bill the CSD order. After all, it was only a matter of fifteen days before the stocks would be physically dispatched from our godown.

As luck would have it, on 31 March, we were missing our budget by a whisker. Therefore, we put our plan into action and billed the CSD order.

Voila, we achieved 100 per cent of our sales budget. We were happy. With momentum behind us, we rolled up our sleeves to start the new FY with a bang.

On 15 April, my sales head informed me that the CSD consignment had been dispatched. I heaved a sigh of relief. An hour later, he came running into my room. Worry was writ large on his face. 'Sir, the truck carrying the CSD consignment has met with an accident.'

I understood the gravity of the situation—on paper, we had dispatched the CSD order from our godown on 31 March. The CSD godown was just a short distance away and it could not take fifteen days to reach it.

Moreover, this consignment had been billed on 31 March and been dispatched on 15 April, and hence was not covered under the insurance policy. If the truck had met with an accident and the goods were damaged, then we would incur a heavy loss.

We rushed to the accident spot. We were relieved to know that it was a minor mishap: the truck tyre had burst, and it had collided with a tree. The goods were not damaged, but the truck was in no condition to move.

I immediately called the head of the transport company. He promised to send a replacement truck within an hour. We waited till the truck arrived and the stock was transferred to the replacement truck, and we then escorted it till it reached the guarded premises of CSD. Only then did we return to my office and heave a sigh of relief.

We had escaped by the skin of our teeth. As I introspected, and wondered if the decision was unethical. With the benefit of hindsight, I can categorically say that it was unethical! I took a vow to refrain from making unethical decisions.

Criteria for Making Ethical Decision

I decided to subject questionable decisions to a 'three-question test':

- Do I have to explain to others that the decision I have made is ethical?
- When I tell my mother about the decision, will it make her proud of me?
- Will I get a good night's sleep?

When I put this decision to the three-question test, I got a disturbing answer:

- I had to explain to my boss that the decision that I had made was ethical. He was not convinced. I promised not to indulge in it again.
- When I explained it to my mother, she said that I should not have done it. My reputation could have been tarnished.
- I would have lost my sleep had the accident become a police case.

I shared this incident with my batchmates from IIM Bangalore. They shared interesting instances from the world of business. Here are two examples.

Increasing Revenue

A product manager was struggling to increase the sales of the toothpaste brand under his watch. Finally, he came up with an out-of-the-box solution: increase the size of the nozzle of the toothpaste tube, so that each time it is squeezed, more toothpaste oozes out. It will result in the toothpaste being exhausted more quickly, leading to faster re-purchase, which will eventually result in increased sales. His strategy was implemented and sales increased.

Let us focus on the nature of his decision. Was it an ethical decision to increase the size of the nozzle to increase sales? You decide.

Increase the Price of Soap

An FMCG company was witnessing soaring input costs for soaps. Due to hyper-competition, it could not pass on the increase in cost to the customers. If it did, sales would be adversely impacted. After brainstorming, a decision was taken to marginally reduce the weight of the soap, but to keep the size of the outer packing and the price the same. To comply with the statutory requirements, the lower weight of the soap was printed on the outer pack.

The customers did not notice the marginal reduction in the weight of the soap since the outer carton size and the price remained the same. They surmised, in good faith, that nothing had changed.

But they were getting less soap for the same price. Was the decision taken by the company an ethical decision? You decide.

When unethical decisions are made, critical thinking is given a pass. These decisions do not solve the problem; they merely postpone the solution. Sooner or later, the unresolved problem will rear its ugly head unexpectedly and can then cause untold harm to you, to the brand and to the company's reputation.

Newspaper Test[122]

Warren Buffet has also proposed a test to help people decide if they are making smart but ethical decisions.

If the decision you have made were to be written about the next day in the local newspaper by a smart but unfriendly reporter, and read by your family, friends and neighbours, how would you feel?

Proud or ashamed? If the former, then go ahead. If the latter, then stop immediately.

Why Making Ethical Decisions Is Important

You should make decisions which are both legally and ethically compliant, each time. Because if you give in to the temptation even once, then the boundary of an unethical decision will keep expanding till it slithers into the illegal turf. Once that happens, then you may even face the prospect of spending time behind bars. That day, you will realize your folly and regret not subjecting the decision to the rigour of critical thinking.

How Can You Transform into a Better Critical Thinker?

Accomplished critical thinkers operate at the intersection point of being an Albert Einstein (read: scientist) and a Sherlocks Holmes (read: detective).

When thinking like a scientist,[123] critical thinkers tend to:

- Look for reasons why they might be wrong, not just reasons why they must be right.

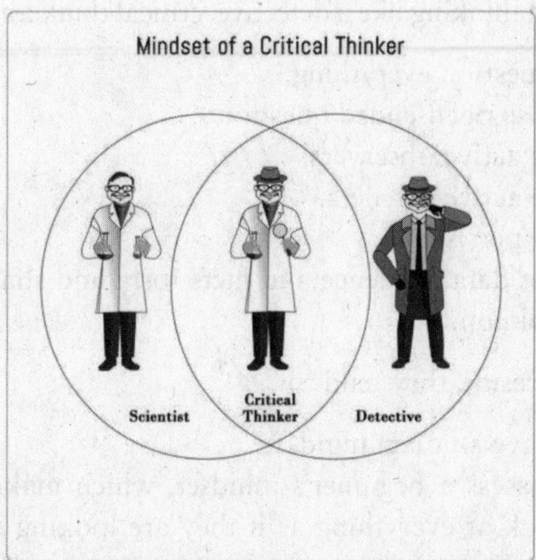

- Hear new points of view.
- Eager to discover new things.
- Listen to ideas that make them think hard and not only to ideas that make them feel good.
- Place curiosity over conviction.
- Seek out evidence that contradicts their opinions.
- View their opinions more as hypotheses in need of confirmation or rebuttal.
- Believe that changing their mind does not make them fickle-minded, but is a sign of progress.
- Put aside their pride and ego while making decisions.
- Favour humility over pride and curiosity over conviction.
- Hold strong opinions, weakly. They are ready to change their opinion when new evidence emerges.
- Seek new ways of looking at the world.
- Surround themself with people who challenge their ideas and not only who support their conclusions.

When thinking like a detective, critical thinkers tend to:

- Question everything.
- Pose open-ended questions.
- Be active observers.
- Be active listeners.
- Be persistent.
- Let data, evidence and facts form and shape their opinion.

As a result, they tend to:

- Have an open mind.
- Possess a beginner's mindset, which makes them look at everything as if they are looking at it for the first time.
- Display unbounded curiosity.
- Be grounded.

A Few More Ways to Sharpen Critical Thinking Skills

Critical thinking is a learnt skill and can be sharpened by making conscious efforts. Here are a few more pointers:

- Surround yourself with critical thinkers who challenge sameness, predictability and familiarity and freely express their thoughts and share their opinions. In this way, you'll be exposed to more sources of knowledge and perspective and will have access to much better ideas, whether they're yours or someone else's.
- Be open to constantly revising your understanding and reconsidering a problem which you thought had already been solved.

- Be open to new points of view, new information, new ideas, contradictions and challenges to your own way of thinking.[124]

Why You Should Become Skilful at Critical Thinking[125]

When you are becoming skilful at critical thinking, you will be motivated to:

- Arrive at an accurate picture of the reality, even if it is unpleasant.
- Arrive at the truth, no matter how unpleasant it may be.
- Get to see the reality as clearly as possible, uncoloured by your biases, deeply ingrained prejudices and more.
- You will not feel threatened when your opinion or beliefs are challenged. Nor will you feel upset when you are proved wrong or disappointed when your decisions are proved to be erroneous.
- You will not fall victim to the banal excuse of too little time, and therefore make better judgements.
- You will be open to new ideas, even when they are at variance with yours, and be delighted when you get new information based on which you may form new opinions.

This will help you make good judgements and arrive at better decisions.

Postscript

Michelangelo sculped the beautiful statue of David from a large block of marble.

Asked why he selected that piece of marble, he replied that he could visualize David residing in the marble block. All he had to do was to remove all unnecessary marble for David to emerge from the marble block.[126]

A critical thinker is like the modern-day Michelangelo. They look upon the problem they are facing like a block of marble. Deep inside the marble block resides the truth. The thickness of the marble is made up of timeless traditions, written-in-stone assumptions and well-established norms. Adding additional layers of thickness to the marble are cognitive biases, crippling emotions, control exercised by reptilian brain, a mighty ego, deep-seated prejudices and falling prey to making unethical decisions.

These layers prevent a normal person from reaching to the truth. Therefore, they arrive at sub-optimal answers and solutions. But critical thinkers remove all the unnecessary marble and let the truth emerge. From this vantage point, they arrive at better judgements, make logical and superior-quality decisions, and solve problems more effectively.

Critical Thinking in a Nutshell

Critical Thinking

Critical thinkers challenge tradition, question assumptions and defy norms. They reason through logic, filter out biases, possess diversity of thoughts and do not fall victim to heuristics. This enables them to arrive at better judgement, think deeply and become skilled problem-solvers.

What Do Critical Thinkers Do?

1. Challenge traditions.
2. Question assumptions.
3. Defy norms.
4. Reason through logic.

5. Question data, information and knowledge.
6. Analyse issues objectively by asking probing questions.
7. Filtering out biases.
8. Posse diversity of thoughts.

Barriers in the Path of Critical Thinking

1. Cognitive biases.
2. Crippling emotions.
3. Too little time.
4. Allowing the reptilian (lizard) brain to be in control.

5. Permitting unhealthy ego to have a free run.
6. Allowing prejudice to colour decision-making.
7. Making unethical decisions.

Advantages of Becoming Skilled in Critical Thinking

1. Arrive at an accurate picture of the reality even if it is unpleasant.

2. Arrive at the truth no matter how unpleasant it may be.

3. Get to see reality as clearly as possible, uncoloured by your biases, deeply ingrained prejudices and more.

4. You will not feel threatened when your opinion or beliefs are challenged.

5. You will not feel upset when you are proved wrong or disappointed when your decisions prove to be erroneous.

6. You will not fall victim to the banal excuse of 'too little time'.

7. You will be open to new ideas, even if they are at variance with yours.

8. You will be delighted when you get new information, based on which you may form new opinions.

Skill 4

Frame the Right Question

The right question will lead to the right answer, which will open up a treasure trove of new business opportunities, which would have remained undiscovered but for framing the right question.

By March 2020, the world was in the grip of COVID-19. The business world was adversely impacted, resulting in large-scale layoffs and a mammoth pullback in investments.

Satya Nadella, the CEO of Microsoft, was asked by reporters how he was dealing with this crisis. He pondered for a moment and replied, 'I am not concerned about the large-scale layoff or the massive pull back in investment. I am focussed on ***how to capture the "new demand" that is created by millions and millions of people going to work from home.***'[127]

By framing the right question, Satya Nadella directed his team's attention to searching for the right answer, which opened up a treasure trove of new business opportunities, which would have remained undiscovered but for framing the right question.

Power of the Right Question

The right question can determine the way we perceive or think about something—and that might serve as a catalyst to bring about change.[128]

It taps into human memory, which is set up so that a piece of information serves as a cue to draw out related information, which can help in arriving at a solution.[129]

Here is an example: if I ask you to imagine a cocktail, you will quickly retrieve information about it, and think about bartenders, spirits, juices, modifiers, glasses, stirrers, margarita, daiquiri and the good time you had. You don't have to expend much effort to recall this information. It surfaces spontaneously because of the initial cue.

If you want to retrieve something else from memory, you need to change the cue. If I now ask you to think about cricket, your mind will recall information about Virat Kohli, T20, Indian Premier League (IPL) or MS Dhoni, even though you were thinking about cocktails just a while back.

The right questions also tap into 'the collective memory of the people who are working on the problem, believing that someone working to solve the problem knows something that will help them find a solution. They just haven't realized yet that they know it.' [130] It is one of the most cost-effective and repeatable problem-solving approaches.

Why Do People Refrain from Framing Questions?[131]

There are many reasons. Here are a few of them:

- Many people believe that they already know the answer. Sometimes they are right, but mostly they are wrong.
- Many people are ignorant about the advantages that a well-framed, right question can offer. So they make no effort to learn the art of framing the right question.
- The education system does not teach students the art of framing the right question. Instead, the system frames the questions and students are expected to provide answers.
- Many people are fearful that they may frame the wrong question, which may invite ridicule and present them in a poor light.
- The 'command and control' style of leadership holds sway in corporations. The 'top' decides and the 'bottom' executes. This style does not encourage employees to question the boss or the system. Those who do are subjugated into submission. Hence, the majority of employees do

not acquire the art and skills to frame the right questions.

How to Frame the Right Question

Framing the question in obvious, conventional ways often leads to obvious and conventional solutions. Framing a more interesting question can help teams discover more original ideas.[132]

Here are pointers to frame the right and more interesting question:

1. Frame a question which challenges the industry rules because the prevailing rule of an industry perpetuates the problem.
2. Frame a question that challenges an expert's opinion. If they had the solution, the problem would already have been resolved.
3. Frame constraints as a creative challenge. It will stimulate the brain to engage in out-of-box thinking to throw up creative solutions.
4. Strive to frame the question so that it is expansive, bold and open-ended. Such questions throw up transformational, not incremental, solutions. Framing a question in obvious, conventional ways will lead to obvious, conventional solutions.
5. Feel the pain of customers. This will inspire you to frame an ambitious question which can result in a solution which will banish the pain from the root.

6. Frame a question such that it motivates people to explore multiple directions while searching for answers.
7. Refrain from framing questions with 'can' and 'should' because they imply judgement:
   - How can we do this?
   - How should we do this?

   Instead, frame questions with 'might': 'how *might* we?'[133]

   - How might we do this?
   - How might this be done?

'Might' opens avenues for possibilities and can generate better solutions.

8. Explore the possibility of framing a question using 'how'.[134] This will change the nature of the conversation and help us understand the reason for the problem that is to be addressed.
9. While attempting to frame the question, add new people into the group because they can look at the issue with a fresh pair of eyes and propose a new, different, bold and 'unexpected' way of framing the question.
10. Frame the problem as a question. It will activate the mind to start working on arriving at a solution.
11. The question should be framed so that it brings to the surface what is not known yet.
12. Framing a question is akin to framing a masterpiece. The frame brings attention to it.

Similarly, frame the question such that it brings attention to the issue to be addressed.

13. After framing the question, play the devil's advocate and ask if the right question has been framed.

Here is an example. A company commands 60 per cent market share. It wishes its team to develop a strategy to garner an additional 5 per cent market share. Here are two options for framing the question for getting the desired result:

- Option 1: We already have a dominant 60 per cent market share. Devise a strategy to gain additional 5 per cent market share.
- Option 2: We have lost 40 per cent market share to competition. How might we gain an additional 5 per cent market share from them?

Chances are that option 2 will motivate the team to come up with an effective strategy, because it frames the task as a 'loss'. Loss looms larger than gain, says Daniel Kahneman, because it is believed that the pain of losing is psychologically about twice as powerful as the pleasure of gaining. And 'might' has the power to generate better ideas.

If you are still struggling to frame a question, then follow physicist Edward Witten's advice: 'Frame a question that is hard (and interesting) enough that it is worth answering and easy enough that you can actually answer it.'[135]

If this also does not help, ask yourself how a ten-year-old will frame it. The answer will give the question you were struggling to frame.

Derailers in the Path of Framing the Right Question

Here is a partial list of derailers that can thwart attempts at framing the right question.

- A question should not have the answer embedded in it. For example, 'We will become the world's number 1 brand.' Here, the answer is present in the question. Such questions will obviate the necessity for a debate. But when it is framed, 'How might we become the world's number 1 brand?' then it will spark discussion, debate, and invite suggestions.
- A question which is designed to identify who committed the mistake will be met with resistance. For example, 'Can we find out who committed the mistake?' or 'Who is responsible for this mistake?'

How to Get the Best Answers?[136]

Once you have accomplished the difficult job of framing the right question, acquaint yourself with guidelines to ensure that you get the best answers.

- Ask the question in a casual way rather than in a formal tone. It will motivate people to be more forthcoming with answers.
- Inform people that they can change their answers at any point. This will encourage them to answer questions honestly and say things which they might otherwise not. It will also get them to open

up more—even though they may rarely change their answer.

- Do not interrupt people when they are answering.
- Learn to listen to them with the intent of understanding them, not replying to them.
- Do not listen in complete silence. Punctuate it with 'yes' or 'hmm' to indicate that you are indeed listening, not merely hearing. If you have not understood a point, ask your colleague to explain it again. At the end, summarize important elements of the conversation to make sure you have understood what was communicated to you.
- Use body language to convey that you are interested in listening to their answer. You can achieve this by:
    - Being close to the person who is answering.
    - Leaning towards the speaker. It will indicate that you're interested in listening to them. On the other hand, leaning backward indicates that you dislike the person and their ideas.
    - Face and maintain eye contact with the person who is answering. This will make you appear interested in their answer.
    - Nod and tilt your head. Both these gestures will indicate that you are giving them an ear.
    - Open your posture by keeping your legs apart instead of crossed; keep your arms open and your palm facing up. These gestures indicates that you are asking them to share their ideas.
    - Make it a point to smile while you are listening. It will encourage them to speak more openly.

If this sounds like Greek and Latin to you, then follow the advice of Dale Carnegie and ask questions the other person will enjoy answering.

Case Studies Illustrating the Power That Lies in Framing the Right Question

Presented below are case studies which will unfold the power of framing the right questions.

1. Identify 'Undiscovered' Revenue Streams Which Lead to Improvement in Top and Bottom Line.

Low-cost carriers (LCCs) operate on wafer-thin margins, causing them to oscillate between profit and loss—more loss than profit.

The founder of an LCC eliminated all seemingly 'wasteful' costs but was still nowhere near profitability. Any further reduction in cost would have jeopardized the safety of the aircraft. Faced with these unsurmountable difficulties, he decided to frame an ambitious question, which challenged the industry status quo: *How can we convert cost to revenue?*

The team began afresh to review all elements classified under cost and explore the possibility of converting them into revenue. They discovered that a cost was being incurred by serving light refreshments to guests. They sensed an opportunity and framed the question to convert it into revenue: *How might we convert light refreshment, a cost, into revenue?*

The answer was self-evident. Stop serving it free and start selling it on board. Voila—a cost became a revenue without in any way jeopardizing the safety of the aircraft.

Having tasted success, the management was encouraged to frame a series of expansive and ambitious questions that challenged the status quo of the industry: *How might we sweat our assets to generate additional profitable revenue streams?*

San Tzu, a Chinese philosopher and military general, had observed an aeon back that opportunities multiply when they are seized. The answer threw up multiple opportunities and multiple revenue streams.

- Charge for aisle and window seat.
- Charge for boarding priorities.
- Strictly enforce the weight of baggage that can be carried on as cabin baggage. Additional weight must be paid for.

This emboldened the team. They posed yet another 'industry challenging' question: *How might we convert 'dead space' into revenue streams?*

The answer opened up additional revenue streams:

- Offer space outside and inside the aircraft to advertisers.
- Offer space on the back of the baggage tag for advertising.

The right questions helped discover new revenue streams, which resulted in an improved bottom line.

2. Convert the Customer's Unreasonable Demand into an Innovative Product

Edwin Land, an American scientist, inventor and businessman, was also an avid photographer. One day, he snapped a picture of his young daughter. She wanted to see her picture instantly.

'You will have to wait until the film is developed in a lab and prints are made,' he explained to her.

'Why do we have to wait for the picture?'[137] she persisted.

This made Edwin Land pose a question to himself: *Why not design a picture that can be developed right away?*[138]

This led him to invent an instant camera, which he called the Polaroid.[139]

For people like Edward Land, challenges and unreasonable demands are a tonic. They re-energize them. They do not get upset when customers make unreasonable demands. Instead, they frame a question that can result in the discovery of a solution. The solution often gives birth to blockbuster products.

3. Convert a Customer's Pain Point into a Megahit Product

Young people oversleep. To reach office on time, they skip breakfast. When asked why they don't carry the breakfast and have it on the way to office, they say, 'How can we carry fried egg, milk and cornflakes or paratha-sabzi in our pocket or inside the bag, and have it on the go? It will be messy, and it will inconvenience others.'

This led to the framing of an ambitious question: *How might a meal be created which can be carried in a pocket or a purse and could be conveniently had on the move, without inconveniencing others?*

It led to the creation of an innovative product, the energy bar, which, like a regular breakfast or meal, contains cereals and high-energy foods. It can be carried in the pocket or purse and can be conveniently munched on the move without inconveniencing others.

4. Convert Your Painful Experience into a Unicorn

Tavis Kalanick and Darrett Camp were standing in the streets of Paris, exposed to the elements of nature and unable to find a taxi.

This painful experience inspired them to frame a question: *What if you could request a ride simply by tapping on your phone?*[140]

The answer led to the birth of Uber. From the comfort of home, an Uber can be ordered by merely tapping on a smartphone. Lo and behold, in double quick time, it would be at our doorstep and would drop us at our destination with pinpoint accuracy. Today, it has become a verb for ride hailing services.

Zoom

Eric Yuan, the founder of Zoom, recollected that as a college student in China, he was tired of taking a ten-hour train ride to visit his now wife. The tiring experience motivated him to focus on video conferencing technology, which eventually led him to invent the communication platform Zoom![141]

Albert Einstein got it right when he said, 'In the middle of difficulty lies opportunity.' Therefore, do not be upset when you find yourself faced with difficulties or having to endure a painful experience. Instead, pose a question to address it. The solution may uncover a gold mine.

5. How to Abandon a Strategy Which Has Outlived Its Utility in Favour of an Untested Strategy Which Holds Promise[142]

In 1985, Andy Grove, then Intel's president, and Gordon Moore (of Moore Law fame), its CEO, faced a dilemma. The company had started out making computer memory chips. This product established Intel's formidable reputation. It came under assault from Japanese memory chips, whose quality level was beyond what Intel thought they could achieve.[143] The computer memory chip business continued to bleed copiously, which led to an all-pervasive gloom at Intel. Finally, the day dawned when the Japanese stole the bulk of the computer memory chip business from right under Intel's nose.

Around this time, a small team working inside Intel had developed a microprocessor which, as luck would have it, was picked by IBM to be the brain of a new personal computer.

Andy Grove and Gordon Moore had to decide whether to shift the focus into new and more promising areas instead of the computer memory chip business, which was responsible for building Intel's formidable reputation.

To arrive at a decision, Andy Grove asked Gordon Moore, *'If we got kicked out and the board brought in a new CEO, what do you think he would do?'*[144]

They felt that the new CEO would not be emotionally attached to the declining computer memory chip business and therefore Moore said, 'He would get us out of memories.'[145]

They did likewise and analysed the business without the burden of legacy—as if looking at it for the first time. With this fresh perspective, they decided to take the radical decision of pulling the plug on the computer memory chip business. This decision made Intel even more competitive and turned it into a technology powerhouse. If they had not acted decisively and taken steps to disturb their existing business, Intel too could have suffered the same fate as Nokia.

When you are facing declining growth or the prospect of getting disrupted, it might pay to pose the kind of question that Grove posed to Moore: *What if a different leader was brought in? What would they do?* This question will force you to jettison your emotional baggage, think afresh and take a decision without the burden of legacy.

6. How Many Ties Did You Break Today?[146]

During the course of my corporate career, I witnessed constant battles among companies' stakeholders:

- Sales team accusing the marketing team of not providing timely support in the market. Marketing team accusing the sales team of focusing on buying sales and not putting enough effort into building brands.
- Sales team accusing the production team of not dispatching sufficient stock in time, which resulted in loss of sales. Production team accusing them of not picking up stocks that they had requested.
- Vendors accusing the accounts team of not releasing payment on time. Accounts team countering by saying that the submitted paperwork was incomplete.

My job was to intervene and break the tie (read: resolve the conflict) in a manner that both sides felt was fair. As a result, productivity shot up. Therefore, at the end of the day, I always asked myself, how many ties did I break today? The more ties I broke, the more the productivity improved.

7. How to Build Relationships with Customers

At a premier coffee shop, baristas were trained to greet their regular customers by name. They were also trained to remember the previous orders of regular customers. This simple act makes the customer feel important and welcome. If a customer is new, then the barista greets them enthusiastically and strives to engage them in conversation. Conversations build relationships. The barista does this by posing open-ended questions.

For example, I was asked once in a Starbucks, 'I saw you going through the menu board. *What kind of coffee do you like?*' This is a much better question than 'Would you like a coffee?' which can elicit a monosyllabic response, 'Yes,' and the conversation would have reached a dead end.

As I answered the question, the barista engaged me a conversation to get a better idea of the type of coffee I desired. It was made accordingly.

When I was leaving, a question was posed to me, '*Hope to see you soon?*'

It is a loaded question. If I had a bad experience, then I would turn around and answer, 'Never again.' In such an eventuality, the barista would have offered to make the coffee again at no cost to me.

This would make me happy since my feedback was accepted and instantly acted upon. Now I would leave the coffee shop, not a dissatisfied customer, but its brand advocate.

But I responded with a smile and said, 'Soon.' The barista smiled and waved back.

You too can frame a 'loaded' question to ensure that you are building relationships with your customers; in case these relationships are broken, have a system in place to repair them post-haste.

8. How to Attract a Superstar to Join the Team

Steve Jobs considered himself to be a product person and focused on building great products. By 1982, he felt the need for a marketing person who could market Apple to the world. His choice was John Sculley, who at that time was CEO of Pepsi.

Let me invite John Sculley to take the narrative forward: 'We got to know each other very, very well, but at the end of it I said, "Steve, I've thought about it and I'm not coming to Apple." Steve paused and thought for a while, and then he was about 18 inches away from me—and in those days he was in his twenties and he had jet black hair, very dark eyes—he said, "*You want to sell sugar water for the rest of your life, or do you want to come with me and change the world?*"'

On 11 April 1983, John Sculley joined Apple as the CEO.[147]

Let me get Tavis Kalanick, founder of Uber, into our discussion. He too framed a question and posed it to people whom he sought to influence: *Do you want to make transportation as reliable as running water for everyone, in every city in the world?*[148] His lure was that Uber would change the way world transported itself. People to whom he posed this question found it irresistible and they gave their consent.

People intrinsically want to do good, desire to improve themselves and harbour a desire to help others. Steve Jobs and Travis Kalanick framed a question which gave hope and offered an opportunity to do good, improve oneself or help others in a meaningful way. In fact, it showed people a clear path of how they could transform themselves into the best, if not the finest, version of themselves. This lure proves to be irresistible to most people.

Let me direct this discussion towards you. How do you recruit people? By luring them with an attractive salary, fat incentives and the promise of a great career? This bait will attract financial mercenaries. But if you wish to draw people who are passionate about helping you achieve your mission, pose a question that will make them realize that by joining forces with you, they are taking a step towards metamorphosing into a finer version of themselves. That would be sufficient to influence them to join forces with you.

9. How to Create a Profitable Product Portfolio

In 1998, Apple was on the verge of extinction.[149]

Among the first decisions that Steve Jobs took was to review the product line. He discovered that multiple versions of the same product were present in the product portfolio. This was done to pander to the demands coming from retailers. The product portfolio needed to be trimmed to save the company. To address this problem, Jobs posed a simple question to the team: '*Which ones do I tell my friends to buy?*'[150]

When he did not get a convincing answer, he reduced (read: subtracted) the number of Apple products by 70 per cent. This 'subtraction' in the portfolio resulted in a greater focus on quality and innovation.

10. What Business Are You In?

Theodore Levitt, the legendary professor at Harvard Business School, had said that knowing what business you are in is important for the success of the business. For example, a drill maker will tell you it makes drilling machines. But people don't want to buy a quarter-inch drill, they want a quarter-inch hole. Therefore, they are in the business of delivering a quarter-inch hole.

- **Luxury Watch**

The head of a luxury Swiss watch company was sipping coffee at a cafeteria. A friend walked up to him and asked, 'How is your watch business doing?'

'I don't know,' he replied.

His friend was aghast and reminded him, 'You are in the watch business, and you do not know how it is doing?'

The head looked up and said, 'We are not in the watch business. We are in the luxury business.'

He was right. If Swiss watches were sold as watches, they would be perceived as being expensive. Since they are sold as luxury items, they do well.

- **Courier Companies**

Ask the best-run and most dependable courier companies about the business they are in. They will tell you that they are not in the courier business but in the 'peace of mind' business, because once the customers have deposited their packet with them, they have 'peace of mind' that their packet will certainly and positively be delivered at the destination. It is for experiencing 'peace of mind' that customers are willing to give their business to courier companies and happily pay a price premium.

- **Automobile Industry**

Automobile companies believe that they are in the business of manufacturing and selling automobiles. But millennials do not want to buy automobiles. Instead, they desire mobility. If automobile companies do not redefine their business as the mobility business, then they will be forced to bite the dust.

You too should pose the question to yourself: 'What business are you in?' The right answer will help you secure the future of your business.

11. North Star for Making Decisions

In 1999, *Fortune* magazine named Jack Welch the 'Manager of the Century'.[151] He was credited with transforming General Electric into a global corporation.[152]

Upon being appointed to the highest office at GE, Jack Welch decided to reach out to management guru Peter Drucker, to seek his opinion on how he should go about doing his job.

Peter Drucker, who had the innate ability to craft deceptively simple questions, framed two questions to guide him in decision-making: *'If GE wasn't already in a particular business, would you enter it today? If the answer is no, what are you going to do about it?'*[153]

Jack Welch took decisions guided by these questions and insisted that every GE business should either be number one or number two in its segment. If not, then those businesses should either be fixed, sold or closed.

'This approach earned Welch the moniker "Neutron Jack", as he abandoned business of GE that which were either underperforming or taking resources away from areas that were GE's best performers,' says Thomas Koulopoulos.[154]

Closer home, J.R.D. Tata also referred to two questions when he had to take tough business decisions:

a. Will it be good for India?
b. Will it be good for the Tatas?

Invariably, it turned out that what was good for India would also be good for the Tatas.[155]

12. Motivate the Team to Take an Aggressive Sales Target Even if the Product Enjoys a Monopoly Status

A cola brand enjoyed monopoly status. This made the team complacent, and they planned to grow the brand at a tortoise's pace. They justified it by saying that they were growing at the market growth rate and hence keeping their monopoly status intact—not realizing that due to their monopoly position, the market grew at the same rate they chose to grow at.

Their boss was convinced that there was ample room for growth. So he decided to pose a question to his team: 'We are a beverage brand. Therefore, our competition is not only with other cola brands or with other carbonated beverages. Instead, we compete with all beverages—water, coffee, juice, smoothies, milk, etc.—which go down the throats of our consumers. **Calculate the "share of throat" for our brand.'**

In the redefined market, the market share of the cola brand dropped to a low-single digit. There was much head room for growth. This realization inspired the team to rework their plan to grow the cola brand to double-digit growth.

No carrot-and-stick approach was required to energize the team! Merely framing the right question re-energized and motivated the team to grow the brand in a muscular fashion.

13. How to Solve an Intractable Problem

In the old days, the loading of a ship commenced when it was docked in the port. During this time, it did not make money. After all, a ship makes money when it is sailing on the high seas, not when it is docked in the port. The industry decided to frame an expansive but oxymoronic question which challenged the industry traditions, assumptions and norms: *How can we load the ships while they are still on the high seas?*

This led to the designing of large, reusable steel containers which are loaded with cargo while the ship was sailing on the high seas. When the ship docked at the port, the containers are expeditiously loaded onto it. The time taken to load the filled container onto the ship was significantly less than the time required to load the cargo after the ship docked at the port. As a result, the time the ships spent in port was shortened and their profitability headed north. Since its introduction, shipping containers have become the industry standard for the movement of goods.

14. How to Anticipate an Impending Storm

Jeff Bezos started Amazon as an online bookseller with a simple business model. It accepted orders and payments and delivered books at the designated address. The business did well.

By the early 2000s, Apple was reviving under the charismatic leadership of Steve Jobs. Bezos surmised that Jobs could come up with a product that could disrupt Amazon.

He did not wait for his prognosis to come true. Instead, he dug the proverbial well before his house was on fire by proactively framing a 'propelling' question, which helped Amazon emerge stronger.

Brad Stone, in his book *The Everything Store: Jeff Bezos and the Age of Amazon*, captured this moment: 'In 2004, Bezos started a secretive Silicon Valley skunkworks with the mysterious name Lab126. The hardware hackers at Lab126 were given a difficult job: *How can Amazon's own successful bookselling business be disrupted with an e-book device while also meeting the impossibly high standards of Amazon's designer in chief, Bezos himself*? In 2007, Amazon unveiled the result of this effort. Kindle.'

Propelling questions[156] are framed to restrain our existing knowledge from restricting our ability to imagine and explore new possibilities. They fast-forward us into the future and prompt positive action in the present.

Here are guidelines which can guide you in framing *propelling questions.*[157]

1. How might we?
2. How could I?
3. What would happen if?
4. Imagine it's 2030. What will your industry look like?
5. If you were rebuilding this business for 2030, what changes would you carry out now?
6. How might we divide our roles and responsibilities between us and a robot?

15. Solve the World's Wicked Problems

Muhammad Yunus[158] was driven by the noble purpose of alleviating poverty. He believed that if small loans could be made available to poor people, particularly women, then the life of the whole family could improve, and they could be lifted out of poverty.

But banks did not lend small loans to poor people, particularly women, because:

- The banks lacked resources to assess the credit-worthiness of 'poor' borrowers.
- The poor people did not possess collateral which they could pledge.
- Even if the bank wanted to offer s small loan amount to the poor, the cost of disbursing it would be higher than the likely profit.

This drove poor people into the clutches of the local village moneylender, who gave them loans at exorbitant rates of interest. Once they took the loan, they found it difficult to get out of his clasp.

These insights and other data points made Muhammad Yunus surmise that an individual may renege on their obligation. But when their behaviour inconveniences their peers, then they would think twice before engaging in such behaviour. Therefore, *why not give loans to a group where every member is responsible for their partner's loan and has the option of choosing their partners?*

Under these circumstances, the group members are unlikely to choose a risky partner. The chosen partners will also take decisions using similar parameters before joining the group. The group thus formed is likely to be safe. Moreover, group members will act as checks and balances to ensure prompt repayment. They will coax and help each other to make sure that, as a group, they do not default.

The loan was offered to a group, not to an individual. Members of a group were asked to find each other and come to the bank together for securing loans. The partner could not be a blood relative. Also, the bank refrained from assigning a member to the group. The group was collectively liable for the entire loan given to the individual members of the group.

Successful execution of this strategy won Muhammad Yunus the Nobel Prize for pioneering the concept of microcredit and microfinance.

16. Get Infinite Returns on Your Investment[159]

Tina Seelig, professor at the Stanford School of Engineering, gave her students the $5 challenge: *What would you do to earn money, in two hours, if all you had was five dollars?* Each team was allocated three minutes to present their project to class.

The teams that earned the maximum money did not use the $5 at all. They realized that $5 is a small sum and decided to redefine the problem: *What can we do to make money if we start with absolutely nothing?*

They set up a stand to measure bicycle tyre pressure for free. If the tyres needed filling, they charged $1. Soon, they changed their strategy. They did not ask for a specific payment; instead, they requested donations. Their income rose sharply, because they had put into play the reciprocal principle—when you do good to people, they respond in equal, if not greater, measure. This team earned a few hundred dollars.

But the team that won framed an open-ended question: '*What is the most valuable and precious asset we have?*' This made them realize that it was not the $5 nor the allocated two hours. Instead, it was the three-minute presentation time during which they would have the attention of students at Stanford University. They sold the 'three-minute' presentation time to a company that wanted to recruit students in the class. They created a three-minute 'commercial' for that company and premiered it to the students during their presentation. They won, because framing the right question made it possible for them to get 'infinite' return.[160]

17. One Central Question to Make Business Decisions

Have you ever wondered how Steve Jobs took decisions? I hear many of you say that his thinking and decision-making process were surreal and beyond our capacity to grasp.

I too thought this way till I understood his philosophy. He believed that everything starts with a great product.

'My passion has been to build an enduring company where people were motivated to make great products,' he said.[161]

Based on this insight, I surmised that Steve Jobs took decisions by framing one question to himself and his team:

- Will it make Apple a great product for customers? If yes, green-light it. If not, junk it.

The cumulative impact of many big and small decisions focused on making Apple a better product was that Apple customers were handed an amazing experience that enriched their lives. In 2018, Apple was crowned the world's most valuable company.[162]

How Can You Frame Your 'One Central Question'?

Always keep the customer at the centre of decision-making and frame the question in such a way that, whenever it is answered, it will further the interests of customers, not the company. The good news is that when companies continuously take decisions in customers' interests, customers reciprocate by displaying a cultish loyalty towards the business.

Framing the Question Matter

In third-world countries, millions of babies are born prematurely. These babies suffer from hypothermia, due to which their body temperature drops below what is required for normal metabolism and other bodily functions. This results in infant mortality. It can be prevented if they had access to incubators. But incubators are expensive, require skilled operators and are expensive to repair. Therefore, they are not easily available in third-world countries.

Two independent groups based in the USA decided to address this problem.

- **Group 1: Stanford University Students**

They decide to focus on the remote villages of Asia, where this problem is severe. To address the problem, they framed the following question:

> *Create a baby-warming device that helps parents in remote villages to give their dying infant suffering from hypothermia a chance to survive.*

This led them to design a tiny sleeping bag which was inspired by the sleeping bags used for trekking. It could be wrapped around an infant. It had a pouch containing paraffin, which, once warmed, could maintain its temperature for up to four hours. The pouch could be reheated by submerging it in boiling water. The sleeping bag solution was intuitive enough to be used at home by mothers, in villages.

This product was christened Embrace Infant Warmer. Compared to the $20,000 price of a traditional incubator, the Embrace incubator was priced at only $25.

- **Group 2: MIT Students**

They decided to focus on Africa. Their analysis revealed that an imported incubator, when it breaks down, remained dysfunctional because the spare parts required for its repair are not locally available and it is prohibitively expensive to import them.

The research indicated that Toyota vehicles are popular in Africa. To keep them running, spare parts are locally available and the local mechanics have acquired skills to repair them using these spare parts.

Armed with this insight, the group framed the following question:

> *Design an incubator using locally available Toyota parts, so that if it goes out of order, then the local mechanic, using locally available spare parts, could inexpensively repair them.*

This led to them to design the Neo Nurture Incubator.[163]

Bottomline: The framing of the question will determine the answer that will be arrived at.

Practised What I Preached

In the earlier part of the book, examples from Blue Riband Duet (BRD) were used to illustrate a range of concepts. Now it is being brought into the discussion to illustrate how framing the right question led to the discovery of a new product category.

In the 1990s, Blue Riband gin was under my watch. We were market leaders. But the gin category had a minuscule share of the total alcoholic beverages market and its was growing at a snail's pace. The business challenge was to grow the gin segment profitably.

Analysis indicated that we should pursue a twin strategy to achieve our objective:

- Solution 1: Induce gin drinkers to drink more.
- Solution 2: Motivate whisky drinkers to consume gin. Since the whisky segment dominates the alcoholic beverages market, even if a fraction of

whisky drinkers migrated to gin, it would increase the gin market size.

We began work on both fronts.

First, we spoke to gin drinkers to understand what might make them consume more gin. The majority of gin drinkers mix gin with lime juice cordial (LJC). Its non-availability prevented gin connoisseurs from savouring more of it. Gin drinkers often lamented: I am in the mood to have gin but cannot due to the non-availability of LJC at home due to any of these three reasons:

- Children have made drinks using LJC and have finished it.
- The lid on the bottle was not properly closed due to which fungus grew on the bottle, making it unfit for consumption.
- I have just exhausted it.

The connoisseurs muttered helplessly: I can have more gin, but make sure that the LJC is never finished.

Next, we spoke to whisky drinkers to find out what would make them consume gin. Here is what they said: it is extraordinarily inconvenient to have it. First, gin must be poured, then LJC must be added. Sometimes there is more gin, and at other times, more LJC. By the time the gin-and-LJC mix is right, the desire to have it has evaporated. On the other hand, whisky is so convenient to have—pour whisky, pour soda or water. The drink is ready! They wanted gin to be made as convenient as whisky for them to occasionally indulge in it!

Based on this insight, we framed the questions:

- *How can we make sure that LJC is never finished?*

- *How can we make gin as convenient to savour as whisky?*

Now, the answer seemed self-evident. Come up with a blend where gin and lime are pre-mixed to perfection. This will kill two birds with one stone:

- For gin drinkers, the lime juice cordial will never be finished.
- For whisky drinkers, it will offer the convenience they are accustomed to. They can pour it, add water or soda to taste, and bingo! The drink is ready. Cheers!

This led to the creation of a new category, premix, and the birth of Blue Riband Duet (BRD). In BRD, gin and lime were premixed to perfection. It was priced premium to the mother brand, Blue Riband gin, which led to improved profitability.

The market gave BRD a rousing reception. Its launch resulted in the gin market growing at a faster clip and an expansion of our profit margin.

Advantages of Framing the Right Question

The are many advantages that accrue from framing the right question. Here are just a few of them:

- Increase top and bottom line.
- Unearth innovative products.
- Convert customers or your pain point into a mega product idea.
- Build and strengthen relationships with customers.
- Influence a superstar to join your team.
- Assist you in creating a profitable portfolio.

- Solve an intractable problem.
- Motivate your team.
- Take proactive actions to nullify an impending storm.
- Provide a North Star for taking decisions.
- Get infinite return on an investment.
- Help you solve the world's wicked problems.

Postscript[164]

Socrates, the Greek philosopher, believed that thoughtful questions result in thoughtful answers, which enable people to learn better. This motivated him to design the Socrates questioning technique.

The Process

The 'teacher' frames the questions and poses it to the 'student', who must answer it. During the process of question and answer, dialogue, discussion, debate and analysis ensue, which ensure that the person answering the question gains deep knowledge and understanding of the topic.

Here are a few guidelines for making the Socrates questioning technique effective:

- Frame questions that provide direction to the dialogue.
- Allow thirty seconds for the person to respond.
- Frame follow-up questions based on the response.
- At regular intervals, summarize the key points of the discussion.

The Socrates questioning technique involves different types of questions.

- Clarification questions:
    - What do you mean when you say this?
    - Could you put your idea in another way?
- Assumption questions:
    - What assumptions are you making?
    - Why have you made these assumptions?
    - Are these assumptions valid?
- Reasons and evidence questions:
    - Can you give us evidence that supports what you are saying?
    - Why do you think what you say should be accepted?
    - What made you reach this conclusion?
- Seeking alternate viewpoints:
    - Any alternate viewpoints?

Benefits of the Socrates Questioning Technique[165]

- Encourages independent thinking.
- Enhances learning from the answers that are given while being engaged in a dialogue.
- Makes you comfortable questioning what is being told.
- Makes you look beyond the obvious.
- Helps you develop critical thinking skills.
- Prepares you to think on your feet.
- Impels you to examine an issue in depth.
- Makes you comfortable while being challenged and gets you to respond cogently when challenged.
- Compels you to organize your thoughts and present them in a compelling manner.

Framing the Right Question in a Nutshell

Frame the Right Question

The right question will lead to the right answer which will open a treasure trove of new business opportunities which would have remained undiscovered but for framing the right question.

Rule of Thumb for Framing the Right Question

1. Challenge industry norms.
2. Challenge experts' opinions.
3. Frame 'constraint' as a creative challenge.
4. Frame an expansive, bold & open-ended question.
5. Frame a question which will inspire the team.
6. Frame a question using 'might' and 'how'.
7. Become childlike when framing the question.
8. Frame a question which will reduce customer's pain point.
9. The question should motivate people to explore multiple directions while searching for answers.
10. Question should not lead to a single answer.

After framing a question, play the devil's advocate and pose a question to yourself: Has the right question been framed?

How to Get the Best Answer

1. Pose the question in a casual way.
2. Inform people that they can change their answer at any point.
3. Do not interrupt when people are answering.
4. Listen with the intent of understanding them, not to answer back.
5. Do not listen in complete silence. Punctuate it with a 'yes' or 'humm'.
6. Be close to the person who is answering
7. Lean a wee bit towards the speaker.
8. Face and maintain eye contact with the speaker.
9. Occasionally nod and tilt your head.
10. Keep an open posture.
11. Smile while listening.

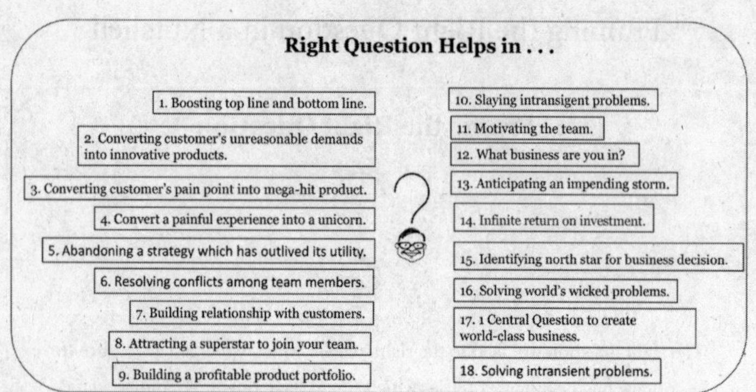
Right Question Helps in . . .
1. Boosting top line and bottom line.
2. Converting customer's unreasonable demands into innovative products.
3. Converting customer's pain point into mega-hit product.
4. Convert a painful experience into a unicorn.
5. Abandoning a strategy which has outlived its utility.
6. Resolving conflicts among team members.
7. Building relationship with customers.
8. Attracting a superstar to join your team.
9. Building a profitable product portfolio.
10. Slaying intransigent problems.
11. Motivating the team.
12. What business are you in?
13. Anticipating an impending storm.
14. Infinite return on investment.
15. Identifying north star for business decision.
16. Solving world's wicked problems.
17. 1 Central Question to create world-class business.
18. Solving intransient problems.

Skill 5

Smart Problem-Solving

The business world is littered with problems. Smart problem-solving skills arm you with perspectives, tools, techniques and frameworks to come up with smart solutions.

King Solomon of Israel faced a dilemma. Two women were claiming the same child as their own. He had to decide who was the real mother. He called for a sword and ordered the child to be cut into two equal parts so one part could be given to each woman. One woman endorsed the king's decision, saying if she could not have the child, neither could the other woman. The other woman, however, broke down and pleaded with the king not to kill the child, but to hand it over to the other woman. She wanted the child to be alive.

King Solomon gave his verdict, saying that the second woman was the real mother because only a mother would wish that no harm should befall her child.

King Solomon applied a lateral thinking technique to solve the problem. It involves solving problems through an indirect approach, using reasoning that is not immediately obvious, and involving ideas that may not be obtainable through step-by-step logic.[166] In contrast, many of us are 'vertical' thinkers—rigid in our thinking—and rely upon traditional and time-tested approaches to solve problems. It acts as a barrier in coming up with solutions to knotty problems.

Smart Problem-Solving Techniques

Lateral thinking is just one of the many time-tested, smart problem-solving techniques. Presented below is a curated list of more smart problem-solving techniques.

1. 5 Why

A member of our sales team always had reasons for not delivering sales numbers. He maintained it was due to 'circumstances' beyond his control. The reality was otherwise. I wanted him to realize it and decided to engage him in a conversation.

- Me (1): Why did you not meet your sales target?
- *He: The stocks were not available with the distributor.*

- Me (2): Why were the stocks not available with him?
- *He: Our company did not supply the stocks to him.*

- Me (3): Why did our company not supply the stocks?
- *He: The distributor had not paid our company.*

- Me (4): Why did the distributor not pay our company?
- *He: Because he was not getting money back from the market.*

- Me (5): Why was he not getting money from the market?
- *He: I focused on selling and not on collecting money from the market!*

I paused for a moment for this realization to sink in and then posed a follow-up question: What will you do now?

'I will do both—sell and collect money,' he said. He came good on his promise and transformed into a star salesperson.

I had employed the '5 Why' technique to make the salesperson realize he was responsible for his poor performance without making him feel cornered.

The 5 Why technique[167] is a simple problem-solving tool. It presupposes that the problem has already been identified and a deeper understanding is required to uncover the root cause. By asking 'why' five times, the nature of the problem and the solution comes up to the top.

When you employ this technique, keep the following points in mind:

- It can be used when the problem is of a moderate level of difficulty.
- It is most effective when the answers come from the person/s who must take action.
- It will hold up a mirror to the person and reveal the source of the problem in a sensitive and non-judgemental manner.
- Once the root cause of the problem is identified, refrain from assigning blame to team members. Otherwise you may not get honest answers the next time.

The 5 Why technique is also referred to as cause–effect analysis because it helps us understand the cause that has resulted in the effect.

Here is a quick tutorial to help you practise this simple but powerful problem-solving technique:

- Assemble people who may be responsible for the problem. It can even be an individual.
- Define the problem crisply.
- Then ask the first why question.
- By repeating 'why' five times, the nature of the problem as well as its solution will become clear.
- If you think you have got to the root cause before the fifth why, then stop.
- Once you have arrived at the root cause, make sure it is addressed robustly. This you can do by

asking the people 'what' should be done. Because the answer (read: solution) comes from them, their commitment to implementing it will be higher.

Let me share an example of how I arrived at the heart of a problem in just 2 whys.

During negotiations with our vendors, I promised them that our company would make timely payments. In return, they reduced the price.

Soon, I started getting complaints from vendors that the payments were being delayed.

I was perplexed. I was approving the release of the payment—then why was this complaint surfacing? I decided to get to the root cause of the problem. I called the accountant and engaged him in a conversation.

- Me (1): Why are the payments to vendors not being released?
- *Accountant: We want to conserve cash in the bank.*

- Me (2): Why do you want to conserve cash in the bank?
- *Accountant: To earn more interest from the bank and to make you happy.*

In this case, two whys brought me to the root cause of why payments were not being released to vendors, despite us having sufficient funds. It was to earn interest and make me happy!

I told the accounts team that I was extremely unhappy with their action. The next time, if they upheld payment for this reason, all hell would be let loose upon them. From then onwards, the payments were released on time.

2. Contrarian Thinking

Our team believed that they had done all they could to keep our customers happy. To make them realize there was still ample scope for improvement, I took a contrarian view and asked them to identify ways to make our customers unhappy with our brand.

They were aghast. On every occasion, I had drilled into them that our job was to make customers happy with our brand. Here, I was asking them to do the opposite!

There was a murmur of protest. But, upon my insistence, they came up with suggestions to get our customers to be unhappy with our brand:

- Offer a bad-quality product.
- Over-promise and under-deliver.
- Never address customers' complaints.
- Make ourselves unavailable to customers who are trying to reach us.
- Speak rudely to them.
- Engage them in an argument and prove them wrong.

Now I posed my pet question to them: What should we do to make our customer fall crazily in love with our brand?

The answer seemed apparent: Just do the opposite!

I. Provide excellent quality products, every time.
II. Under-promise and over-deliver.
III. Address customers' complaints—within twenty-four hours.
IV. Make it easy for customers to reach and talk to us.

V. Speak politely to customers.
VI. Our job is not to win an argument with our customers.

Now I asked them to rate our existing service, on a scale of 1 (very poor) to 5 (excellent), on the above six parameters.

Contrarian Thinking					
Statements	Ratings				
	1 Very Poor	2 Poor	3 Fine	4 Good	5 Excellent
Provide excellent quality. Every time.				✓	
Under promise and overdeliver				✓	
Always answer customers complaints—within 24 hours			✓		
Make it easy for customers to reach and talk to us			✓		
Speak politely to customers				✓	
Our job is not winning an argument with our customers			✓		

Voila! The graph pictorially showed them there was enough room for improvement. The team got down to improving the services we offered our customers. Soon, we had more of our customers falling more crazily in love with our brands.

3. What Is Not Going to Change?

Jeff Bezos used the 'what's not going to change' technique to make investment decisions that made the flywheel of Amazon spin faster. Let me hand over the stage to Bezos to explain his strategy. 'Most people take decisions based on the question: What's going to change in the next five to ten years. But rarely do they ask: What is not going to change over the next five to ten years? For Amazon, three things that are unlikely to change are—wide selection offered, low price and faster delivery. I cannot imagine that ten years from now customers are going to say—I really love Amazon, but I wish their prices were a bit higher, they offered less selection to choose from and take took longer to deliver. If these are the things that the customers will continue to value ten years down the line, then we take decisions to come good on them.'[168]

Coming to your business, identify those attributes of your business which customers are unlikely not to want ten years down the line. Then take decisions to come good on them.

4. Change the Label

During World War, German Shepherds were extensively used by both sides. When the war ended, it was believed that the word 'German' would harm the breed's popularity, due to the anti-German sentiments prevailing at that time. So they changed the name to Alsatian. When the negative sentiments passed, the name was changed back to 'German Shepherd' globally in 1977.

A similar strategy is followed by terrorist organizations which constantly face the spectre of a being banned. When that day comes, they do not stage a protest. Quietly, they bring down their signboard, put a lock on their official premises and move to new premises. Here, they restart their operations under a new name from the new premises.

To solve a problem, identify the cause which is responsible for it. Remove it. The problem is thus smartly solved.

5. Reframe the Problem

The office staff complained that the elevator crawled, not climbed, and they had to wait a long time for it.

The HR team proposed that a new and faster elevator should be installed. But that was vetoed since it involved large capital expenditure.

The marketing team was asked to pitch in with a creative solution. They decided to reframe the issue: *Why not 'distract' the passengers by playing music and installing mirrors in the elevator?*

As a result, while waiting for the elevator and riding in it, people would start crooning the musical numbers and admiring themselves in the mirror. Now the wait and travel time passed in a jiffy.

The initial framing of the problem was not necessarily wrong, of installing a new high-speed elevator. But it was an expensive solution. Reframing the problem gave an entirely new perspective. It led to the discovery of a more elegant solution.[169]

Here is another example: Americans love dogs, and many families keep them as pets. But it has a downside. Many pets are put up for adoption. Alas, not all get adopted. This puts pressure on the shelter homes. The obvious solution to address this problem is to get more families to adopt. That is easier said than done.

Downtown Dog Rescue is in Los Angeles. Lori Wiese, its founder, conducted an analysis which indicated that 30 per cent of pet owners surrender their pets because they do not have financial resources.

Armed with this insight, she reframed the issue and posed a question to the family when they bought their pet to the shelter home: *Would they prefer to keep the pet?*

Almost 75 per cent wanted to continue keeping the pet. But the pain point was finance. So Weise offered them $60 per pet to get them to continue keeping the pet. Many took up this offer and returned home with their pet.

When faced with an intractable problem, reframe it. It may lead you to discover an elegant solution.[170]

6. Think Backwards

Amazon gets any team working on developing new products to write future press releases (PRs) announcing a finished product well before it is launched.[171] The PR announcement lets the team know, in advance, what is expected from them and what outcome they must deliver. Once the goal is clear, then the team can channelize their energies to *work backwards* to achieve them. This document is not meant for the public, but for internal use.

Here are more advantages of opting for future press releases:

- It sets the deadline for when the initiative must hit the market.
- It mentions the features and the corresponding benefits the product will offer.
- It outlines why the product will improve the customers' experiences.
- It describes the hurdles that were overcome to make the initiative see the light of the day.
- It articulates why the new initiative will create value for customers.

Uber

When I open the Uber app, it asks, 'Where to?' I key in the destination. It 'works backwards' to show me the fare, time to destination and the route it will take to reach the destination.

Not just Amazon and Uber, even Steve Jobs was a proponent of this strategy. He said, 'You have to start with the customer experience and work backwards to the technology.'[172]

Briefing the R&D Team to Make a Blend Which Delivered 'Good Mornings after Great Evenings'

We followed a variant of this strategy to get the R&D team to work backwards to craft an alcoholic blend which delivered the promise we were going to make to customers.

Our research had uncovered a wicked problem faced by connoisseurs: while they were having a 'good evening', their concern was for the next morning! We briefed the advertising agency to communicate this benefit. They came up with a clutter-breaking tagline: Good Mornings After Great Evenings!

We briefed our R&D team to develop a blend which could deliver 'Good Mornings After Great Evenings' to connoisseurs.

The R&D team was taken aback by this innovative style of briefing. But it must have inspired them. They worked backward and developed a blend which indeed delivered 'Good Mornings after Great Evenings'.

Gold Riband Prestige Whiskey was launched with the promise of 'Good Mornings After Great Evenings'. The market loved the benefit promised by the brand and the brand was off to a good start.

7. Perpetual Beta

Companies build new brands in secrecy, so that competitors do not get a whiff of it. Prior to launch, they show it to select customers and get their feedback. But this feedback is difficult to incorporate since the product is almost ready to be launched. No wonder 95 per cent of new products fail.[173] The same is true for start-ups: 75 per cent of them fail.[174]

To overcome this problem, companies have altered their strategy. They launch a 'minimum viable product (MVP)' with enough features to get the attention of users. Real users use the product. The company continuously collects their feedback and keeps on incorporating it into the product, making it better and better. This strategy is also called 'being in a state of perpetual beta'—a continuous state of improvement. Being in a state of perpetual beta offers multiple advantages:

- It takes the guesswork out of decision-making.
- It also cleanses decision of cognitive bias.
- It favours experimentation over elaborate planning and customer feedback over intuition.[175]
- The speed of problem-solving increases.
- The time to market is reduced.
- It involves lower upfront commitment of cost.

8. Thinking through Analogy

In the 1970s, mini mills entered the steel business by making cheap concrete-reinforcing bars known as rebar. Industry giants did not seem to mind their entry since this segment was unprofitable for them. This gave mini mills access to an uncontested market, where they tasted success. Bolstered by their success, they gradually moved up the value chain. In due course, they ended up disrupting the giants of the steel industry.

In the 1990s, Intel was resisting entering the cheap microprocessor market for inexpensive PCs. Intel's CEO at the time, Andy Grove, alluded to the steel analogy, referring to cheap rebars as 'digital rebar'. He argued, 'If we lose the low end today, we could lose the high end tomorrow.' Intel soon began to promote its low-end Celeron processor more aggressively to makers and buyers of inexpensive PCs.[176] This enabled Intel to maintain its hold over the market.

You too can benefit from the power of reasoning through analogy, and influence people to agree to do what is thought to be impractical, undoable or unworthy.

9. Reasoning through First Principles[177]

Elon Musk believes that thinking through analogy has a drawback. It presupposes that what has not happened in the past is unlikely to happen in the future. After all, he was a victim of this thinking. When he started thinking of bringing down the price of electric batteries, people pointed out that past efforts to reduce the price came to naught and a similar fate awaited him.

Musk embraced reasoning from 'first principles' to overcome the limitation of thinking through analogy. It involves boiling things down to the most fundamental truths and then reasoning up from there.

Let me hand over the stage to Elon Musk to take the narration forward: 'Battery packs are expensive. Historically, it costs $600 per kilowatt-hour. Using first principles, the question to ask is, "What are the material constituents of the batteries? They are cobalt, nickel, aluminium, carbon, and some polymers for separation, and a steel can?"

'Now if these items were bought on a London Metal Exchange, it would merely cost $80 per kilowatt-hour. Now the task is to think of clever ways to take these materials and combine them into the shape of a battery cell, and you can have batteries that are much, much cheaper than anyone realizes.'[178]

Here are other benefits that accrue from reasoning through first principles:

- It liberates us from dogma, cognitive bias and the crippling thinking that if it has not happened in the past, it cannot happen in the future either.
- It helps us to get to the bottom of what we know, as of now, to be the truth, and then work up from there.
- It also gets us to test current assumptions, and check if they still hold water.
- It helps us remove complexity and ambiguity surrounding a problem.

Next time you face an intractable problem, boil things down to the most fundamental truths and then reason up from there. That takes a lot more mental energy, but if you use this technique, you have a chance of earning the sobriquet of being the Elon Musk of your industry.

10. Skin in the Game[179]

The Tata Group set up a factory near Pune for manufacturing trucks and buses. One night, a group of agitated villagers gathered at the factory gate. They claimed that the effluents from the factory had been discharged into the stream flowing by their village and had poisoned the water. Their buffaloes were dying after drinking it.

The management acted with alacrity. They gave full compensation to the villagers for the loss of their animals and ordered an investigation to identify the fault. Following the investigation, the effluent disposal system was upgraded. To make the system foolproof, decisions were taken to change the direction of the fully treated water. Instead of it flowing out towards the stream passing through the villages, it would be directed into the company's lake.

Simultaneously, a decision was also taken to hold the officers' monthly meeting in the guest house located near the lake. During lunch, the officers would be served fish caught from the lake. Now the team had to be doubly sure that harmful effluents that could harm the fishes, and therefore themselves, were not being discharged. The problem never reared its ugly head again.

- **Family First**

I was the president of an FMCG company. We were in the last quarter of the financial year and wanted to close the year with record sales. We decided to come up with a scheme for the sales team which would motivate them to give their best shot.

We designed a scheme not for the sales team, but for their families, and called it 'Family First'.

In the Family First scheme, every product in the company's portfolio carried points. Premium-priced products that yielded high margins were allocated more points, while lower-priced products which had lower margins were assigned fewer points. Then we selected a mix of household items and gadgets which would appeal to the family:

- Toaster
- Food processor
- Dinner set
- TV set
- Personal computer

An attractive brochure was designed in which each of these items were prominently displayed along with the points next to them, which would be required for getting them.

We briefed the sales team about this scheme and showed them the brochure. They were excited and wanted a copy.

You will get it soon, we told them.

We had no intention of handing the Family First brochure to them. The brochures were couriered to their homes. When they reached their homes, they became a hot topic of conversation. By the time the salesperson reached home, every family member had made up their mind which product they wanted from the brochure.

- Wife: Food processor, toaster, dinner set
- Son: Personal computer
- Daughter: TV set

The family members bombarded the salesperson with their choice. To pacify them, he nodded, which the family members took as consent.

The salesperson realized that he would have to put in an extraordinary effort to get the sales numbers that would enable him to earn sufficient points to get the items his family members wanted. From that day onwards, when he reached home, the family members did a daily sales review. God forbid, if there was a shortfall in sales, he was told in no uncertain terms that he had to make it up. He was no longer working for the company. Now he was working for his family.

Our work was taken over by the families of our sales team and the family review system proved to be more effective than our sales review system.

We closed the year with excellent sales numbers.

If you too wish to solve a problem, then design a programme in which the skin of the people who must deliver the results is in the game.

This strategy was also followed in ancient times by the Romans when they built an arch. The people who had built it stood under it as the scaffolding was removed.

11. Pre-mortem[180]

A post-mortem allows health professionals and the family to learn what caused a patient's death. Everyone benefits except, of course, the patient. The business fraternity has evolved a system which benefits the 'patient' (read: business). It is called 'pre-mortem'.

A typical pre-mortem begins with briefing the team on the big idea.

Then the leader informs everyone that the big idea has failed spectacularly. Over the next few minutes, people must independently write down every reason they can think of for why the big idea failed, even before it is implemented.

Next, the leader asks each person to read one reason from their list of reasons why the big idea failed. This ensures that many possible reasons of failure are identified before they occur, instead of learning them when the business is autopsied, when precious little can be done. After the session is over, the leader reviews the list and draws up plans to eliminate likely causes of failures.

Pre-mortem works on the principle that forewarned is forearmed. It improves the chances of the success of the big idea.

12. Value Migration

Till not very long ago, customers wanted to be transported in the quickest time and in the most cost-effective manner. Not anymore. Now people, particularly millennials, want to be transported in a 'clean' way.

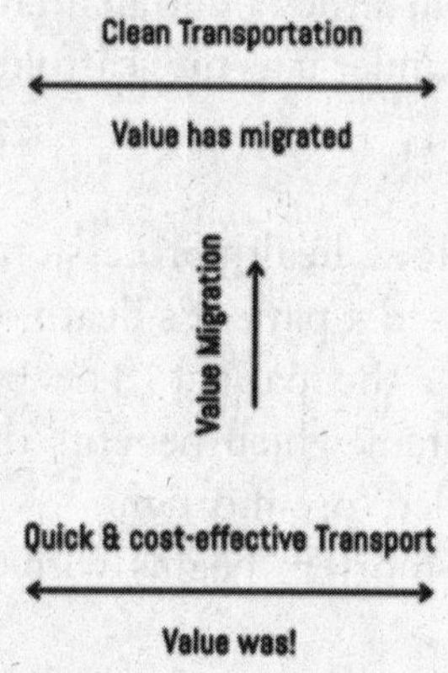

Traditional automobile companies operate where the value was, building automobiles which run on fossil fuels and damage the environment. But Tesla operates where the value has migrated, and therefore, it has been successful in dethroning the traditional automobile companies to become the world's most valuable automobile company.

Patanjali Dant Kanti Toothpaste

Until recently, customers bought toothpaste made using chemical ingredients. Now, customers want toothpaste made from natural ingredients.

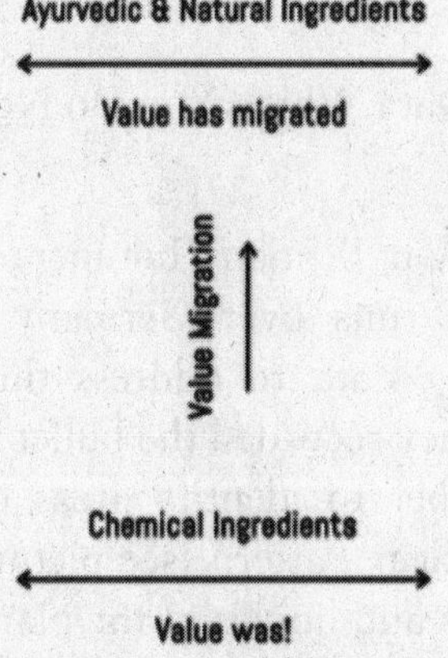

Patanjali Ayurved, co-founded by Baba Ramdev, launched Dant Kanti toothpaste, made using natural and ayurvedic ingredients, and it operates where the value has migrated. As a result, it has stolen the market share from under the nose of blue-blooded MNCs.

Why Are Market Leaders Wilfully Blind to the Value Migration That Happens in Their Industry?

Bill Gates summed up the plight of these companies by observing, 'Success is a lousy teacher. It seduces smart people into thinking they can't lose.' Companies are run by smart people who believe that past success is a guarantee of future success, not realizing that it is akin to driving while looking in the rear-view mirror. Accidents are bound to happen.

Let us bring the discussion to you. Is your company operating where the value was or where it has migrated? If it is the former, take immediate steps to move to where the value has migrated. Else, you face the spectre of becoming irrelevant.

13. Look for Data Which You Do Not Have to Solve a Problem[181]

During World War II, many bombers were getting shot down while on runs over Germany. The researchers started collecting data to address this problem. After every mission, they recorded the bullet holes and damage from each bomber to identify areas of weakness. The data showed a clear pattern (see picture). Most damage was to the wings and bodies of the plane.

The solution seemed obvious: increase the armour on the wings and the body, where the bomber had received the most hits.

Before this decision could be implemented, a Hungarian-Jewish statistician named Abraham Wald scrutinized the data. He detected a fatal flaw in the analysis. The researchers had analysed data available

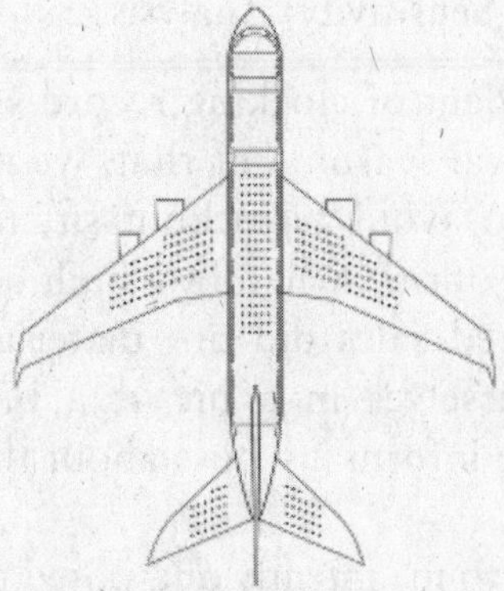

from bombers that had returned to base. Absent was the data of every plane that had been shot down.

The data showed that the bombers that returned had minimal damage in the tail section, the cockpit and the engine areas. It was not because these areas were strong enough to survive a bomb hit. In fact, they were the weakest areas. If hit in these parts, they could not survive.

Ironically, the plotted data had identified the strongest parts of the bomber, which could survive a bomb hit. Other areas of the bomber were vulnerable.

With the new insight into the vulnerable areas of the planes, the tail section, the cockpit and the areas around the engine were strengthened. This action resulted in more bombers returning to base after successfully carrying out their missions.

Many times, it is not the available but the missing data that holds the key to solving the problem. Search for it and take it on board before making a decision. Otherwise you will feel that you have solved the problem, but it would have remained unsolved.

14. 'What If' (Sensitivity) Analysis

We were confident of clocking record sales during the upcoming festival season. For that, we needed to build up inventory to avoid a stockout situation. But there was an element of risk: what if we built up the inventory and the expected sales did not materialize? Then we would find ourselves in a bit of a bind. Therefore, I felt obliged to inform my boss about the risk we were taking.

He listened to me intently and posed two questions:

- What is your confidence level that the expected sales will materialize?
- 'What if' the sales did not materialize? Then what will you do with the excess stock?

'Sir, our confidence level is over 80 per cent that we will do the expected sales. In case they do not materialize, then we will offer additional schemes to incentivize our channel partners to pick up the excess stock. The extra cost of the scheme will be funded by the quantity discount we have negotiated with our manufacturer for supplying this "extra" stock,' I said, and continued, 'If the expected surge in sales happens, then the morale of our team will go up. If it does not, then we can liquidate the stock at no extra cost to the company.'

My boss greenlit the plan.

As luck would have it, our worst nightmare came true. Sales did not materialize as per our expectations. In this moment of crisis, the 'what if?' question of my boss came to our rescue. He had made us mentally plan for this contingency. The extra stock was liquidated by offering attractive schemes to our channel partners, without adversely impacting our bottom line.

Bulletproof Monthly Sales Target

At the beginning of each month, I would pose a question to the sales head: 'How do you propose to achieve this month's sales target?'

He would share with me the detailed plan he had drawn. I would study it and pose a question: 'What if' three customers who have promised to give sales orders go back on their word? How would you make up for the loss?

The situation was hypothetical. But it forced my sales head to think of strategies for recouping this 'hypothetical' loss in sales.

He would give me three options for recouping it. We would debate till it was not just an idea but a plan capable of delivering sales, if the situation demanded it. This strategy ensured that we met our sales target with monotonous regularity.

15. Scenario Planning

The 'what if' analysis can bulletproof a scenario that has a chance of going wrong by identifying areas of weakness and vulnerability and proactively planning for overcoming them. But it falls woefully short when it comes to anticipating a Black Swan event, a term popularized by Nassim Nicholas Taleb in his book *The Black Swan: The Impact of the Highly Improbable.* It is characterized by three attributes:

a. It is unpredictable.
b. Its repercussions are far-reaching.

c. After the event, people assert that the event was predictable and foreseeable.
d. Nothing in the past can help us prepare for it.

The Scenario Planning exercise provides a technique for anticipating a Black Swan event.

It directs us to create implausible scenarios and then come up with possible responses to them. It has many benefits.

- Since the event has not happened, there is no precedent of how to tackle it. This forces people to put on their thinking caps and think afresh. There is more free flow of thoughts and exchange of ideas.
- During brainstorming sessions, there is a greater acceptance of contrarian voices.
- It expands the thinking of the team.
- It makes the team 'proactive, not reactive'.
- It prepares them to come up with a response to a Black Swan event so that they are not paralyzed into inaction if it materializes.
- Groupthink is averted.

Scenario Planning Exercise for Anticipating a Black Swan Event

As a first step, identify the heart of your business, which is unique to your business and imparts it a competitive advantage.

Now pose a question to yourself and to the team:

- What if the 'heart' of our business disappears overnight, without a warning?

The answer to this question will help you in anticipating a Black Swan scenario and motivate you to proactively start planning to tackle it!

How Did We Plan for a Black Swan Event?

The heart of our FMCG business was our extensive distribution muscle. It contributed nearly 95 per cent to sales. I posed a hypothetical question to myself: What if our extensive distribution system disappeared overnight? That meant that overnight, 95 per cent of our sales would disappear. It would threaten the existence of our company.

In anticipation of this Black Swan Scenario, we decided to identify new revenue streams which were independent of the existing distribution system. Here is what we came up with:

- List our products in Canteen Stores Department (CSD). It is a retail chain owned by the Government of India under the Ministry of Defence. It has a presence in all major military bases in India and listing here would ensure that our products were available for sale across CSD stores.
- List our products in modern trade stores, like Big Bazaar, Reliance Retail, etc. This would ensure that our products were available for sales in their stores across the country.
- Develop 'institutional' business through which we could sell our products directly to pharmaceutical and alcoholic beverages companies, who would run promotional schemes using our products to promote their products among their stakeholders.

- Focus on export markets in SAARC and Middle Eastern countries.
- Develop a 'private label' for modern trade stores, the hospitality industry, etc. It involved making products under the retailer's or the hospitality company's brand name and supplying it to them.

Instead of waiting for a Black Swan event to strike us, we proactively took steps to implement these new revenue streams that we had identified. As a result, we de-risked our business and made our company stronger.

16. Funnel Analysis

The world is witnessing double disruptions caused due to the pandemic and increasing automation. As a result, McKinsey & Company has predicted that 'while some jobs will be lost, many others created, but almost all will change'. Are you prepared to face double disruption?

If you are keen to prepare yourself to face the future shaped by these double disruptions, then 'funnel analysis' can come to your rescue. It involves several steps:

- Step 1: Frame the question you wish to get answers to. In this case, the question would be: *How do I prepare myself in a world double-disrupted by the pandemic and increased automation?*
- Step 2: Meet experts from this area and stakeholders who are likely to be impacted by double disruptions, pose the above question to them and record their statements. Refer to column 1.
- Step 3: Sub-group statements with similar thoughts (column 2).

- Step 4: Sub-group statements with similar thoughts and club them under one skill (column 3).

FUNNEL ANALYSIS

How to be future ready in a double-disrupted world caused due to pandemic and increasing automation?

COLUMN 1	COLUMN 2	COLUMN 3
STATEMENTS	SUB-GROUP SIMILAR STATEMENTS	SUB-GROUP SIMILAR STATEMENTS AND CLUB THEM UNDER ONE SKILL
Challenge traditions.	1. Coming up with big ideas to solve wicked problems.	*Creativity*
Converting customer complaints into blockbuster products.	2. Getting best ideas from outside my industry and adapting it to my industry.	
Coming up with big ideas to solve wicked problems.	3. Executing the big ideas so that they are profitable.	*Innovation*
Question assumptions.	4. Challenge traditions.	*Critical Thinking*
Discover hidden business opportunities.	5. Question assumptions.	
Transform commodity into a brand.	6. Defy long standing norms.	
I want to share my ideas with the world.	7. Discover hidden business opportunities.	*Frame Right Question*
Getting best ideas from outside my industry and adapting it to my industry.	8. Converting customer complaints into blockbuster products.	
Defy long-standing norms.	9. Coming up with smart solution.	*Smart Problem-Solver*
I want people to use their cognitive skill to solve company's problems.	10. I want people to have aspiration greater than the available resources.	*Entrepreneurial Spirit*
Executing the big ideas so that they are profitable.	11. I want people to work with a sense of ownership.	
Coming up with smart solution.	12. I want to share my ideas with the world.	*Skilful Storyteller*
I want people to work with a sense of ownership.	13. Transform commodity into a brand.	
I want to persuade people with my ideas.	14. I want to persuade people with my ideas.	*Influence People Without Authority*
How to keep myself abreast with the latest knowledge?	15. I want people to support my ideas.	
I want people to have aspiration greater than the available resources.	16. I want people to use their cognitive skill to solve company's problems.	*Humanness*
I want people to support my ideas.	17. How to keep myself abreast with the latest knowledge?	*Lifelong Learner*

The funnel analysis indicates that you must acquire four basic types of skills:

1. Higher-level cognitive skills
    - Creativity
    - Innovation
    - Critical thinking
    - Framing the right question
    - Smart problem-solving
    - Entrepreneurial spirit
2. Social skill
    - Storytelling
    - Influencing without authority
3. Emotional skill
    - Humanness
4. Self-management skill
    - Lifelong learner

If you acquire them, you will be better prepared to face this double-disrupted world.

Funnel analysis is omnipotent and has the power to give directions to overcome any and every problem you face.

17. Design Thinking[182]

Design thinking (DT) is a popular tool used for solving problems. It keeps the people for whom the solution is designed at the centre of decision-making. Therefore, DT comes up with solutions best suited to them. Other problem-solving techniques place the company or the brand at the centre, and not necessarily their customers.

Therefore, they arrive at solutions that benefits the latter and leave the customers disappointed.

Design thinking involves the following steps:

- Team composition: The team that is charged with solving the problem has diversity of gender, nationalities, cultures and functional expertise. This ensures that diverse experiences and views are brought to the table. This facilitates coming up with creative solutions.
- Conducting ethnography research: The team observes, listens and engages with people to gain first-hand understanding of the problems they face. As a result, the team members start empathizing with the people for whom they are designing solutions.
- Framing a driving question: Based on research, a driving question is framed which will inspire team members to generate ideas by pushing past obvious solutions to get to breakthrough ideas and solutions.
- Ideation phase: During this phase, team members adopt a 'divergent' approach to come up with as many creative ideas as they can. Once this is done, then they take the 'convergent' approach to zero in on a specific big idea. While arriving at it, the team adopts an integrative and holistic perspective by seeking to understand how the recommended idea will integrate with the existing larger system.
- Prototyping: The shortlisted idea is prototyped, and feedback is sought. Every feedback leads to a fresh round of iteration. Every iteration leads to

refinement of the idea and the experiment moves forward.

- Execution: The final idea that surfaces through iteration is executed.
- Communication: The idea is communicated by crafting a compelling story which inspires action.

PillPack[183]

PillPack followed the design-thinking process to transform the nightmarish experience that elderly people had to endure in getting their prescription filled into a pleasurable one. They developed a prescription home-delivery system which delivers prescribed medicines to their doorstep.

Ethnography research identified that elderly people find it difficult to buy prescribed medicine and have it on time due to a variety of reasons, which include:

- Difficulty in visiting a pharmacy.
- Waiting at the pharmacy to fill out the prescription.
- The medicine finishes or expires without warning.
- Missing having it on time.
- Unable to understand which medicine must be taken in combination with which one.

PillPack designed a system through which the doctor sends the prescriptions straight to the pharmacists, who organize the medications into pre-sorted, personalized packets. These tidy little packets are labelled by date and time and delivered to the customers' doorsteps. Every fourteen-day supply of medication is delivered at home.

Pharmacists at PillPack's are available any time via phone or email to answer questions, should one wish to speak with them.

PillPack transformed a painful experience for elderly people into a pleasurable experience by following the tenets of design thinking.

Problem-Solving Mindset[184]

McKinsey Quarterly[185] has identified problem-solving mindsets for very uncertain times. It starts with good news. Great problem solvers are made, not born. You too can become great at problem-solving by inculcating a mindset which encourages curiosity, tolerates ambiguity and remains humble, taking a dragonfly-eye view of the problem and tapping into the collective intelligence of the crowd.

Let us unpack them to gain deeper insight into each one.

- **Be Curious and Frame Questions with 'Why'**

To generate more curiosity, put a question mark after the initial hypothesis or first-cut answers.

- Why is this so?
- Why is this solution better? Why not that one?

'The small artifice is surprisingly powerful: it tends to encourage multiple solution paths and puts the focus, correctly, on assembling evidence,' say Charles Conn and Robert McLean in 'Six Problem-Solving Mindsets for Very Uncertain Times', in *McKinsey Quarterly*.[186]

- **Tolerate Ambiguity and Stay Humble**

Problems-solvers realize that their knowledge 'is always provisional and incomplete and that it might require revision considering new evidence,' warn Charles Conn and Robert McLean.[187]

Humble people know that problem-solving involves a lot of trial and error. They 'challenge solutions that imply certainty by asking questions such as "What would we have to believe for this to be true?" This brings to the surface implicit assumptions about probabilities and makes it easier to assess alternatives.'[188]

- **Take a Dragonfly's-Eye View**

'Dragonflies have large, compound eyes, with thousands of lenses and photoreceptors sensitive to different wavelengths of light . . . This enables their eye to take in 360 degrees of perception,' say Charles Conn and Robert McLean.[189]

A problem-solver adopts a dragonfly's-eye view by 'widening the aperture on a problem or viewing it through multiple lenses. The object is to see beyond the familiar tropes into which our pattern-recognizing brains want to assemble perceptions. By widening the aperture, we can identify threats or opportunities beyond the periphery of vision.'[190]

- **Tap into Collective Intelligence and the Wisdom of the Crowd**

Chris Bradley, co-author of Strategy *Beyond the Hockey Stick*, observed, 'It's a mistake to think that on your team you have the smartest people in the room. They aren't there. They're invariably somewhere else. Nor do they need to be there if you can access their intelligence via other means. In an ever-changing world where conditions can evolve unpredictably, crowdsourcing invites the smartest people in the world to work with you.'[191]

Derailers in Problem-Solving

Be warned: these are invisible enemies which can subliminally thwart your attempts to solve a problem!

- **Heuristics**
  Heuristics alludes to a mental shortcut that allows an individual to decide, pass judgement or solve a problem quickly and with minimal mental effort. It is a rule of thumb used by our brain to make decisions. But it can also prove to be costly when individuals miss critical information or act in a biased manner. Here is an example: in judging distance, for example, our minds frequently rely on a heuristic that equates clarity with proximity. The clearer an object appears, the closer we judge it to be. The fuzzier it appears, the farther away we assume it must be. This simple mental shortcut helps us to make the judgements about distance required to navigate the world. Yet, like most heuristics, it is not foolproof. On days that are hazier than normal, our eyes will tend to trick our minds into thinking that things are more distant than they appear.[192]
- **Subconscious Decision-Making**
  Most of the time, our brain makes decisions subconsciously. We are not even aware of the process our brains follow to make decisions.

It seems that our brain does not follow a step-by-step process to make decisions. Therefore, we cannot review the process of the brain. In many cases, it serves us well. But at times, it can let us down. Many times, we end up making suboptimal decisions. Whether the decision turns out to be right or wrong becomes clear only after the decision has been taken and implemented.

- **Pattern Recognition Bias**

  Pattern recognition is deeply ingrained in our DNA. It helped us survive. As we read in the chapter on storytelling (Skill 7), our forefathers believed that the swaying of the grass was an indicator that a predator was hiding behind it to ambush them. Thereafter, whenever they noticed this pattern, of swaying grass, they surmised that there could be a predator and moved in the opposite direction. In most cases, the predators would not be present. It could be wind that was gently swaying the grass.

  Even in business, we take decisions based on our past experiences (read: pattern recognition). Taking decisions based on pattern recognition is akin to driving a car while looking into the rear-view mirror. Accidents are likely to happen.

- **System 1 in Control**[193]

  System 1 thinking is thinking that operates automatically and quickly. It takes little or no effort and is heavily influenced by context and past experiences. Therefore, it is prone to error.

- **Wilful Blindness**[194]

We choose to be wilfully blind to information which can unsettle our fragile egos, challenge our long-cherished beliefs or our worldviews and most importantly, which evokes our fear of change. We opt for this strategy because it makes us feel better not to know.

- **Bounded Rationality**[195]

  Bounded rationality is a human decision-making process in which we seek a decision that will be good enough, rather than the best possible decision. Therefore, because of cognitive and temporal limitations, we do not gather all the necessary information that would be required to make a rational decision.

  Bounded rationality causes us to make satisfactory choices, but that does not mean that those choices are optimal. We make 'good enough' decisions instead of the best ones.

- **Cognitive Biases**

  We are blind to the obvious and we are also blind to our blindness, warns Daniel Kahneman. This blindness is manifested as cognitive bias. Here are two cognitive biases that many of us fall victim to:

- Self-love bias: Most of us are in love with our solutions and want them to win. This obsession prevents us from evaluating other options or listening to other views. We become ardent salespersons of our own ideas and solutions. We defend them with the tenacity of a bulldog. We are unwilling to change our position, even when additional data is provided. Our aim is to defend it and if nothing else works, push it down the throats of others. We are not open to dissent or feedback.

- Ownership bias: We believe that our solutions are far superior to other people's, and we fight tooth and nail to implement them.
- Illusion of attention: We believe that while we were solving the problem, nothing escaped our attention. The reality is very different, as this experiment conducted at Harvard University proves.

In this experiment, people were shown a video of a basketball game and were instructed to count the number of times the ball was passed. In the video, six people—three in white shirts and three in black shirts—were passing the basketball among themselves. While the game was in progress, a gorilla walked across the middle of the court, thumped its chest and exited; in the process, it spent as many as nine seconds on the court.

When the subjects were asked if they had noticed the gorilla, the results were shocking. It was discovered that merely half of the participants had noticed the gorilla! The others were so focused on the task of counting the number of passes that they had not spotted something as conspicuous as a gorilla on the court.

This experiment revealed that when people are single-mindedly focused on a goal, they tend to miss what is happening in the environment. The interesting part is that they have no idea that they have missed the obvious.

- Outcome bias: We focus on arriving at a solution and overlook systems and processes that need to be followed to arrive at it.

- Illusion of skill: We tend to believe that we have considerable expertise in problem-solving. The reality may be otherwise.

Postscript

If you find all this too complicated, then it would be wise for you to follow the strategy pursued by ancient Persians to solve problems. Herodotus, the Greek historian, reported that the ancient Persians tended to deliberate on important problems and coming up with solutions while they were drunk. They then reconsidered their solutions the following day when they were sober. If a solution was approved both drunk and sober, the solution held; if not, the Persians set it aside.[196]

Smart Problem-Solving in a Nutshell

Smart Problem-Solving

The business world is littered with problems.
Smart problem-solving skill arms you with perspectives, tools, techniques and frameworks to come up with smart solutions.

Problem-Solving Techniques

1. Lateral thinking.
2. 5 whys.
3. Contrarian thinking.
4. What is not going to change?
5. Reframe the problem.
6. Think backwards.
7. Perpetual beta.
8. Thinking through analogy.
9. Reasoning through 1st principles.
10. Skin in the game.
11. Pre-mortem.
12. Value migration.
13. Look for data which you do not have.
14. 'What If' (Sensitivity) Analysis.
15. Scenario planning.
16. Funnel analysis.
17. Design thinking.

Problem-Solving Mindset

1. Be curious and frame question.
2. Tolerate ambiguity and stay humble.
3. Take a dragonfly view.
4. Tap into collective intelligence and the wisdom of the crowd.

Derailers in Problem-Solving

1. Heuristics.
2. Subconscious decision-making.
3. Pattern recognition bias.
4. System 1 thinking in control.
5. Wilful blindness.
6. Bounded rationality.
7. Cognitive biases.

Self-Management Skill

Skill 6

Lifelong Learning

In a volatile, uncertain and complex world disrupted by technology, people need to be lifelong learners. It increases employability, accelerates career advancement, enhances self-confidence, and helps to remain relevant and face the unexpected with aplomb. In brief, it is a passport to being a lifelong winner.

Proudly, I presented a copy of my book, *The New Rules of Business*, to Adi Godrej, chairman of the Godrej Group.

As we waited for tea to be served, I requested, 'Sir, please share a life lesson that has stood you in good stead.'

'Never stop learning,' he said softly.

Growth Mindset

Godrej, at seventy-seven, displayed an insatiable desire to learn, making him eminently qualified to be described as a lifelong learner. Such people possess a growth mindset, which makes them believe that no matter how much they know, it is less. This feeling of inadequacy motivates them to keep learning. They worry less about looking smart and put more energy into learning.[197] They tend to achieve more than those with a fixed mindset, who believe that they are innately talented and know almost everything. As a result, they whittle away their energy in trying to prove that they are always right.

Satya Nadella, the CEO of Microsoft, hit the nail on the head when he said, 'The learn-it-all (read: growth mindset) will always do better than the know-it all (read: fixed mindset).'[198]

In addition, they possess many more laudable traits:

- They believe that it is fine not to have all the answers and are comfortable saying, 'I do not know!' They rationalize it by saying that 'now' does not mean 'never'. Later, they direct their efforts towards discovering (read: learning) the answers to fill the gaps in their knowledge. New knowledge increases their confidence.

- They consciously cultivate the habit of continuous learning by following the five-hour rule.[199] No matter how busy they are, they devote at least an hour a day—or five hours a week—learning, reflecting or practising. They do this throughout their lives. By relentlessly following this seemingly simple rule, they set into motion the law of compounding: small actions that we consistently undertake, every day, which by themselves do not make any noticeable impact, but when they are done regularly over time, the compounding effect is a mammoth one. For example, if you get 1 per cent better each day for one year, you will end up thirty-seven times better by the time you are done.[200]

Let me explain with an example. You decide to build your running stamina. You start running. On the first day, you will not notice any increase in your stamina. Even by the end of the first week, you are unlikely to notice any difference. But if you persist for six months, then you are sure to notice the difference. By now, the law of compounding would have come into play!

Why Do We Stop Being Lifelong Learners?

During childhood, our learning curve is steep because 70–80 per cent of our dialogue consists of asking questions: 'why', 'how' and 'what'.

As we grow up, the rate of asking questions drops to between 15 per cent and 25 per cent.[201]

Why do adults refrain from asking questions, despite knowing that the answer will help fill the gap in their knowledge?

The fear of being ridiculed, shamed and laughed at! Such people wilfully ignore the sagacious advice of Confucius: By asking a question, you may appear a fool for a minute, but by not asking the question, you remain a fool for life.

Strategies for Turning into a Lifelong Learner

Here is a curated list for you to metamorphose into a lifelong learner.

1. Read–Reflect–Teach

To secure a seat at the prestigious Indian Institute of Technology (IIT), I had to ace the Joint Entrance Examination (JEE). I reached out to my uncle, who was then a professor at IIT Bombay, for advice. He said I should read about the topic I wished to understand. 'Then close your eyes and reflect and recall what you have read. If you can recall what you have just read, then you can claim to have understood the topic,' he said.

I followed his advice and started to experience the benefits. But I felt that to get a good JEE rank, I needed to gain mastery over those subjects.

Once again, I sought my uncle's advice. His mantra: teach what you have learnt.

Forthwith, I implemented his advice. My sister was one year senior to me in college. I offered to teach her and her friends physics, mathematics and chemistry. Although they were in a higher class, my level of understanding was better and therefore, I was able to fluently explain concepts to them. If they posed a question I could not answer, it did not embarrass or disappoint me. I would go back to my notes to seek an answer, return forthwith and explain it to them. This strategy made me gain mastery over those subjects.

Teaching can be a powerful force for learning. It compels us to gain a deeper and more cogent understanding of the topic. It also helps us discover gaps in our knowledge. We build confidence in what we're passing along, which in turn leads to learning.[202]

By pursuing the strategy of reading–reflecting–recalling–teaching, I was able to realize my dream of securing a seat at IIT Kanpur. I used the same strategy during my stay at IIT and later, while preparing to take the Common Admission Test (CAT) to secure a seat at IIM Bangalore!

Albert Einstein had proposed a variant of this strategy: Explain what you have learnt to a six-year-old. If you can do it successfully, then you can certify yourself as having mastery over the subject.

2. Read a Lot[203]

The brain is a muscle. Reading develops it and keeps it healthy and strong.

Warren Buffet follows this strategy. He spends 80 per cent of his working day reading and thinking. He says, 'I just sit in my office and read all day. That is how knowledge builds up, like compound interest.'

There are many more benefits of reading:

- It fills us with facts, information, ideas and knowledge.

- Reading requires focus, concentration and attention. These are critical skills for learning. When we engage in reading, they improve.
- It improves our analytical thinking because it rouses our brain to think in unusual ways.
- It impels us to think and reflect.

How much should we read? 'Till our children call us a book with legs,' says Charlie Munger, the long-time business associate of Warren Buffet.

3. What You Know Is Key to New Learnings

Work took me to France and Russia. During the few days I spent in Paris, I was able to add many French words and phrases to my vocabulary. I spent an equal number of days in Moscow, but picked up fewer Russian words. This happened because in school, I had learnt basic French. Therefore, I already had an existing, though meagre, vocabulary in French. This old learning acted like a magnet to which new French words and phrases got attached. But I had no prior exposure to the Russian language. Therefore, there was no existing base of knowledge (read: magnet) to which new words or phrases could get attached.

In this resides an insight into learning—what you know is key to new learnings, because new learning will get 'attached' to your existing learning. In this way, your body of learnings will keep growing.

You can execute this strategy by:

- Taking online courses.
- Cultivating an eclectic taste in books.

- Cultivating a diverse set of acquaintances and engaging with them in discussions.
- Seeking new experiences.
- Opting for career rotation.

These activities will broaden your width of 'knowing'. Now, whenever you are exposed to new learnings, they will get attached to the little you already know. This way, the little that you know will keep on growing.

4. Learning though Observation

Our company had sponsored a cricket Test match between India and the West Indies, held in Mumbai. As a result, I got a VIP pass. The West Indies batted for a day and a half. Then it was India's turn to bat. Three Indian players, one behind the other, were walking out to open for India. I was puzzled—how could three batsmen open for India? Soon, the puzzle was resolved—two players walked out to the middle, while the third player, wearing full cricketing gear, sat on a chair in the scorching sun, near the boundary. I asked an official, 'Who is the person sitting in the scorching sun?'

'Sachin Tendulkar!' he answered. I was surprised. In Test matches, Sachin batted at number four.

'He bats at number four, so why is he sitting in the scorching sun, wearing complete cricketing gear?' I asked the official.

'To acclimatize himself!' he replied nonchalantly.

I was dumbfounded by Sachin Tendulkar's work ethic. His turn to bat would come later. But he was acclimatizing himself, while the batsman who was due to bat next was sitting in the air-conditioned comfort of the players' dressing room.

This sight of Sachin Tendulkar got etched in my heart. It motivated me to adopt his work ethic. Since then, I started preparing for meetings and presentations much before the scheduled dates. On the appointed day, I would arrive before time for meetings and presentations, well prepared.

Unknown to me, I learned work ethics through observation. It entails learning by mindfully observing the behaviour of others.

5. Shadow the Leader

Organizations have tried to institutionalize the process of learning through observation by instituting a programme titled 'Shadow the Leader'. In it, a youngster is attached to a senior member of the company with the mandate of shadowing them. This provides an opportunity to the youngster to learn from observing how the leader makes decisions, engages with people and generally conducts themselves. The youngster seeks to memorize and then exhibit these behaviours, or versions of them. This strategy ensures that the work ethics and learnings of the seniors are transferred to the juniors.

6. Learning through Discovery

My son Kautuk and I were watching the finals of the 2006 FIFA World Cup. Zinedine Zidane, the French captain, in a fit of anger, head-butted Italian defender Marco Materazzi. He was red-carded. Kautuk was devastated.

'He cannot be red-carded!' he screamed, even as Zidane was leaving the field.

When the match ended, I asked him, 'Where did the idea of the red card come from?'

'I don't know,' he replied. But the question intrigued him sufficiently to ask me, 'Tell me where it came from.'

'I will,' I said, 'but first, try to discover it. If you cannot, then I will tell you.'

In double quick time, he 'discovered' the answer and shared it with me for validation.

'A referee had dismissed an Italian player. But due to the language barrier, the player was not able to understand that he was being asked to leave the field. This frustrated the referee. One day, he was driving in London, and he saw the traffic light turn red. He stopped. In a moment of serendipity, it struck him—yellow means caution, 'take it easy' and red means 'stop—you are off'. He intelligently adapted this idea to the game of football and proposed it to FIFA, the governing body for football. It was accepted and has now become an integral part of the game,' said Kautuk triumphantly.[204] Since he learnt it himself, he has not forgotten it since.

When learning is through self-discovery, it makes us more interested in learning[205] because:

- We are not bored of learning because we are learning what interests us.
- In this state of mind, we learn to understand and not merely to memorize.
- We learn at our own pace. Therefore, we can grasp the content better.
- Self-learning takes a meandering path to what is sought to be learnt. In this journey, we are exposed to a variety of other topics that were not on the agenda.

Therefore, if you do not know an answer and somebody offers to tell you, request them to give you time to discover it. By this simple act, you will be putting into play 'learning through self-discovery'. The learning you acquire through this process will be more durable and you will be exposed to many more new topics as you undertake this journey.

7. Learn without an Agenda[206]

'I had dropped out (of Reed College) and didn't have to take the normal classes. So, I decided to take a calligraphy class. None of this had even a hope of any practical application in my life. But 10 years later, when we were designing the first Macintosh computer, it all came back to me. And we designed it all into the Mac. It was the first computer with beautiful typography,'[207] reminisced Steve Jobs while delivering the 2005 commencement address at Stanford University, and added, 'Again, you can't connect the dots looking forward; you can only connect them looking backward. So, you must trust that the dots will somehow connect in your future. This approach has never let me down, and it has made all the difference in my life.'[208]

I too have intuitively followed the strategy to learn without an agenda, believing that these learnings will somehow help me in later years.

Opting for Psychology Course at IIT Kanpur

At IIT Kanpur, we were studying to be engineers. As a part of the programme, we also had to take courses in Humanities and Social Sciences (HSS). I chose to do courses in psychology. When my friends asked me the reason for taking these courses, I could offer no rational answers, except to say that I wanted to understand why people behave the way they do. They would shake their heads in disbelief, muttering something about wondering how understanding people's behaviour would make me a better engineer.

Later, I joined IIM Bangalore, and stared to specialize in marketing management. The psychology courses I had taken in IIT Kanpur stood me in good stead. They gave me a deeper understanding of consumer behaviour, about how they think, feel and make decisions about what they buy and how they will respond to new products. These insights enabled me to create many successful whisky brands which won the hearts of customers. Here is an example.

Drinkers Sip the Image of a Brand, Not Just the Blend

While working in the alcoholic beverages industry, I was assigned the responsibility of managing whisky brands. To offer them a competitive edge, I made a conscious effort to gain a deeper understanding of how consumers thought and felt about this product category.

I decided to conduct a mini-dipstick study.

I bought a popular brand of Indian whisky and the world's best-selling scotch, broke the seals of both bottles and interchanged the blends. I poured the Indian whisky into the bottle of the world's best-selling scotch whisky, and the best-selling scotch into the Indian whisky bottle.

At this time, the one-way pourer cap, which is the first line of defence against counterfeiting, had not been introduced in India.

Now, I invited three self-proclaimed whisky connoisseur friends for a tasting session.

In front of them were placed empty glasses, cheese, soda, water and ice.

I started by pouring the best-selling Scotch whisky from the Indian whisky bottle into everyone's glass. They made their drink to taste by adding water or soda and ice. Having got their drinks ready, they all roared a collective 'Cheers' and took a sip!

I sought their feedback. Unanimously, they gave it a thumbs down, saying that the whisky was harsh and it burned their throats.

I asked them to take a bite of cheese to cleanse their palates.

Now, from the bottle of the world's largest-selling scotch whisky, I poured the Indian whisky. They added soda or water and ice to taste, raised their glasses and said 'Cheers'.

'What is your feedback?' I asked.

Everybody unanimously voted it to be of excellent quality.

This dipstick indicated that drinkers consume the image of a brand and not just the blend.

Based on this consumer insight, I concluded that investment should be made into ensuring that the quality of the blend was excellent. But a larger investment, if not an equal investment, should be done into crafting the image of the brand. After all, connoisseurs consume image, and not just the blend.

I leveraged this insight to give a competitive advantage to alcoholic brands that were under my charge.

8. Learn from Your Failures

Every failure provides us with a teachable moment. Then why do we fear failures?

Stigma is attached with failure. People who fail are perceived to be losers and less gifted, and they do not wish that label to be ascribed to them. Failure also triggers the release of stress-causing hormones like cortisol. Therefore, people tend to justify their failures with reasons ranging from bad luck to non-preparation—everything except themselves. By pursuing this strategy, they fritter away precious opportunities for learning.

Henry Ford hit the nail on the head when he said that the only mistakes (read: failure) we make are those from which we learn nothing.

- **Learning from My Failure**

We launched a premium whisky in the 750 ml pack size. This decision was based on hard data that in the premium segment, the 750 ml pack size sold the most. But the market gave the new brand a lukewarm response.

Research conducted to understand the cause of the lukewarm response indicated that premium whisky drinkers indeed preferred the 750 ml pack size, but of their favourite brand. They did not wish to take the risk with a new brand and preferred to buy a smaller pack size—375 ml or 180 ml. Upon trial, if the new whisky was found to be good, then they bought the larger pack size. This failure taught me an important lesson: data should not be used blindly.

- **Learn from the Failures of Others**

Life is too short to make all the mistakes (read: failures) ourselves. It pays to learn from the failures of other people, too. I have learnt from the failures of others. Even of my boss.

I was working in a conglomerate. In a meeting, the discussion centred on the cash crunch in the flagship company, which was adversely impacting its business.

The chairman looked at the group CFO and asked for suggestions to alleviate the problem.

'A group company has recently raised money from the market. It is still not deployed, since the project for which it was raised is delayed,' informed the group CFO, and then suggested a solution, 'They can provide a bridge loan to our flagship company.'

The chairman liked the idea; he looked at the president of the company, who had raised the funds, and asked him, 'Can you give a bridge loan?'

The president looked at the chairman and said, 'Sorry, sir. This is public money. It has been raised for a specific project. Using it for any other purpose would mean violating the terms for raising it.'

The chairman looked a wee bit disappointed, and he guided the discussion towards exploring other ways of raising funds to help the flagship company.

After the meeting was over, I walked across to the president, who was also my mentor, and said, 'Sir, you should not have refused the chairman point-blank in front of all of us. You should have done it in private.'

'Yes, Rajesh, I realized my mistake. After the meeting, I went to his office and apologized to him,' he said.

'But by then the damage was done,' I said.

He nodded his head in agreement.

Soon, he was transferred (read: demoted) to another position, which entailed fewer responsibilities.

This incident taught me an important lesson. Do not disagree with your superiors in public. If required, do it in private. Also, I used a variant of it while dealing with team members: praise in public. Reprimand in private. I have strictly followed these learnings and have won people's support for my actions.

9. Peer Learning

An Italian proverb reminds us that if we live with cripples, then we will soon learn to limp. Empirical research lends credence to this axiom—we become the average of the five people we choose to spend our time with.[209]

Guided by this insight, I make a conscious effort to have diversity in my network of friends on multiple dimensions—gender, nationality, age, profession and those who are more knowledgeable and smarter than me.

Since they came from varied backgrounds, they brought refreshingly different experiences and divergent points of view. To accept varied viewpoints is an important part of learning.

While in their company, I do not feel a sense of shame or inadequacy in admitting:

- I am sorry, but I do not seem to know. Please explain it to me.
- Please tell me something new. You always seem to know interesting things.

- What do you think? I would love to hear your take on it.
- This sounds so interesting. Please tell me more.

These questions give people cues about what I wish to learn. Since I have posed them, the person assumes that I am genuinely interested in learning. This motivates them to open up and provide answers.

I actively listen with the sole intent of understanding the narrator's viewpoint. At regular intervals, I pose questions, not to challenge them, but to gain a better understanding of their viewpoints.

If I have still not understood, then I do not feel any shame in saying: I am sorry, but I have not understood. Can you explain it again?

A word of caution—pose questions so that they sound like a request, not an order. This you can achieve by prefixing them with 'please' or another affirmative word.

The list of benefits that accrue from asking questions and seeking clarifications is long. But the result is the same—it fills the gap in our knowledge, and we progressively become better.

If there is an abundance of benefits, then why do people refrain from having a diverse circle of friends and acquaintances?

Because they are victims of affinity bias,[210] which makes us connect with people like us, who share similar interests, experiences and backgrounds. This prevents conflict and unpleasantness. But it acts as a barrier to learning.

10. Learn from All

Galileo Galilei had observed an aeon back that he had never met a man so ignorant that he couldn't learn something from him.

'Humble people recognize you can learn from anyone and everyone,' confirm Adam Grant and illustrates it with an example, '. . . a student who was admitted to Yale . . . asked his school's janitor to write his recommendation letter. The appreciation and curiosity that the student showed toward somebody who's literally at the bottom of the totem pole in that high school. That's humility.'[211]

I too believe that everyone, in some way, knows more than me. Therefore, I can learn from everyone. Here is what I have learnt from my driver, caretaker, Uber driver, a stewardess and others.

- **Driver: Never Be Late**

During my corporate stint, I depended on my driver to drop and pick me from the airport and to get me to meetings on time. Never once was he late. In fact, he was ahead of time. Intrigued, I asked him about his secret recipe.

'Sir, when you tell me to report at 6 a.m., you have already added half an hour as a buffer. On top of it, I add another half hour buffer. I plan to reach by 5.30 a.m. Even if things go wrong, and they do, I have an hour of buffer to ensure that I am always ahead of time.'

I embraced his strategy and have acquired a reputation for being ahead of time for appointments.

- **Caretaker: Serve with a Smile**

I frequently visited Dubai. Instead of staying in a hotel, I opted to stay in an apartment. The caretaker of the apartment always wore a smile while greeting, serving food or when asked to run an errand. One day, I asked him how he managed to always serve with a smile.

He replied, 'Sir, I have two options: to serve you with a frown or with a smile. If I serve you with a frown and you get upset and complain, then I could lose my job. That would be a monumental tragedy for me and my family. But if I serve you with a smile, then you are likely to say good things about me to my superiors. This will make them happy, and my job will be safe.'

Since then, I have always approached any job assigned to me with a smile.

- **Uber Driver: Compassion and Generosity**

It was a hot day. I was taking an Uber back home. After covering some distance, the Uber driver asked with deference, 'Sir, can I take a break?'

'Yes,' I nodded.

He parked the car, darted out and returned in a jiffy. After settling in his seat, he turned around and gave me a chilled bottle of water.

'Sir, for you. You must be thirsty,' he said with a gentle smile.

I was touched by his gesture. He needed to save every penny. But he spent it to refresh a rider whom he might never meet again.

It dawned on me that we do not have to be rich to practise compassion and generosity. Also, no act of generosity, no matter how small, ever goes waste. It gets paid forward.

I have paid it forward by offering counselling to my students and to people in my network whenever they have reached out to me for help. My only condition is that they pay it forward. In this way, acts of kindness, generosity and compassion are perpetuated.

- **Steward: Power is Not Given. It Is Taken to Delight Customers**

I was invited by an MNC to conduct a workshop in Bengaluru. They put me up at the Marriott. Every day, I had breakfast at the coffee shop. A young lady would enthusiastically serve me. On the last day of my stay, I had breakfast and was about to leave when I heard her say, 'Sir, please wait.'

I did as I was told. Moments later, she returned holding a plate with a pastry. On it was written in chocolate sauce 'Bon voyage'.

I was speechless, but soon found my voice to thank her for her delightful gesture.

Apologetically, I told her, 'I have just finished my breakfast. I cannot have this wonderful pastry.'

'No problem,' she said. 'I will pack it so that you can have it later.'

'I am travelling back to Mumbai and it will be difficult to carry it,' I informed her.

'Sir, wait,' she said, sprinting away, and returned a moment later with the pastry safely ensconced in a container. 'Now you can carry it. It will not inconvenience you.'

From the young lady, I learnt critical lessons in management:

- When the actions are time-sensitive, then empower yourself. Do not escalate the issue to your boss. They will respond but, by then, it could be too late.
- Practise the art of addressing the customer's concerns on the fly. It will delight them, and that will transform them into a brand advocate who show a high degree of loyalty towards your company.
- Your actions should do the talking for you, not your words.

A word of caution: Acts of generosity and compassion should come from your heart. Do not do them for brownie points.

11. Learning from the Experiences of Others[212]

The retail food business suffers from shrinkage. This is caused due to spoilage, employee theft, shoplifting or being cheated by suppliers in some way. But Whole Foods, known for selling nutritious eats, did not track it systematically. They believed that it was the cost of doing business.

In 2017, Amazon bought Whole Foods. Amazon has vast experience in collecting data and making decisions based on it. They prevailed upon Whole Foods to track all the shrinkage and compare it across stores so that they could get the data to identify where the problems are, and then try to reduce them. Whole Foods started followed this advice, and reduced shrinkage. It had a positive impact on the bottom line.

12. Reverse Mentoring

We inhabit a world powered by technology. In this world, senior people find themselves feeling like fish out of water. But millennials, the digital natives, are comfortable in this world. They have sufficient dexterity to 'teach' senior people how to navigate this world.

Many organizations are leveraging this insight by getting younger people to become teachers to senior members of the company. This is called 'reverse mentoring'.

I have been a beneficiary of reverse mentoring.

Till 2009, I was not active on social media. In contrast, my son, Kautuk, was hyperactive on it. He offered to help me. I became his student, and he became my tutor. In a jiffy, he opened my dormant Facebook account and asked me to identify an issue about which I felt deeply.

The Indian Premier League was on and as a marketing person, I was at a loss to understand why CEAT Tyres was sponsoring the strategic time out. After all, there was no connection with the brand and the property it was sponsoring. The only benefit it could garner would be brand recall. He heard me and with the speed of lightning, keyed in my thoughts and posted them. Immediately, I started receiving responses. I was soon flooded with dopamine, the pleasure hormone. I felt elated. Since then, I have been active on social media. As a result, I have been able to get in touch with my students across the world. The credit goes to reverse mentoring.

13. Learn through Purposeful and Deliberate Practice

Malcolm Gladwell is the author of many *New York Times* bestsellers, including *Outliers*, in which he introduced the concept of '10,000 hours of practice' for becoming an expert in any field. His postulation found widespread acceptance. But there was a caveat—the practice should be deliberate, purposeful and coupled with high-quality feedback.[213]

Here is an example. If I wish to learn to drive a car, and practise driving on an empty road for 10,000 hours, will I become a skilled driver? Maybe no, because when I drive on city roads, they are unlikely to be empty. There will be other vehicles on the road, and pedestrians who will be coming from all sides. Under such circumstances, merely practising for 10,000 hours will not skill me to drive in real-world conditions.

Therefore, I should undertake deliberate and purposeful practice under the varying conditions that I am likely to encounter on the road, and seek high-quality feedback, which I should incorporate in the next round of practice. Then, at the end of 10,000 hours, I can certify myself as being a skilled car driver.

The same is true for learning. Commit yourself to 10,000 hours of deliberate, purposeful practice coupled with high-quality feedback. In the end, you will be tired but will have the satisfaction of certifying yourself as being an expert in the area.

14. Learn through Physical and Mental Practice

When deliberate and purposeful practice, coupled with a high standard of feedback, is done at two levels, physical and mental, then the quality of learning skyrockets.

Let me get elite tennis players into our discussion. When they 'physically' practise, their coach gives them high-quality feedback. Back in the hotel room, while lying on the bed, they engage in 'mental' practice by playing the game on the ceiling of the hotel room (read: in their mind). Even when they play the game mentally, the brain forms the same neural connections as it does when they are physically practising. This dual strategy of practising both physically and mentally results in the formation of muscle memory. During the actual match, then, they can reproduce shots automatically.

What is true for elite sportspeople is also true for us. The combination of deliberate, purposeful practice which is both physical and mental will result in greater improvement in learning.

I followed this strategy while teaching a brand management course at IIM Indore. I would go through the teaching material (physically) in the evenings. At night, while lying on the bed, I would close my eyes and recollect the content (mentally). By practising physically and mentally, I was able to deliver a flawless performance in class. I almost always got excellent student feedback!

15. Learning, Unlearning and Relearning

In 1985, while studying at IIM Bangalore, we learnt many principles of management ('darlings'), which were written in stone. For a long time, they proved to be true. But as the twenty-first century dawned, many of them were proving to be ineffective. To stay relevant, I had to kill those darlings which had outlived their utility and acquire new 'darlings'.

- **Darling 1: Leaders Speak First**

Over time, I discovered that some people in my team, to please me, would hear my opinion and when asked for an opinion, parrot a variation of it.

To get their honest opinion, I reversed the order. The team members spoke first. I spoke last.

- **Darling 2: Leaders Have All the Answers**

On numerous occasions, I was bereft of answers to the many business challenges facing us. I admitted to my team that I did not have answers and sought solutions from them. The team rose to the occasion and suggested solutions that helped us surmount those challenges.

- **Darling 3: Keep Customers Happy**

We had learnt that our job was to keep customers happy. But much to my amazement, I realized that I had to keep employees happy, because they make customers happy and happy customers give repeat business. So I replaced keeping customers happy with keeping employees happy.

Become adroit at discarding the 'darlings' which have outlived their utility. Substitute them with new darlings. Keep repeating this process.

16. Express Yourself in Multiple Mediums

Express what you have learnt in multiple mediums.

- Twitter: It will compel you to present the learning in 280 characters.
- Instagram: You will have to present your learning pictorially.

- Podcast: You will have to share the learnings through the audio medium.
- YouTube: You will have to use your ingenuity to present the learning in an audio-visual format.
- Facebook: You will have to craft a post so that the learning appeals to your friends.
- LinkedIn: You will have to craft your post such that the learnings appeal to professionals.

When you share your learning through all the above mediums, then you have earned the right to be called a subject matter expert.

Enablers for Turning into a Lifelong Learner

There are a multitude of enablers which will help you transform into a lifelong learner. Here is a curated list:

- Be curious. It makes your brain more receptive to learning.
- Reclaim your natural tendency to ask questions: 'why', 'how' and 'what'. This will enhance your learning.
- Do not pretend that you know everything. This feeling of inadequacy will motivate you to keep learning.
- Be ready to be challenged.
- No matter how much you know, be consumed by an insatiable desire to know more!
- Stop berating yourself if you do not know. In fact, get comfortable saying 'I don't know'. Follow this by asking 'Can you please explain it to me?'

- Become comfortable moving out of your comfort zone and trying something new, at regular intervals, if not every day. In short, seek new experiences; they are an important and invaluable source of learning.
- While learning, when you concentrate, your mind consumes an inordinately large amount of energy. This makes you feel enervated. In this frazzled state, your ability to absorb and retain learning goes down. It is advisable to learn in short bursts and with periodic breaks. A rule of thumb is to learn for an hour and a half and then take a break for fifteen minutes.
- Learning is best when it is slow and accompanied by pauses, during which you should engage in reflection on what you have learnt.
- Reading and reflection are great ways of learning.
- Learn through debates and discussions where your learnings and points of view are challenged.
- No matter how busy you are, devote an hour to learning, every day, five days a week.
- Before settling down to learning, get into a positive mood. Learning is enhanced when you experience positivity.
- Learning through self-discovery is an effective way of learning.
- Learn without an agenda.
- Do not be ashamed of failure. Look upon it as an opportunity to learn. Also, learn from the failures of others.

- Make it a habit to learn from peers. Also, develop a high-quality network. Then make a conscious effort to learn from the network.
- When learning gets appreciated, you will be motivated to continue to learn more. Keep the company of people who are supportive and appreciative of your proclivity to learn.
- Learning is an iterative process. Keep going over what you have learnt and reflecting on what you have learnt. In this way, you will absorb what you have learnt and make the learning your own.
- Engage in purposeful and deliberate practice and actively seek feedback. Incorporate it in the next round of learning.
- Practise what you have learnt at two levels: physical and mental.
- Permit yourself to change your opinion if new information surfaces.
- Learning can only be internalized when it is applied. Therefore, at every opportunity, practise applying it. Here are a few ways:
    - Offer workshops in your areas of competency.
    - Write blogs and articles in your industry journal.
    - Seek out opportunities to be a speaker at industry forums.
    - Teach what you learn to your network. It is best to teach children. If they understand what you have taught them, then you can certify yourself as having truly gained mastery over the subject.
- In the Internet era, you can learn almost everything through tutorials offered on YouTube or by doing

a Google search. This will help you keep filling the gaps in your knowledge. Assign the responsibility of learning to yourself.

- Create a learning community or join a club or an organization focused on the topics you wish to learn. Or even join a degree programme. Massive Open Online Courses (MOOCs) offers opportunities to learn from the world's best teachers. In addition, take time out to listen to podcasts and audiobooks.
- Different people learn differently. Some learn by listening, others by reading, some by doing and some by watching demonstrations. Identify the learning style which suits you best and adopt it.
- Get yourself reverse mentored by getting younger people to become your teachers.
- Seek opportunities to 'shadow an eminent person' and learn by observation and imitation.

Derailers in the Path of Becoming a Lifelong Learner

You will encounter many roadblocks as you embark on the journey to transform yourself into a lifelong learner. Beware of them.

- Many learners embark on the learning journey when survival is at stake.[214] In such cases, learning is done with the sole objective of warding off the threat. The downside is that when the threat recedes, the learning evaporates.

  Here are a few examples when learning is done under duress:

- ○ To pass an examination.
- ○ To get a degree because without it, getting a job would be difficult.
- ○ To ace a job interview because it would mean getting a job.

As soon as the threat recedes, the learning that happened under duress also evaporates.

To retain learning, refrain from learning under threat. Learn because you want to learn and do it of your own volition.

- Nurturing a fixed mindset which makes you believe that you are innately talented and know almost everything and do not need to engage in learning. To banish this malice, adopt a growth mindset.
- Allowing distractions, like mobile phones and laptops to be in proximity with you. Eliminate distractions by keeping the mobile phone on airplane mode and turning off all notifications.
- Engaging in multitasking by switching among tasks. This leads to distraction, and it impairs learning. To get rid of this evil, discipline yourself to focus on one task at a time.
- Going on learning without unlearning and relearning. To ward off this derailer, follow the mantra 'Learn. Unlearn. Relearn.'

All these strategies for learning will come to naught if we do not guard against unconscious biases. They come in the way of learning. Here are just few of them:

- Curse of knowledge: Once we feel that we know something, it is difficult to imagine not knowing it. It can result in a professional tumble.[215]
- Gender bias:[216] We tend to learn from one gender over another gender.
- Blind spot bias: Believing that you have none of the biases, but other people are likely to be infected by them.

How Will You Know If You Have It in You to Transform into a Lifelong Learner?[217]

To determine if you can transform into a lifelong learner, pose two questions to yourself.

- Do you want to keep learning and getting better?'
- Are you willing to feel the discomfort of putting in more effort and trying to learn new things that will feel weird and different and won't work right away?

If the honest answer is an unequivocal 'yes' to both questions, then you can certify yourself as possessing the mindset for being a lifelong learner.

Postscript[218]

Charlie Munger started his career as a lawyer, making $20 an hour. He thought to himself, 'Who's my most valuable client?' And he decided it was himself. So he decided to sell himself an hour each day.

He used that hour to read and learn. Today, he is Warren Buffet's right-hand man and vice chairman of Berkshire Hathaway.

Let us bring the discussion to you. You are your most valuable client. Sell yourself an hour a day. But do not fritter that hour on social media or binge-watching Netflix. Instead, invest it in learning. You will transform yourself into a learning machine and prove Charlie Munger's observation right: 'I constantly see people rise in life who are not the smartest, but they are learning machines.'

If this sounds difficult to follow, then follow a simpler piece of advice from Charlie Munger, 'Go to bed every night a little wiser than when you woke up.'

Lifelong Learning in a Nutshell

Lifelong Learner

In a volatile, uncertain, complex and uncertain world, which is disrupted by technology, people need to be lifelong learners. It increases employability, accelerates career advancement, enhances self-confidence, helps to remain relevant and face the unexpected with aplomb. In brief, it is a passport for being a lifelong winner.

Strategies for Transforming into a Lifelong Learner

1. Read – Reflect – Teach.
2. Read a lot.
3. What you know is key to new learning.
4. Learn through observation.
5. Shadow the leader.
6. Learn through discovery.
7. Learn without agenda.
8. Learn from failures—yours & others'.
9. Peer learning.
10. Learn from all.
11. Reverse mentoring.
12. Purposeful and deliberate practice.
13. Physical and mental practice.
14. Learn. Unlearn. Relearn.
15. Express in multiple mediums.

Enablers for Transforming into a Lifelong Learner

1. Be curious.
2. Ask questions.
3. Do not pretend to know everything.
4. Be ready to be challenged.
5. Get comfortable saying, 'I don't know' & follow up by asking, 'Can you explain it?'
6. Become comfortable moving out of your comfort zone.
7. Learn in short bursts.
8. Learn. Reflect. Teach.
9. Choose slow, deliberate and reflective way of learning over learning fast.
10. Every weekday devote an hour to learning.
11. Before learning get into a positive mood.
12. Self-learn through self-discovery.
13. Take on the onus of learning on to yourself.
14. Be self-motivated to learn.
15. Learning is an iterative process. Keep revising.
16. Permit yourself to change your opinion.

Derailers in the Path of Becoming a Lifelong Learner

1. Learning under threat.
2. Fixed mindset.
3. Surrounded by distractions.
4. Plagued by anti-learning biases.
5. Keeping on learning without unlearning.
6. Multitasking.

Social Skills

Skill 7

Storytelling

Storytelling is the most powerful way to put ideas into the world.[219] *Those who have mastered the art of storytelling win.*

In 2009, the 'Significant Object' experiment was conducted to determine if associating stories with 'insignificant' objects increased their value.

For this experiment, a bunch of trinkets was purchased for $129. Storytellers were approached to invent a story for each of them. These trinkets, along with the invented stories, were put up on eBay. They sold for $3612, fetching an eye-popping return of 2700 per cent.[220]

Merely associating stories with insignificant objects made them valuable because stories arouse us emotionally.[221] In this state, rational thinking is crippled, while emotion gain the upper hand, and we act in a manner which is emotionally fulfilling.

Psychologists also support this empirical evidence.[222] They say that there are two sides to our brain: the emotional side and the rational side. The emotional side can be considered an elephant, while the rational side can be seen as the rider sitting atop the elephant. Stories that touch our emotions arouse the elephant. Then the rider (read: rational part of the brain) has little control over it. The elephant almost always has its way (read: emotion wins!).

Why Is Storytelling Effective?

We have been communicating through stories for more than 20,000 years.[223] Wisdom and knowledge have been transferred from one generation to the next through oral storytelling. It took many forms, like songs, poems, chants, prayers, proverbs and more. This has made us proficient at listening, remembering and retelling stories. Only later were they written down and much later, printed, after the invention of the printing press.

Benefits of Storytelling

Storytelling offers plenty of benefits. Here is a partial list.

- **Pass on the Storyteller's Experiences to the Listeners**

Let me take you back in time to when our ancestors would sit huddled around campfires to share their day's experiences.

Today, a hunter is narrating his day's experience (read: his story). 'I noticed a slight movement of grass. On closer scrutiny, I noticed a lion. I shot an arrow in his direction. Taken by surprise, he ran for his life, and I for mine. Do not go alone to the place where I sighted a lion. Many lions are roaming there in search of prey.'

As the story was being narrated, neural coupling occurred between the storyteller and the listeners' brains. This resulted in his experience getting passed on to the listeners and they started to feel as if they had experienced the event.[224]

- **Heightened Focus, Attention, Trust and Meaningful Connections among Listeners**

Neural coupling causes similar hormones to be released in the listeners' brains to those released in the hunter's brain when he was experiencing the event.

Let us go back to the story and track the release of hormones in the listeners' brains:

- Cortisol, the stress hormone, would have been released when the lion entered the story. This would also have resulted in heightened focus and attention on the story.
- Adrenaline, the flight or fight hormone, would have been released when the hunter took to

his heels. Events which cause the release of this hormone tend to be well remembered.

- Dopamine, the happiness hormone[225] which makes us feel more hopeful and optimistic, would have been released when the hunter reunited with the tribe and the story had a happy ending.
- Oxytocin, the feel-good, trust hormone, would have been released as the story progressed. It would have built empathy, connection and trust between the narrator and the listeners.[226]

- **Help People Remember Patterns That They Later Use to Make Decisions**

The hunter mentioned that the swaying of grass (read: a pattern) meant a predator could be hiding in the grass. This pattern would be stored in the listeners' memories. In future, when they notice the swaying of grass (read: pattern), they will deduce that a predator could be lurking behind it to ambush them. They will refrain from venturing in that direction.

Pattern recognition involves making a connection between memories and information that is being received. It helps to predict what is likely to happen.

- **Stories Are Remembered over a Longer Time**

When we hear intensely emotional stories, hormones like adrenaline and dopamine are released. It facilitates formation of declarative memories, which can be consciously recalled or declared. These memories stick around for a considerable time and are considered long-term memories.[227]

- **Facts Are Boring. Stories Make Them Interesting and Memorable.**

Let me narrate a story in two ways.

Narration 1: The master died. His pet Alsatian died soon after.

Narration 2: The master died. His pet Alsatian died heartbroken.

Which narration did you like? Most people vote for the second, because it has emotion embedded in it. Emotions makes stories memorable. Narration 1 merely stated a fact, which is staid and boring.

As human beings, we are hardwired *not* to remember facts nor understand logic for long. But we understand, remember and recall stories [228] because stories emotionally arouse us, and emotional arousal and memory are closely linked.[229] Stories go where logic and rational thinking are denied admission: our hearts. Therefore facts, when communicated in the form of an interesting story, are twenty-two times more likely to be remembered,[230] because our brain decodes visual information 60,000 times faster than text (read: data).[231]

Instead of presenting data and logic to influence people, use the power of storytelling. It will pay good dividends.

- **Complex Ideas Can Be Explained through Stories**

Storytelling is an age-old technique to communicate complex ideas in ways that it is easily understood and acted upon. There will also be many listeners who may not understand the story. But all are likely to remember the message the story sought to communicate and act upon it.

Case Studies Illustrating the Power of Storytelling

During my corporate career and later as an educator, a trainer and an author, I did not solely rely on data, logic, 'carrot and stick' approach or the power of my chair to influence corporate team members, students and readers to my way of thinking. Instead, I relied on the soft power of storytelling to influence them. It paid rich dividends.

Presented below are case studies which will educate you about the power of storytelling.

1. Transform a Commodity into a Brand

I was teaching the brand management course at IIM Indore. A student raised his hand and asked me, 'Sir, how can we convert a commodity into a brand?'

When he raised his hand, I noticed that he was wearing an engagement ring.

'Are you wearing your engagement ring?' I asked.

'Yes,' he said.

'An engagement ring is a commodity. Monsieur Louis Cartier, the brilliant jewellery designer, converted it into a brand by associating an emotional story with it,' I said, and proceeded to narrate the story.

'The Trinity de Cartier[232] ring has three different colours of gold, intertwined in an eternal embrace. Each colour represents a timeless emotion:

- Pink for love.
- Yellow for fidelity.
- White for friendship.'

When this 'story' is narrated to men, they get emotionally aroused. In this state, they purchase it to gift to their lady friend, praying that their relationship should be bound in an eternal embrace of love, fidelity and friendship till death do them part. The ring stirs similar emotions in the lady receiving it. As a result, the Trinity ring has transcended from being merely a ring to a brand capable of stirring oodles of emotions.

2. Create Preference for a Brand

Nestlé launched 'the Cocoa Plan' with the twin objective of improving the lives of cocoa farmers and ensuring an uninterrupted supply of good quality cocoa.[233]

This plan offered literacy schemes for women and children, believing that when they have access to education, cocoa communities have a bright future.[234]

These initiatives won Nestlé the goodwill of farmers and it ensured an uninterrupted supply of good quality cocoa, which went into manufacturing its various brands of chocolate, including KitKat.

When this story is narrated to consumers, that the chocolate that goes into making KitKat is from 'the Cocoa Plan', which plays the role of a catalyst in brightening the future of the cocoa community, it ceases to be merely a chocolate brand. It is transformed into a compassionate brand and Nestlé into a compassionate company.

Buyers prefer to buy KitKat, believing that through the small act of buying it, they are also supporting the cocoa farmers and their families to live better lives.

Nestlé associated a story of 'do well by doing good' with its brand to create a preference for it.

3. Motivate the Team to Work Hard

The year had ended. We had turned in an excellent performance. Throughout the year, we had worked with unmatched passion to re-energize our company. Green shoots were starting to become visible. Still, a lot more was to be done to turn the corner. A meeting was called to share the achievements with the employees and prepare them for the struggle ahead. As I got up to speak, a chorus greeted me, 'Let's celebrate! Let's celebrate!'

I looked at my people and asked, 'May I tell you a story?'

'Yes! Yes! Yes!' they chanted!

This lore is about Henry Ford. He revolutionized car manufacturing by introducing the assembly line. The first assembled car rolled down the ramp and stopped a few feet from the assembled group, comprising top team members, including Henry Ford. The team broke into spontaneous applause.

'Mr Ford, we have created history. We should celebrate,' chorused the team members.

Mr Ford acknowledged the applause, looked at his watch and said, 'Gentlemen, we have exactly 60 seconds to celebrate. And then we get back to work.'

Friends, we have taken the first tentative step towards re-energizing our company. We still have a long way to go. If we continue to work together, we will truly be out of the woods. Then we will celebrate for days on end. But, today, we have exactly 60 seconds to celebrate and then we get back to work.'

As if on cue, the team went back to work. The company went on to repeat its good performance over the next two years and turned the corner.

Why did the team return to work?

Our brain is hardwired for survival. Therefore, we are motivated to behave and act in a manner that ensures our safety and survival. The story underscored an important point: for us to survive, we need to get back to work. They did.

4. How to Manage Up?[235]

Students and participants who attend my workshop often ask me to suggest a toolkit to 'manage up' (read: manage bosses). But the toolkit I provided them proved to be ineffective. This made me take the route of storytelling to show them the path to follow to manage up. I narrate the following story to them.

Michelangelo sculpted the marble statue of David. When it was about to be completed, prominent people from the republic of Florence were invited to preview it. Piero Soderini, protector of the arts, was among them. He expressed his misgivings about the proportions of the nose of the statue.

Michelangelo had a reputation for being temperamental. But in this case, he strangely consented to do the correction. He bent down to collect the hammer and chisel and, strangely, picked up some marble fragments and marble powder which were lying on the floor.

He began the charade of correcting the nose by tapping at appropriate places and keeping the hands slightly open for the marble fragments and marble dust to fall. This gave the impression that Michelangelo was carrying out the suggested changes. This charade convinced Piero Soderini that the statute had become perfect.

I would end the story by saying, 'Do not dissent with your boss in public. It will make them more vindictive. Instead, think of a clever strategy to manage their ego while protecting the authenticity of your effort.'

Students and participants would happily nod their head to indicate that they now had a toolkit to 'manage up'.

5. Leave a Distinctive Mark in Your Career[236]

Many of my students besiege me with the same question: 'Sir, what should I do to leave a distinctive mark in my corporate career?'

To them, I narrate a story from the life of Bollywood star Rishi Kapoor.

On the first day of shooting of the film Bobby, *the song 'Main Shayar Toh Nahin' was to be filmed. Rishi Kapoor arrived early on the set to practise the steps before stepping in front of the camera. He enquired if the choreographer (then the dance master) had arrived.*

He was informed that no dance master had arrived yet! This made him nervous. Soon, Raj Kapoor, Rishi Kapoor's father and the producer and director of the film, arrived on the set and instructed that the lights be turned on. Turning towards Rishi Kapoor, he told him to take his position and start moving from there while lip-syncing to the first line of the song.

Rishi nervously enquired about the dance master.

Raj ji got angry and said, 'Why do you need a dance master?'

'I have never enacted a song in my life,' replied Rishi.

Raj ji heard him and said, 'It is fine. Now stand there and start performing the song.' He did as he was told.

After the shot, Raj ji told Rishi Kapoor, 'If I had called a dance master, he would have shown you the same steps that he had been showing to current superstars like Dharmendra and Rajesh Khanna. You would do the same thing. The public will say that you are copying them. Tum apni chhao banao—*make your own distinctive identity.'*

I would end the story by advising students, 'Strive to be distinctive and establish your own unique identity. It should be so original that others should be inspired to imitate you. Then you are sure to leave a mark in your career.'

6. Overnight Success Is an Illusion

Students want to achieve overnight success. I caution them to be patient. But my advice was like water off a duck's back. This made me change my strategy. I started narrating a story about Pablo Picasso to highlight that overnight success is an illusion and enduring success takes time.

One day, while enjoying his evening meal at a restaurant, Pablo Picasso was interrupted by a fan who handed over a napkin and said, 'Could you sketch something for me? I'll pay you for it. Name your price.'

In response, Picasso pulled out a charcoal pencil from his pocket and swiftly sketched an image of a goat.

The man reached out to collect the napkin, but Picasso withheld it, saying, 'You owe me $100,000.'

The man was outraged. '$100,000? Why? That took you no more than 30 seconds to draw!'

Picasso then crumpled up the napkin and stuffed it into his jacket pocket. 'You are wrong,' he said. 'It took me forty years.'[237] [238]

I would look at my students and pose a question to them: 'If it took Picasso forty years to sign his name, then will it not take lesser mortals like us some time before we achieve success?'

They would nod in agreement.

To further drive home this point, I would recite the words of the Chinese philosopher Confucius (551 BC–479 BC):

Do not be desirous of having things done quickly.
Do not look at small advantages.
Desire to have things done quickly prevents their being done thoroughly.
Looking at small advantages prevents great affairs from being accomplished.

The story of Picasso, supported by the wisdom of Confucius, would strike an emotional chord with the students. They would resolve to work diligently and patiently to earn their success.

7. How to Keep Work-Related Stress at Bay

Work-related stress has become an integral part of life. Unchecked, it can cause insomnia, depression, anxiety and more.

'What should we do?' I am often asked.

With such people, I share words of wisdom given by M.S. Dhoni, former India cricket team captain, who has earned the sobriquet of 'Captain Cool' because even during the most tense moments on the cricket field, he would be unruffled.

'Do not think about the results. It is results which puts pressure on us. It gets us thinking, "what if we do not win the game? What if we do not get selected?" The moment we start to worry about result then fear grip us. When we act out of fear, failure is a likely outcome.

'Think about what is under our control. If we take care of them then we can get the desired result. If we do not get the desired results, then we can learn from the failure and improve. In both cases we gain,' says Dhoni.[239]

I reinforce Dhoni's advice by quoting from the Bhagavad Gita, that we have control over our actions, but not over the results of those actions. Therefore, we should act and not worry about the result.

M.S. Dhoni's advice and the lesson from the Bhagavad Gita prove to be irresistible. Many people embrace this advice and successfully keep work-related pressure at bay.

8. Tell Inconvenient Truths, without Ruffling Feathers

I was invited by an MNC to conduct a customized training programme. For that, it was imperative for me to speak to the participants to gain a deeper understanding of the challenges facing them. But whenever I called, they would be busy attending meetings. I felt it was not a good sign. I wanted to communicate this bitter truth to them. But I dreaded giving this unpleasant feedback, fearing that it may in result in strained relationships. This prompted me to choose the medium of storytelling to communicate this inconvenient truth. On the last day of the programme, I narrated a story to the participants.

A horse was galloping at breakneck speed. As the horse turned a corner, an old man enquired of the man riding it, 'Where are you going, young man?'

'I do not know, ask the horse!' screamed the rider.

I looked around the room. I noticed many smiling faces.

'Why are you smiling?' I asked a participant.

'Most of us are like the rider. We are astride the proverbial horse which is galloping at full throttle. Unfortunately, it is not under our control,' he replied.

Another participant said, 'We should be in control of the most precious resource we have: time. Unfortunately, we are allowing someone else to control it.'

As more and more participants shared their takeaways, a consensus seemed to be building up—they must reclaim control over their time.

I had communicated a bitter truth to the participants. But it did not ruffle feathers since the medium that I had chosen was a story. But the message had hit home.

9. Renounce Bad Habits

During my corporate career, I noticed a smattering of salespeople were addicted to 'buying' sales by offering deep discounts, extended credit periods and indiscriminately dumping stocks in the market. When confronted, they would say that it was second nature to them to get sales at any cost.

I bluntly told them that certain death awaited our company if they continued to buy sales. But to no avail. Finally, I leaned on the power of storytelling to get them to abdicate this deeply ingrained pernicious habit. At a sales meeting where all the erring salespeople were present, I narrated a story:

A scorpion wanted to cross the river. But a strong current made it difficult for him to cross. Looking around, he noticed a bird.

'Can you carry me across the river on your back?' he asked.

'If I do and you bite me, then it will mean certain death,' replied the bird.

'It will also mean certain death for me,' argued the scorpion, and continued, 'Why would I want to kill myself?'

The bird saw merit in his argument and invited him to hop on to her back. Soon, they were airborne.

While they were cruising over the river, the scorpion bit the bird. The bird started to lose consciousness and began to plunge down to her death. In a semi-conscious state, she asked the scorpion, 'Why did you bite me? I am going to die, but so will you.'

The scorpion ruefully looked at the bird and said, 'It is my habit to bite. I cannot help it.' Both plunged to their deaths.

'What lesson did you get out of this story?' I asked the assembled sales team.

'Our bad habit will be the cause of our downfall. It may also trigger the downfall of the company which supports us,' said one salesperson. Most of the team members agreed with him. The sales team took a pledge to abdicate this bad habit of buying sales.

Storytelling was able to achieve what a carrot and stick policy could not!

10. Motivate People to Give Their Best at Work

I was invited to conduct a workshop with a mandate to motivate company employees to give their best at work. During the workshop, I shared frameworks, tools and techniques which could help the participants deliver a superlative performance every day. I concluded the workshop by narrating a story.

Every morning, a lion wakes up and resolves to kill a deer for breakfast. Every morning, a deer also wakes up, wanting to stay alive by outrunning his predators.

'Do you know who wins this race?' I ask the participants.

'Lion,' said a participant.

'Why?' I asked him.

'The lion is stronger and more powerful than the deer,' said the participant.

'Yes, the lion is more powerful and stronger. It should win. But most of the time, the deer wins. Because the deer is running for his life, while the lion is running for his breakfast.'

There was a stunned silence in the room. I looked at the participants, and posed a question to them, 'Every day, at work, do you run (read: work) to save your life, like the deer, or merely work to earn your salary, like the lion? The mindset you display every day at work will determine where you stand at the end of your career.'

'Lion and deer mindset' became buzzwords among the participants. They referred to it when they wanted to remind people to pull up their socks at work or compliment a colleague on their way of working. There was a definite improvement in people's performance.

11. Guidelines for Desirable Behaviour

Stories have the power to guide employee behaviour. Therefore, companies hire 'business historians' to discover stories that are lying undiscovered in the company. They are polished and narrated to the employees. These curated stories inspire employees to act in a manner the organization desires.

- *Story 1*

The founder of a five-star hotel was taking a stroll in the lobby of his hotel. He noticed a guest sleeping on an ottoman. He took his shawl and ever so gently, covered the guest and continued his stroll. Unknown to him, some staff members had observed him draping the guest with his shawl.

The night staff narrated this incident to the staff who came in the morning to replace them. In this way, this story was retold countless times to remind employees that one should go beyond the call of duty to ensure the comfort of the guests of the hotel. Over time, the property earned the reputation of anticipating even the unstated needs of their guests.

- *Story 2*

In 1995, Samsung's chairman Lee was dismayed to learn that the cell phones he gave as New Year's gifts to his associates were found to be defective. He issued an order that all cell phones lying in the godown should be made into a pile. They were piled up and over 2000 staff members gathered around it. It was set on fire. When the flames died down, a bulldozer was brought in to raze to the ground any phone that may have survived the fire. Chairman Lee, who was present on the spot, issued a warning to his people: If you continue to make poor quality products like these, I'll come back and do the same thing.

Fast-forward seventeen years. In May 2012, three weeks before the new Galaxy S III was to be shipped, a Samsung channel partner informed the company that the back covers of the smartphone looked cheaper than the demo models which were shown earlier. Upon checking, it was found that the feedback was correct—the grain wasn't as fine.

There were large number of covers of inferior quality in the warehouse. This time, there would be no bonfire—all the defective pieces were scrapped.[240]

12. Get People to Decode a Complex Idea and Act upon It

The design head of a luxury car company was facing a challenge. His team was unable to design a car with which buyers would fall in love at first sight. No matter how he explained it, his team failed to come up to his expectations.

In a moment of serendipity, he remembered a story from the company's history. He narrated it to his team.

A middle-aged couple visited the company's showroom. The salesperson presented a line-up of cars to the husband. One car caught his fancy and he decided to buy it. Upon the completion of formalities, the key was handed to him. Happily, he got into the car and was on his way home. The driving experience was so exhilarating that he forgot everything. Upon reaching home, he looked at the passenger seat. Lo and behold—it was empty!

It dawned on him that in the excitement of buying the car, he had left his wife in the showroom.

Sheepishly, he made the trip back to get his wife, who was waiting to unleash her wrath on him.

'This is the kind of car I want you to design. Men should fall in love with it so intensely that they should forget the love of their life—at least momentarily,' concluded the design head.

The design team understood what was expected from them and they got down to designing cars with which men fell hopelessly in love.

Each designer would have decoded the story in their own way. But they understood what was expected of them!

13. Fighting Local Competition

Local competition had mushroomed. They were posing a threat to our growth. A national strategy was proving to be ineffective in checkmating them. The solution lay in getting the local team to craft a strategy and execute it with alacrity. I wished to communicate this message to the team. I choose the route of storytelling to deliver it.

A man was heavily steeped in debt. The moneylender magnanimously offered to write it off if he gave his daughter's hand in marriage to him.

The father was reluctant. Noticing this, the moneylender revised the offer. He said, 'The ground is littered with pebbles in two colours—white and black. I will pick two pebbles, one white and one black, and put them in a bag. Your daughter will pick a pebble from it. If it is black, she must marry me; if it is white, your debt is pardoned, and she does not have to marry me.'

The daughter agreed to his proposal.

The wily moneylender bent and picked up two black pebbles, believing that no matter which pebble she picked, it would be black. The daughter noticed his deceit.

The moneylender asked her to pick a pebble from the bag. She picked a pebble, but purposely dropped it. It was impossible to identify which one had fallen.

With contrition written on her face, she said, 'How clumsy of me! But we can still learn the colour of the pebble I picked from seeing the colour of the pebble in the bag. It will be the opposite to the one I had picked.'

The pebble in the bag was found to be black. It was concluded that the white pebble had been picked. The moneylender did not dispute it. The daughter had outfoxed the wily moneylender!

'The local competitors are like the cunning moneylender. They want to defeat us. But you can come up with simple strategies to outsmart them, just like the daughter did in this story,' I said and asked, 'Can you do it?'

'Yes,' they roared back!

They came up with strategies to successfully strangulate local competition. Our growth was back on track.

Story 2.0: Stage Drama Which 'Actively Immerses' Listeners

Storytelling is a powerful tool to put ideas into the world and influence listeners. Many times, it involves them passively. But when stories are staged as drama, it has the power of 'actively immersing' the listeners, making the story more memorable.

An alcoholic beverages company narrated a story in the form of an unforgettable drama.

On the eve of the annual sales conference, the grapevine was abuzz that a revolutionary idea was to be unveiled, which would take the market by storm.

The conference was scheduled to start at 9 a.m. People were already in their seats by 8.55 a.m. The president walked in minutes before the clock stuck 9 and took his place at the head of the table. He was flanked by the heads of sales and marketing, manufacturing, etc.

In front of the president were displayed bottles of the best-selling whisky brands.

The sales conference commenced at 9 a.m. sharp. But a regional manager (RM) was late. He knew the danger of entering the venue late. So he took all precautions to slip into the hall unnoticed.

But the sharp eyes of the president noticed him sliding into the room.

'You are late!' boomed the voice of the president. Saying this, he picked up a bottle of whisky from the display in front of him and threw it at the RM, who took evasive action to dodge the missile hurled towards him. Most people closed their eyes, expecting the missile to hit the target. But luckily, it missed the target and fell on the floor with a loud thud. People expected the whisky bottle to break into thousands of pieces. But to everyone's utter amazement, it did not break.

'Get the bottle,' commanded the president. The RM picked up the bottle and handed it to the president.

The president's face was awash with a beaming smile. Holding the bottle in his hand, he declared, 'This is a PET bottle. Unlike a glass bottle, it does not break. It is convenient to carry . . .' He kept sharing the benefits of a PET pack over a glass bottle. The team lapped up every word.

The 'drama' which had been enacted in front of the sales team had effectively communicated the benefits of a PET pack to them. With a spring in their step, they introduced the PET pack to the market and received a positive response.

Narrating a story by staging a drama actively immerses listeners. It will be better remembered than merely narrating a story in which listeners are passively involved.

I Leveraged the 'Soft Power' of Storytelling to Establish My Competency and Land My Dream Job

'Recruiters may *think* they make decisions based purely on logic, but their *feelings* play just as large of a role.

It's human nature. Emotions drive how connected we feel to other people, and those connections lead us to perceive someone in either a positive or a negative light. The quickest way to land on the "positive" side of that equation is simple: Tell a good story on your resume, in your cover letter, and during your interview,' say Janine Kurnoff and Lee Lazarus in *Harvard Business Review*.[241]

During my corporate career, I followed their advice and narrated stories to get my dream jobs. Later, as an educator, a corporate trainer and an author, I narrated stories to establish my professional competency. This strategy proved to be more effective than presenting hard data to establish my competencies.

Here are the three stories I narrated:

Story 1: I Am Creative

As the marketing head of McDowell & Company, I was charged with the responsibility of proposing a name for a premium whisky. While flipping through a magazine, I came across an advertisement for Signature Bindi. I thought to myself, 'Signature' seems such an inappropriate name for a bindi but an apt name for a whisky. Thus, 'McDowell Signature' got its name.

Creativity involves making connections between dissimilar ideas that seem independent or even in tension with one another, in a new and meaningful way. I had successfully made the connection between women's cosmetics and whisky and therefore I believe I am creative.

Story 2: Grow the Market 100 Times

In 2002, the size of the deodorant category was less than Rs 100 crore. I wanted to re-energize the category. Based on my experience, data analysis and judgement, I reimagined the deodorant as perfume. This re-energized the deodorant category and it has since then grown to over 100 times. Today, perfume has become a generic benefit of the deodorant category. I believe I have the competency to grow a market exponentially.

Story 3: Create a New Segment

In 1990, we launched launch Blue Riband Duet, a premix gin, which had gin premixed with lime. This led to the birth of a new segment, premix gin, and was priced at a premium to Blue Riband gin.

I would conclude by saying that I considered myself to be:

- Creative.
- Possessing skills to grow a market to 100 times its size.
- Having the expertise to create a new and profitable segment.

I would unfailingly succeed in establishing my professional competency.

You too can leverage the power of storytelling to get your dream job and to establish your competency.

DNA of a Compelling Story

There are myriad ingredients that go into making a compelling story that can motivate, inspire and arouse people to action. Here are a few of them:

- Stories should be relatable and emotionally engaging so that they excite the metaphorical elephant, who will then pay scant attention to the rider sitting atop it.
- Emotionally engaging stories tend to be better remembered than simply stating facts.
- Stories laced with metaphors and analogies activate other parts of the brain along with the language part. Here is an example. When I say that at Starbucks the aroma of coffee is mesmerizing, the aroma part of your brain gets activated along with the language part.
- Avoid using clichés and other words and phrases done to death. The brain will be so used to them that it may even overlook them.
- The best stories are not preachy. Leave sufficient scope for interpretation so that people reflect upon the story, arrive at their own conclusions and act upon them.
- Contextualize your story. Then the message will hit home with greater impact.
- Do not manufacture or fabricate compelling stories. Once the fraud is discovered, it will alienate listeners. To paraphrase a popular saying, hell hath no fury as people who are misled.

- A simple, straightforward and heartfelt story will be more impactful than a complicated story. Therefore, refrain from populating it with too many facts, data and characters.
- Each story should drive home a single message.

Transform into a Mesmerizing Storyteller

Here are a few pointers which can help you transform into a mesmerizing storyteller:

- Believe that you have the makings of a mesmerizing storyteller. After all, we all are born storytellers.
- Do not try to copy somebody's narration style. You are likely to fail miserably. Perfect your style of narration.
- Practise narrating stories at every opportunity. The more you practise, the more natural you will become at narrating them.
- Successful storytellers often focus listeners' minds on a single important idea.[242]
- Start building a story bank. Populate it with stories from your personal experiences. Audiences love to hear personal stories.
- Use pauses, eye movements, hand movements, body postures and voice modulations to make the story engaging.
- Narrate stories dramatically. You are sure to score a bull's eye.

Postscript[243]

In 1999, two Stanford students, Larry Page and Sergey Brin, narrated an eleven-word story to a legendary Silicon Valley venture capital investor called John Doerr: Google exists to '*organize the world's information and make it universally accessible and useful*'.

The story inspired him to buy a 12 per cent stake in the company for $11.8 million. Today, it's worth billions.

Storytelling in a Nutshell

Storytelling

Storytelling is the most powerful way to put ideas into the world. Those who have mastered the art of storytelling win.

Benefits of Storytelling

1. Timeless technique to pass on and preserve knowledge.
2. Stories pass on the storyteller's experiences to the listeners.
3. Leads to heightened focus & attention, establish trust, and meaningful connections among the storyteller and the listeners.
4. Stories build empathy and compassion.
5. Stories help people remember patterns which they use to make decisions.
6. Stories are remembered over longer periods of time.
7. Facts and figures are boring. Stories make them interesting & memorable.
8. Complex ideas can be explained better through stories.

Power of Storytelling

1. Transforms a commodity into a brand.
2. Create preference for a brand.
3. Motivate the team.
4. Manage up!
5. Leave a mark in your career.
6. Overnight success is an illusion.
7. How to keep work-related stress at bay.
8. Tell inconvenient truth without ruffling feathers.
9. Renounce bad habits.
10. Motivate people to give their best at work.
11. Guideline for desirable employee behaviour.
12. Communicate complex idea.
13. Fighting local competition.
14. Stage drama which 'actively immerse' listeners.

DNA of a Compelling Story

1. The stories should be relatable, emotionally engaging and arousing.
2. Use metaphors and analogies.
3. Avoid using clichés and done-to-death words and phrases.
4. The best stories are not preachy. Leave sufficient scope for interpretation.
5. Stories told in a context, hit home.
6. Do not manufacture or fabricate compelling stories.
7. Select straightforward and authentic stories with which the audience can relate.
8. The story should be short and simple.
9. Each story should drive home a point.

Transform into a Mesmerizing Storyteller

1. Believe in yourself that you are a born storyteller.
2. Do not try to copy somebody's narration style. Create your own style.
3. Practise narrating stories at every opportunity.
4. With each story, focus on making one important point.

5. Start building a story vault. Populate it with stories from your experiences.
6. Use body language and voice modulations to make the story engaging.
7. Narrate the story dramatically.
8. Enjoy narrating them and do it with unmatched passion.

Skill 8

Influence without Authority

It will enable you to bring others to your way of thinking, motivate them to support your initiatives and adopt your idea of their own free will. This will get you noticed, get you promoted and help you rise in life.

By the early 1990s, Bagpiper whisky was India's largest selling brand of blended whisky. Now, we were determined to make it the world's largest-selling brand of blended whisky.

That would entail sizeable investments in re-energizing the brand. My immediate boss did not have the authority to green-light this. This could only be done by our chairman, Dr Vijay Mallya. I was entrusted with the responsibility of influencing him.

At the annual budget meeting, held that year in Bengaluru, I made the presentation to Dr Vijay Mallya. Looking towards him, I said, 'Sir, we will make Bagpiper the world's largest-selling brand of blended whisky.'

I expected a positive response from him. But there was none. This did not dishearten me. I reframed my proposition and presented it to him with greater vigour: 'Sir we will make Bagpiper the world's largest-selling brand of blended whisky. Do you know what will happen to you?'

This question must have intrigued him. He looked towards me with raised eyebrows, as if asking me, 'What will happen?'

I put the next slide on the screen. It had a picture of Dr Vijay Mallya on the cover of *TIME* magazine. The headline read 'Vijay Mallya, the Man Behind the World's Largest-Selling Whiskey'.

Senior members of the group, in attendance at the meeting, broke into spontaneous applause. Dr Mallya blushed. He kept staring at the screen, soaking in the *TIME* cover. Slowly, his gaze turned towards me, and he posed the million-dollar question that I was waiting for: 'Can it happen?'

'Yes, sir,' I said confidently.

'What is to be done?' he asked.

I told him the investment figure that would be required to realize 'his' dream. Turning towards our president, he asked, 'What do you think?'

Our president, faced with a Hobson's choice, replied, 'We will make it happen.'

Thus started the journey of Bagpiper to becoming the world's largest-selling brand of blended whisky, because I was successful in influencing Dr Vijay Mallya to commit a king's ransom.

Influence can be defined as the ability to affect the character, development or behaviour of someone by tapping into the emotions that drive them to action, and also developing a strong emotional connection with them.[244]

Why Is Influencing People without Authority a Critical Skill?

If you aspire to lead people or drive change, then you will need to master the art of influencing—a skill which, like any other, can be learned.[245] When you have mastered this skill, you will be able to influence people without coercion to:

- Your way of thinking.
- Getting them to support your ideas.
- Adopt your way of thinking.
- Help you in achieving your goals.

This will get you noticed, get promoted and rise higher in life.[246]

How to Influence People

There are myriad ways to influence people. A curated list is presented below:

1. 'Inside–Outside' Strategy

Let us bring the discussion back to my presentation. I had deployed the 'inside–outside' strategy to influence Dr Mallya. To understand it, you will need to gain insight into the workings of our brain. It can be visualized as being made up of three layers:

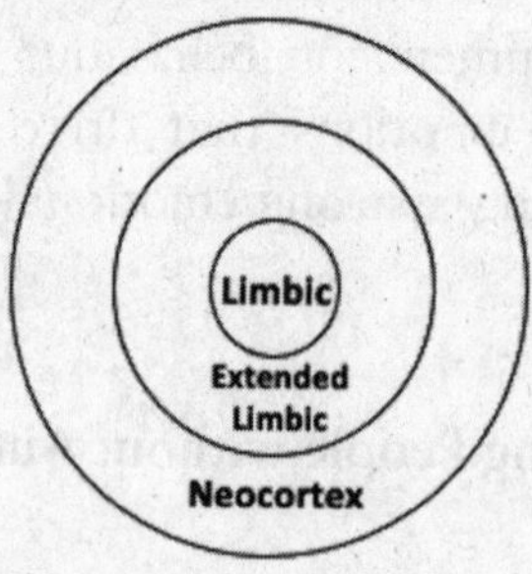

- Inside layer: Limbic brain, where emotion and feeling reside.
- Middle layer: Extended limbic, where behaviour resides.
- Outer layer: Neocortex, where rational thinking and intellect reside.

Let's go back to the presentation. I had framed a rhetorical question whose answer would always be 'yes' because it favoured Dr Mallya: Do you wish to be on the cover of *TIME* magazine? The question must have touched his emotions (read: limbic brain). Emotions determine how we think. Thinking dictates how we feel. Feeling determines how we behave and act.

His intuitive answer, to himself, would have been 'Yes, of course!' The moment that happened, I had won the battle. His behaviour (read: extended limbic layer) towards me changed and he asked me: What is to be done?

I gave him the investment figure which would have activated the rational and analytical part of his brain (the neocortex). Intuitively, he must have greenlit the investment figure because his emotions must have been in control of his thinking process. But he followed the protocol of asking the president for his opinion.

Now let me attempt to influence Dr Vijay Mallya by following the traditional strategy of presenting data, facts and figures to him. This strategy would have activated the rational part of his brain (neocortex), which would have cautioned him to be circumspect. He would have responded along these lines, 'The investment figure is large. Let my office study it and revert.'

His office would have done a rational analysis and advised him: It is better to invest the money where returns are assured rather than in taking a punt on making Bagpiper the world's largest-selling brand of blended whisky, which may or may not happen. In the bargain, our dream would have died a premature death.

Successful politicians also deploy the 'inside–outside' strategy for influencing voters.

Ache Din Aane Wale Hain. Chahiye?

Let us bring the prime minister of India into our discussion.

During the 2014 election campaign, as a PM aspirant, he posed a rhetorical question to the voters which was in their interest: *Achhe din aane wale hain. Chahiye?*

It must have touched their emotions and intuitively, they would have said to themselves, 'Yes, of course!' The moment that happened, Mr Modi won the battle. Their behaviour towards him would change and they would ask him: What do we have to do?

'Vote for me!' he said. Voters did. He won.

Make America Great Again

In 2016, Donald Trump too seemed to have used this technique. He posed a rhetorical question to American voters, which was in their interest: Do you want to make America great again? The answer was 'yes'. As a result, their behaviour towards him changed and they asked him: what do we have to do?

'Vote for me!' Many did. He won the election.

A word of caution: do not use this strategy to manipulate people.

2. Earn Trust

In 2008, I was invited by IIM Indore to teach the brand management course. A well-wisher warned me that I would not be able to control the students. But I had a framework in mind which I was sure would help me influence them.

On day one, I introduced myself, saying, 'Friends, I was lucky to secure a seat in IIT Kanpur. But by the third year, it dawned on me that I would make a bad engineer. I decided to do what all of you have done—join an

IIM. I graduated from IIM Bangalore and worked with unmatched passion to create and build brands which I hope has entertained and given you limitless pleasure. May I mention a few of them?'

'Yes,' said the students.

'McDowell's Signature—I gave it its name,' I said.

A roar greeted this disclosure.

I waited for it to die down before continuing, 'Friends, I am going to say three words from an advertisement. If you can complete it, then I deserve to teach the brand management course.'

The class waited in pin-drop silence for me to utter those three golden words:

'*Khoob jamega rang* . . .' I began.

'. . . *jab mil baithenge teen yaar—aap, main aur Bagpiper*,' the class completed in a chorus.

Now, I posed the third question to them, 'Do you guys use deodorant?'

'Yes,' they said.

'Friends, I reimagined the deodorant category as perfume. Since then, the category has grown multi-fold!'

There was a stunned silence in the class. It told me that I had won their admiration.

What framework did I follow?

Look at the below graph.[247] During my introduction, I had subtly communicated that I was high on competency. And, through my body language, choice of words and style of speaking, I came across as a 'warm' person. As a result, I entered the 'admired' quadrant.

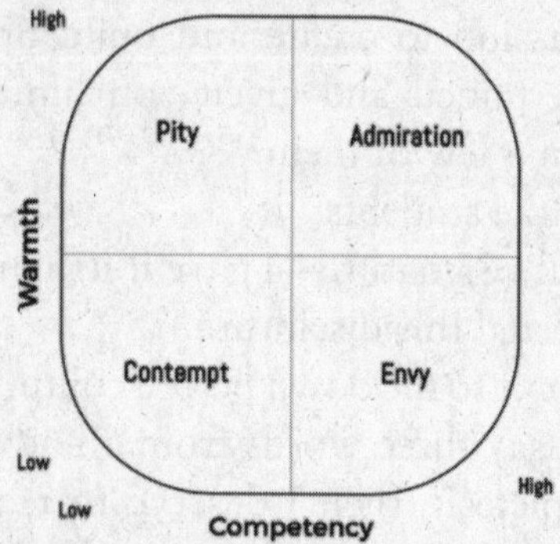

All through the course, I continued to score high on:

- 'Competency' due to the high quality of content I presented to them and the cogent answers I gave to the questions posed to me.
- Warmth because I addressed students by their names. In case I did not know them, I addressed them as 'sir' or 'madam'. I was always polite and respectful towards them, listening to them with patience and responding, not to prove them wrong, but to offer my perspectives. Lastly, I always gave sincere compliments!

As the course progressed, admiration turned into respect and finally into trust. Once I won their trust, then I was able to influence them.

3. Build Connection and Rapport

A highly decorated officer belonging to the elite Special Forces bid au revoir to the forces, and decided to pursue a career in the private sector.

His sterling reputation preceded him, and he was snapped up by a large private-sector company. The chairman of the company was to hand over the letter of appointment to him. At the appointed hour, the colonel was ushered into his presence. Over tea, the chairman said, 'I wish to point out a difference between the services and the private sector. In the former, people follow your command because it has the backing of the headquarters. Unfortunately, here, there will be no backing from head office. Therefore, people may not follow your command.'

The colonel thought for a moment, and then looking into the eyes of the chairman, replied, 'Sir, in the services people followed my command not because it had the backing of the headquarters, but because they had faith that I would put my life in danger before putting theirs. If they were to be injured, then I would not desert them, but put my life at risk to get them to safety. Most importantly, if they made the supreme sacrifice for the country, then I would move heaven and earth to ensure that their mortal remains reached their families.'

As expected, the appointment letter was withdrawn.

But in the response of the colonel lay embedded strategies followed by officers to influence the people they lead. They live by the motto set forth by Field Marshal Chetwode.[248]

> *The safety, honour and welfare of your country come first, always and every time.*
>
> *The honour, welfare and comfort of the men you command come next.*
>
> *Your own ease, comfort and safety come last, always and every time.*

This motto inspires the officers to put the interests of their people ahead of their own, not merely in words, but through deeds and actions. This enables them to build a deep connection and rapport with their people. Once built they desist from misusing it to serve their narrow self-interest. If they did so and it was discovered, then they would find it difficult to earn it back.

Lao Tzu, the Chinese philosopher, had also offered similar advice: Avoid putting yourself before others and you can become a leader among men.

I can sense a question stirring in you: What strategy should you follow to build a connection and a rapport with your team so that you are able to influence them without exercising authority? Here are a few pointers:

- Gain a deep understanding of every member of your team. You can do this by posing open-ended questions to them:
    - *Describe yourself in one word.*
    - *What is the best compliment you have received?*
    - *Which talent of yours has not yet been discovered?*
    - *What are the challenges you are facing at home?*
    - *How do you relax?*
    - *What saddens you?*
    - *A memorable experience which you remember with pride.*
    - *How will your friends describe you?*
    - *What words would you like inscribed on your tombstone?*
    - *To whom do you attribute your success?*
    - *What makes you special?*

- o *What drives and inspires you at work?*
- o *What gets you disengaged at work?*
- o *What are the barriers you are facing at work?*

Their answers will give you directions for building a connection and a rapport with them.

Make Your People Feel Psychologically Secure

When COVID struck, Ajay Banga, Mastercard's then chief executive, made a promise to the company's 19,000 employees that there would be no layoffs because of the economic destruction wrought by the virus.[249] This assurance made the employees show deeper commitment and put in greater effort.

You too can make your people feel psychologically secure by demonstrating that you care for them by following two rules:

- o Golden rule: Treat your people as you would like to be treated.
- o Platinum rule: Treat your people as they would like to be treated.

To implement this strategy, pose two questions to your team members:

- Which actions of yours and of other people did they like and want you to display?
- Which actions of yours and of other people would they not like and do not want you to display?

Use your best judgement to tailor your behaviour, deeds and actions to conform to the answers you have received.

Here are more pointers to help you build connections and rapport:

- Do not issue instructions from the comfort of your office. Get into the trenches with your team and put your shoulder to the wheel.
- As far as possible, explain to your team, in a transparent manner, why you acted in a particular way or have taken a particular decision.
- Desist from asking your team to do what you are unwilling to do.
- Do not be afraid to be vulnerable in front of your team. Seek their help.
- Listen to your team with the intention of understanding what they are trying to communicate. Do not listen with the intention of answering them back. This simple act will make people feel that their voice is being heard.
- Do not indulge in favouritism or act in a biased manner or act upon hearsay.

Did I Form a Deep Connection and Rapport with My Team?

One evening, I was feeling exhausted. I put my mobile phone on silent and went off to sleep. Soon, my wife woke me up, saying, 'There are ten missed calls. Someone is trying to reach you. It must be urgent.'

The missed calls were from my eastern India regional manager, Mr M, based in Calcutta (now Kolkata). I called him back. He was on the verge of tears. 'Sir, my son is in Bangalore (now Bengaluru) and he has dengue. His fever is not coming down. I am very scared. I have to be by his bedside.' His voice reflected pain, fear and helplessness in equal measure.

'Please go to Bangalore. I am approving your leave,' I replied.

'Sir, it's puja time in Calcutta. All flights are full. Please help me reach Bangalore,' he pleaded.

'I will arrange for your air tickets to Bangalore,' I promised him. He sounded relieved.

After disconnecting the phone, I spoke to our travel agent to arrange for the ticket and share the details with Mr M. Next, I spoke to our Bangalore distributor and instructed him to do the following:

- Get a good doctor and take him to examine Mr M's son.
- Pick up Mr M tomorrow morning from the airport and drop him at his son's hostel.
- Provide help to Mr M during his stay in Bangalore.

I assured him that the company would take care of these expenses. The distributor happily consented.

The next morning, Mr M reached Bangalore. His presence made his son feel better.

Two days later, I got a call from Mr M. 'Sir, I wish to return to Calcutta with my son. I am not getting tickets. Can you help?' he requested.

I got our travel agent to arrange for two tickets for Mr M and his son to return to Calcutta.

This story of this episode spread like wildfire in the company. People noticed that the company went out of its way to help Mr M—not just him but his family member too, without once considering the cost incurred in offering them this assistance. In fact, the company bore the entire cost. This incident built faith and belief in me and in the company. They started to believe that under my leadership, no one would be left to fend for themselves if calamities came knocking on their door. This incident also indicated to the team that I keep the interests of my people ahead of the company's and my own.

A few weeks later, I was on a market visit to Calcutta. Mr M came to my hotel to accompany me to the market. As I came out of the elevator, he walked towards me. Upon reaching me, he started to bend down to touch my feet, saying, 'You saved my son's life. You are like a god to me and my family.'

I was close to tears. I held him close and said, 'I am so happy that your son is safe! I am so happy that I was of help to you.'

This and other similar acts on my part earned me the faith and belief of my team and I was able to form deep connections and relationships with them. Therefore, I was able to influence them.

4. Transactional Analysis

Kautuk, our son, is a writer and a stand-up comic. His working hours are from 7 p.m. to midnight. On weekends, he reaches home around 1 a.m. As parents, we were deeply worried about his safety. Just a message from him would reassure us. But, unfortunately, it would not come. In a state of worry, we would fall into a fitful sleep.

Finally, the doorbell would ring. Seething with anger, I would open the door and ask him, 'Is this the time to come home?'

Kautuk would not say a word. But his expression did the talking for him: 'Papa, do you want me to give up on my dream for the sake of your sleep?'

He would angrily stride towards his room and shut the door in my face. Tension would prevail the next day too!

I decided to change my strategy and sought to influence Kautuk to change his behaviour.

Now, when Kautuk reached home, I opened the door with a smile and asked him, 'How was your show?'

He was taken aback by the unexpected empathy. He took it in his stride and responded animatedly, 'Papa, there were several spontaneous claps and three whistles. On one occasion, I had to wait for the applause to die down before I could resume.'

'I am so happy, Kautuk,' I said and sensing it to be an opportune moment, said, 'Can I make a request?'

'Of course,' said Kautuk with a smile which was spread all over his face.

'As parents, we are worried about your well-being. To keep us from needlessly worrying, can you message us your whereabouts?' I said.

'As soon as the show ends, the audience surround me and then, later, all of us comics sit down to dinner. As a result, I forget to message you. But from now on, I will try not to forget,' he promised.

Then onwards, Kautuk did keep us informed about his whereabouts . . . most of the time.

I employed transactional analysis to influence Kautuk.

It states that we have three 'ego states' residing in our personality: Parent (P), Adult (A) and Child (C). Our behaviour is decided by which personality becomes dominant during our interactions with other people.

Let me apply TA to my interaction with Kautuk.

Initially, when I opened the door, my 'parent' state was dominant, which made me pose a parent-like question to him, 'Is this the time to come home?'

Kautuk, likewise, has three ego states (read: personalities) in him. As soon as my 'parent' questioned him, his 'child' became dominant and he responded like one: 'No matter what I do, you are never satisfied. In fact, you find fault with everything that I do. For the sake of your sleep and peace of mind, you want me to give up my dream career.'

When 'cross' communication happens, conflict follows.

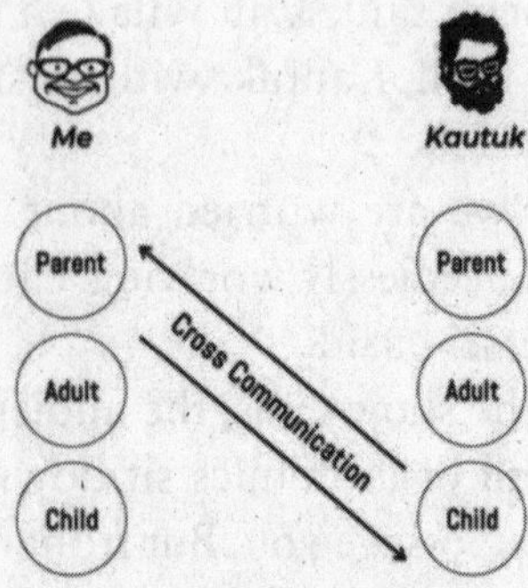

To avoid conflict with Kautuk, I changed my strategy. Now, when I opened the door, I got my 'adult' personality to become dominant and asked him how his show was. This brought to the fore Kautuk's 'adult' personality, and he promised to keep us informed. Now, our conversation was 'adult to adult' and it was devoid of conflict. Moreover, it was productive.

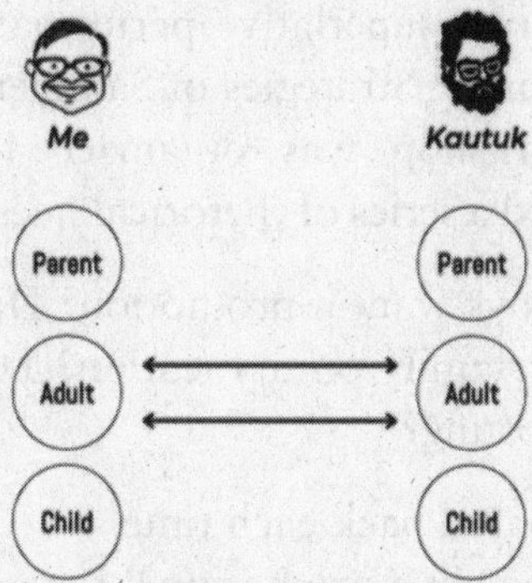

To influence people, strive to maintain 'adult to adult' conversations with them. In this way, your chances of influencing people go up.

5. Make Desirable Behaviours Easy

My CEO friend narrated his woes to me: 'Only a minuscule number of people in our sales team work with commitment and deliver superlative performance. The majority put in only the minimum effort required to get by.'

He paused and then articulated the challenge he wanted me do address, 'How do I influence the majority who put in only minimal effort to get by, to consistently deliver superlative performance?'

I asked him to introduce me to the high performers he was alluding to. I requested them to share ten strategies they used to deliver high performance.

I used funnel analysis to analyse the information. It threw up ten unduplicated strategies that they were following to deliver superlative performance. I labelled them as 'Ten Winning Strategies of Salespersons'.

Now, a workshop was organized for the entire sales team. I posed a series of rhetorical questions to them:

- Do you guys want a promotion? Do you want to take your family on a vacation? Do you want a foreign posting?

'Yes,' they roared back each time.

'How will you get a promotion?' I queried.

'By delivering top-quality performance,' they replied.

'Do you want to know a simple roadmap for delivering top-quality performance?' I asked.

'Yes,' they thundered.

'Sitting among you are your colleagues who are high performers. They work in the same environment as you, face similar difficulties and challenges as you. Despite that, they deliver top-notch performance.' I paused for a moment to allow this thought to sink in.

'In collaboration with them, I have done an analysis to identify ten common strategies which help them deliver top-notch performance. May I share them with you?' I asked.

There was pin-drop silence. Curiosity got the better of them and they said 'Yes!'

I put on the slide containing the ten winning sales strategies of the star performers, which I had culled out using funnel analysis. They were:

I. Deep understanding of customers' needs.

II. Being exceptionally responsive.
III. Ability to present a compelling value proposition to customers.
IV. Up-to-the-minute market intelligence.
V. Display sense of ownership and accountability.
VI. Excellent at internal collaboration.
VII. Exemplary listening skills.
VIII. Skilful in thinking out of the box.
IX. Meticulous execution.
X. Strong references from customers.

Now, I invited the top performers who were sitting among the participants to share their stories about how they had applied these winning strategies to win in the marketplace.

The whole team listened to them in pin-drop silence. Then I posed a question to them, 'Do you believe that by implementing these strategies, you can deliver superlative performance in the marketplace?'

Most people nodded in agreement.

'Do you wish to gain mastery in them?' I asked.

Almost everybody in the room said in one voice, 'YES!'

So a training programme was organized where everybody underwent training on how to become skilled in these ten strategies. Concomitantly, a reward programme was introduced to reward adherence to these winning strategies.

Skilled in them, many more sales team members started delivering superlative performance in the marketplace.

What strategy did I deploy to influence the sales team?

I refrained from issuing a threat to the laggards: Shape up or you will be shipped out. Neither did I share with them case studies of how salespeople in Amazon and Apple deliver superlative performance. They would have dismissed those, saying that those could not be applied in their organization.

Instead, I shared with them a list of proven strategies which their own peers were following to deliver superlative performance in the marketplace. Hence my recommendation had credibility. Many bought into it and started practising it.

To influence people to change their behaviour, do the following:

- Communicate to them why changing their behaviour will be beneficial for them.
- List out the new behaviours they must adopt.
- Outline the simple steps they need to take to adopt the desirable behaviours.
- Make these desirable behaviours easy to adopt and undesirable behaviours hard to perform.[250]
- Reward the new behaviours.

6. Change the Context

In rural areas, people go to the fields to answer nature's call, even women! One reason why this practice has endured can be the lack of stigma attached to it. But this age-old practice is fraught with risk, particularly for women. It leads to the spread of disease and can result in women getting into embarrassing situations. Despite these drawbacks, this habit is deeply ingrained and has continued unabated.

The challenge was how to influence people to:

- Give up the habit of answering nature's call in the open.
- Build a toilet at home and get them to use it, particularly women members of the family.

A study indicated that in rural homes, the mother-in-law controls the daughters and daughters-in-law. If winds of change had to blow in the household, she must be positively influenced.

Let me take you to rural India to visit a typical family, and pose a question to the mother-in-law: Why are female members of your family still going to the fields to answer the call of nature? Is it not wrong?

Her reply: this has been the practice for generations. If it was not wrong then, how has it become wrong now?

While she was speaking, a picture of her was clicked on a smartphone. When she paused, her picture was shown to her.

She was surprised. A smile lit up her face and she said, 'When did you take my picture? I did not notice you taking it.'

'*Mataji*, your picture was taken using this inexpensive mobile phone. It has a camera in it. Most boys in the village have it. Bad boys can take bad pictures of your daughters and daughters-in law while they are in the fields, without them realizing it. Then, not just the village, but the whole world can see these pictures. Do you want the world to see these bad pictures?'

The mother-in-law was shaken at this revelation.

'No,' she murmured, and asked, 'What should I do?'

'Build a toilet in the home and do not allow the girls of your family to go to the fields!'

The mother-in-law nodded in agreement.

What influenced her?

It was brought to her notice that the context had changed due to the widespread availability of mobile phones fitted with cameras, which can take pictures of people without them noticing it. This shook her and she became open to being influenced.

The bottom line: when the context changes, the barriers that stand in the path of getting influenced melt away. In their absence, people are open to being influenced.

7. Stage a Drama and Cast the People to Be Influenced as Actors

Two luxury car brands competed fiercely in the marketplace. But the market seemed to be giving an edge to Brand B.

This worried the sales team of Brand A. They did a market survey and arrived at the conclusion that the engine of Brand B was better than theirs.

They brought this to the attention of their engineers, who refused to pay heed to their feedback. This frustrated the sales team. To prove their point, they invited the engineers to test drive and experience the difference themselves.

On the appointed day, the engineers came to the venue for test driving. Standing next to each other were the two cars—theirs and the competitor's.

The engineers drove their own car and found the engine to be in top condition. They said so proudly.

Then they took the wheel of the competitor's car and took it for a spin. The engine performance was markedly inferior.

Upon returning to the base, they gave their verdict: the engine performance of Brand A (their own brand) was markedly superior to the competing brand's.

'That is what we are also saying,' chorused the sales team.

Saying this, they opened the bonnets of both cars. Nestled inside the hood of Brand A was the engine of Brand B, and vice versa. The sales team had swapped the car engines.

The engineers were red-faced. They went back to the drawing table, determined to improve the performance of their engine to beat the competitor hollow. They delivered on their promise.

The sales team influenced the adamant engineers to change their opinion through demonstration, not words and arguments.

The next time you wish to influence people and find yourself wanting, stage a drama (read: demonstrate) in which you cast them in the title roles. Soon, they will be singing your song along with you.

8. Bring Behavioural Sciences into Play

During my career, I have influenced people by liberally using principles of behavioural science. Here are a few examples!

- **Social Proof**

In late 1980s, Bagpiper whisky become India's largest selling whiskey. We celebrated this achievement by proudly proclaiming that it was 'India's largest-selling whisky'. This acted as a social proof. For brand loyalists, it reassured them that their choice of Bagpiper was indeed correct. For whisky connoisseurs who patronized competing brands, this message would make them think—if it is India's largest selling whisky, then many people must be consuming it. So many people cannot be wrong. Let me also try it.

E-commerce companies also follow this strategy. They encourage shoppers to post ratings and reviews of the products that they have bought. It acts as social proof for potential shoppers. More and better reviews and ratings are likely to result in more sales. Potential shoppers surmise that if so many people have given a product a positive review and rated it so highly, then it must be good. This influences them to vote for it with their wallets.

- **Scarcity Effect**

Towards the end of the month, when salespeople are short of achieving their sales target, they approach their distributors for more orders. During the ensuing conversations, they subtly drop a hint that in the coming month, the fast-moving brand is likely to be in short supply. The distributors can stock up now, they suggest, because there is no guarantee that it will be available next month. Often, the threat (read: fear) of scarcity makes the channel partners place additional orders.

- **Influencer Marketing**

In advertising lingo, it is called celebrity advertising, and in digital marketing, it is referred to as influencer marketing. Here is how it works: a brand gets an influencer like Shah Rukh Khan to endorse it. These influencers put into motion this thought process: I love Shah Rukh. Shah Rukh loves Pepsi. I love Pepsi.

Pepsi thus succeeds in influencing people to try Pepsi.

Postscript

If you find the toolkit for influencing people to be about as easy to understand as Greek and Latin, focus your energies on building a formidable reputation in the area where you wish to influence people, like Jonty Rhodes did in fielding.

'We were not only wary of Jonty Rhodes, but, if the truth be told, scared of him. Even if he was positioned a little deeper, we would avoid taking a run if the ball was hit in his direction. He put the fear of god in batsmen,' reminisces Ravi Shastri.[251]

Influence without Authority in a Nutshell

Influence without Authority

It will enable you to bring others to your way of thinking, motivate them to support your initiatives and adopt your idea of their own free will. This will get you noticed, get you promoted and help you rise in life.

Strategy for Influence without Authority

1. Inside–outside strategy.
2. Earn trust.
3. Build connection and rapport.
4. Transactional analysis.
5. Make desirable behaviours easy.
6. Change the context.
7. Stage a drama and cast people to be influenced as actors.
8. Put into play the principles of 'behavioural science'.

Emotional Skills

Skill 9

Humanness

The Fourth Industrial Revolution is upon us. It is leading to a proliferation in 'thinking jobs'. This requires people to be engaged and motivated at work. The traditional ways of motivating people by the carrot-and-stick approach and through financial incentives are proving ineffective. The new approach requires the adoption of a people-first policy, which views people as humans who must be treated with 'humanness'. This approach has the potential of unlocking the unlimited potential of people to give their best on the job.

In 1986, I joined Herbertsons Ltd, a United Spirits Group company (now Diageo India). Soon, tragedy struck our family. My father departed for the other world. My mother, sister and I were devastated. After completing the rituals, I returned to work.

My president, the late Mr Naaz Rovshen (NR), stopped by my workstation and enquired compassionately, 'How is your mother coping?'

My silence would have given him the answer. With compassion in his voice, he said, 'You can take as much leave as you need to take care of your mother. For additional help, let me know.'

I was overwhelmed with emotion. My president showed care and compassion towards me and my family. I had difficulty in holding back my tears. I thanked him profusely.

As luck would have it, very soon, my immediate boss left for greener pastures. Under his stewardship, detailed plans had been drawn up for the launch of a new brand. Those plans were executed in his absence.

A few months into the launch, bad news started to trickle in from the market. The new product was besieged with quality problems. After extensive deliberation, a decision was taken to withdraw it from the market. As the product executive of the brand, I was tasked with the responsibility of coordinating the recall.

Soon, I got a message from the president's office that I should share the total loss incurred due to the recalled brand.

I did the maths and arrived at the loss. To put it mildly, it was humongous. I was scared. I knew that no amount of luck would save me from a verbal lashing. After all, I was the product executive in charge of the now failed brand.

To mitigate the severity of the drubbing I was going to get, I did some research to determine NR's preferred time for leaving the office. He had studied in the USA. At heart, he was still an American who believed in a work-life balance. Every day, he would leave the office at the closing hour, 5.15 p.m.

I took an appointment for 5.10 p.m.

At the appointed time, I entered his office. He was absorbed in his work. He waved at me to sit down. I was happy that a few more minutes would tick by. Finally, he looked up and said with a smile, 'Hi, Rajesh. How are you? Why did you want to see me?'

'Sir, you wanted to know the loss that was incurred due to the recalled brand,' I reminded him.

He nodded. I shared the figure with him and handed him the note on which I had done the detailed calculations.

He studied it and remarked, 'It is substantial!'

'Yes,' I said, feebly, looking down at the floor. I was waiting for the verbal lashing to start. Instead, he resorted to the Socratic method of questioning and posed a series of open-ended questions to me:

- Why did the brand fail?
- Could this failure not have been prevented?
- What lessons did I learn from it?
- How might we prevent such lapses from happening in the future?

As I started to answer his questions, I gained a deeper understanding of the issue. I felt a sense of gratitude towards him for opening my eyes to the various dimensions of this failure which had escaped my attention. As I got up to leave, I thanked him for being compassionate towards me, but felt morally responsible for the loss the company had incurred and said, 'Sir, I am sorry!'

He looked surprised and said, 'Why are you sorry? You are not to be blamed. You have joined us only recently. But if you have learnt the lessons from this failure, then the group will make crores from you.'

Saying this, he got up from his chair to leave. While going past me, he patted me on the shoulder and gave me a reassuring smile to express his confidence in me.

His gesture inspired me. Unknown to him, he had put into motion the Pygmalion effect. It is a psychological phenomenon wherein high expectations lead to improved performance. In other words, it is a self-fulfilling prophecy, and it motivates people to live up to the expectations others have from them.

My president, through his words, deeds and actions, had placed people over profit. He treated me like a human being by showing compassion towards me. It motivated me to work with unmatched passion to meet the expectations he had from me.

Over the years, I contributed immensely to United Spirits. I was part of the team which scored innumerable wins in the marketplace:

- Bagpiper became the largest-selling brand of blended Scotch whisky in India.
- Bagpiper Gold was conceptualized.
- India's first white rum, Royal Treasure White Rum, was launched.
- Gold Riband Prestige whisky, with the promise of 'Good Mornings After Great Evenings', was

launched. It was for the first time in India that a whisky was launched as a solution to a problem consumers faced.

- Blue Riband Duet, India's first premix gin, which promised 'Gin and Lime Premixed to Perfection', was launched. It created the premix segment.

During one of our company's overseas conferences, I spotted NR strolling by himself. I struck up a conversation with him. 'Sir, years ago you had told me that if I have learnt lessons from my failures, then the group will make "crores" from me. I am happy to say that I did internalize the lessons from those failures and your words have come true!'

A smile lit up his face. He shook my hands and said, 'See? I was right!'

My president was humane, and he treated me with humanness. His words and actions showed caring, kindness, empathy, compassion, deep respect, belief and faith in me. Under such leaders, my morale and performance soared.

Command-and-Control Style of Working

I have also worked under leaders who used the 'command-and-control' style of working. They tended to be authoritative, abrasive and expected their directives to be followed without question. Under their leadership, my performance suffered. I became disinterested at work.

Research done by Gallup supports my experience: a paltry 13 per cent of the workforce is passionate about their work, while 80 per cent is less than fully engaged at work.[252] Gallup refers to this high level of disengagement as a 'stunning amount of wasted potential'. The lion's share of the blame can be attributed to the command and control style of working, which was required by the earlier 3 Industrial Revolutions (3IRs).

- 1IR: mechanized production using water and steam power.
- 2IR: powered mass production using electric power.
- 3IR: automated production using electronics and information technology.

These three IRs required people to:

- Perform physical labour.
- Carry out repetitive jobs.
- Follow instructions without question.
- Follow a set procedure for making decisions.

To get people to perform these tasks required the command-and-control style of working. This style treated people as human automatons. In turn, people bought their bodies to work while leaving their brains and hearts at home.

Why Is 'Humaneness' Imperative Now?

Industry 4.0, also called 4IR, is upon us. It is driven by extraordinary technological advances, which are resulting in the merging of the physical, digital and biological worlds, and is powered by AI, robotics, the Internet of Things (IoT), 3D printing, genetic engineering, quantum computing and other cutting-edge technologies.[253]

This is leading to a proliferation in thinking jobs where people have to think while doing their jobs. This requires them be engaged and motivated at work.[254] The traditional ways of motivating people by the carrot-and-stick approach and through financial incentives are proving ineffective. The new approach requires adoption of a people-first policy which views people as human and treats them with humanness. This approach unlocks the unlimited potential of people[255] and motivates them to give their best on the job.

Is It Possible to Be Humane and Still Be Effective?

Take solace from the fact that humane leaders who practised humanness have won our admiration and our hearts. Now it is your turn to emulate them and win the respect of your team.

A word of caution: do not be humane and practise humanness to manipulate people. Instead, do it with the intention of engaging, inspiring and motivating them to transform into the finest versions of themselves.

How to Be Humane

Presented below are case studies of humane leaders who practised humanness to get the best out of people. Their way of working will give you directions to practice humanness at your workplace.

1. Lead with Your Heart

A theft was reported at the Taj Mahal hotel.[256] The investigation pointed towards two employees being the culprits. This incident was brought to the notice of J.R.D. Tata. He meticulously studied the investigation report and gave his verdict: terminate their services. In the same breath, he asked his manager to find out if these employees had schoolgoing children. If yes, then the Tatas and the Taj Hotel would take care of their education.

'Why should the children pay a price for their fathers' follies?' he reasoned. Through this simple act, J.R.D. Tata displayed humanness.

J.R.D. Tata ran the Tata Group with his mind but led with his heart.

Dalia Lama too advocates this strategy—cultivate a tough mind but a warm heart.

2. Preach What You Practise

'My son is addicted to sugar. Can you ask him to stop indulging in it?' a women said to Mahatma Gandhi, pointing towards her son.

Gandhiji thought for a moment and asked them to visit him a few days later.

On the appointed day, they presented themselves in front of Gandhiji. He looked at the boy and advised him to give up the addiction of sugar. The boy nodded.

The mother was puzzled. 'You could have given this advice when we were here last time. It would have saved us this trip,' she rebuked Gandhiji.

'Last time when you were here, I too was addicted to sugar,' confessed Gandhiji. He paused and added, 'Before I advised your son, I had to make sure that I could give up this addiction.'

Eleanor Roosevelt was right when she declared that it is not fair to ask of others what you are not willing to do yourself. Humane leaders follow Roosevelt's advice.

3. Convert Your Critics into Your Friends

President Abraham Lincoln spoke kindly about his critics. A female critic asked him how he could speak so kindly of his enemies when he should destroy them.

'Why, Madam,' replied Lincoln, 'do I not destroy them when I make them my friends?'[257]

Humane leaders do not take revenge or settle scores on gaining power. On the other hand, they use it to convert their critics into their friends by displaying humane qualities such as sensitivity, empathy, compassion, kindness and honesty.

Here is how Lincoln lived these qualities: when something went well, Lincoln always shared the credit. When something went wrong, he shouldered his share of the blame. When he himself made a mistake, he acknowledged it immediately.[258]

4. Self-Penalize for Mistakes Committed by Others

Mahatma Gandhi undertook fasts to establish peace, communal harmony and to prevent further violence.[259] This act of self-penalization would have pricked the conscience of the perpetuators of violence and nudged them to behave responsibly. And it did.

M.S. Dhoni also applied a variation of this strategy to get members of the Indian cricket team to be punctual.[260] Let us start at the beginning. In 2008, when Anil Kumble was the captain of the Test team, it was decided that latecomers would be fined Rs 10,000. This deterrent did not have the desired effect. The fine amount was peanuts for the cricketers.

M.S. Dhoni, who was then the captain of the ODI team, also felt that there should be consequences for coming late. He kept the same quantum of punishment, but with a twist. If somebody came late, then everybody else was fined Rs 10,000!

This strategy worked because we do not mind being penalized for our mistakes. But if others are penalized for our mistakes, then it pinches our conscience. We at once modify our behaviour so as not to inconvenience others.

Humane leaders are like M.S. Dhoni. They do not resort to the carrot-and-stick policy nor the power of their position to command obedience. They intelligently use principles of behavioural science to make people behave the way they want without having to fire a single bullet.

5. Kiss Down

During a weekly meeting, a worker complained to the chairman that the hygiene of the worker's toilets was terrible. But the executive toilets were clean and hygienic.

The chairman asked his executive how much time he would need to set it right.

'A month,' he replied.

'I would rather do it in a day. Send me a carpenter,' commanded the chairman.

The next day, the carpenter was ordered to swap the signboards. The signboard of the workers' toilet was changed to 'Executives' and that of the executive toilets to 'Workers'. The quality of both toilets became the same in a few days.

The chairman did not pay lip service to their problem but acted upon their grievance at the speed of light. In the process, he displayed humanness towards those further down the food chain by treating them as humans. He did this by kicking up and kissing down.

6. Share the Pain Equitably[261]

In 2008, the St Louis-based manufacturing company Barry-Wehmiller lost a large chunk of its orders overnight due to recession. The company needed to save millions, so the board and the company's CEO Bob Chapman got together to discuss layoffs.

In the end, Chapman refused to let anyone go, so he and the board devised a furlough programme, through which every employee would be required to take four weeks of unpaid vacation. Bob announced the programme in a humane manner, saying, 'It's better that we should all suffer a little than any of us should have to suffer a lot.'

This meant that everyone was safe. The team's morale went up and trust and cooperation soared.

Humanness demands that we treat people like we treat our family members. During tough times, we do not let them go. Instead, we all come together and suffer a little so that no one member endures a lot of hardship. This builds trust and cooperation among family members.

When employees are treated like family members, it also leads to building of trust and cooperation among team members, and morale and productivity soar.

7. Demonstrate Care

When I was president of J.K. Helene Curtis, on most Sunday mornings, around 11 a.m., I would call the sales managers. As soon as they realized that I was on the phone, they would start updating me on business. I would interrupt them, saying, 'I have called you not to discuss business, but to find out about you and your family.' Hearing this, they would invariably say that they and their families were doing well. After exchanging some more pleasantries, I would disconnect. Each phone call would last maybe three minutes. Since I made these calls on Sundays, my wife could overhear my conversations.

'Do these phone calls serve any purpose?' she would ask me.

'Of course, they do,' I would reply. But I could see from her expression that she did not believe me.

'How would you feel if Mr Gautam Singhania, our CMD, called on a Sunday morning, not to discuss business, but to enquire about our family's welfare?' I asked her.

'Delighted,' she said. 'After all, he is such a busy man. And if he takes time out, that too on a Sunday, then it shows he really cares for us,' she replied.

'For my team members, I am their Gautam Singhania,' I told her. 'When I call them, their family also feels that the company cares for them.'

A simple phone call energized the salespeople, and they worked with renewed vigour.

A word of caution: indulge in such behaviour to demonstrate genuine care and not to manipulate your team to work harder.

8. Express Appreciation and Gratitude

'Indra Nooyi, the former CEO of PepsiCo, wrote more than 400 letters each year to the parents of her senior executives,' says Marguerite Ward.[262] In the letters, she expressed her appreciation and gratitude by writing a paragraph about what their child was doing at PepsiCo, and she thanked them for the gift of their child to the company.

Indra says, 'These letters opened a floodgate of emotions. Parents wrote back saying that they were honoured and shared the letter with friends and family.'[263]

What purpose did one paragraph in the letter serve? It served two, actually. It made the employees feel appreciated and evoked a sense of gratitude in them. It also made their families feel proud of them. This motivated the employees to work with greater commitment and engagement.

You may wonder if this seemingly simple act of humanness delivers business results.

Take yourself. Would you like your CEO to write a personal letter to your parents expressing their appreciation and gratitude about you? Will it make your parents feel proud of you? Will you be emotionally charged and work with extra commitment?

If the answer is yes, then you too should emulate this habit of Indra Nooyi's.

9. Make People Aware of Their Potential

Chennai Super Kings won the Indian Premier League (IPL) championship thrice. But in the 2020 season, they fared badly. M.S. Dhoni, the captain, was asked how he would motivate his players to perform. He replied, 'I will ask each player to assess for themselves and determine if they have played to the potential they have got! In short, have they done justice to their potential?'[264]

By asking this question, Dhoni was getting the players to introspect and visualize the potential they possessed. After all, that was the basis of their selection for the team. Once the realization would dawn that they were not doing justice to their potential, they would be motivated to start on the journey to live up to their potential.

Humane leaders do not scream or bully people when their performance falters. They create an atmosphere in which employees can introspect and re-energize themselves to start on the journey to live up to their potential.

10. A 'Giver', Not a 'Taker' or a 'Matcher'

Adam Grant, the renowned psychologist and best-selling author of *Give and Take: A Revolutionary Approach to Success*, alludes to three types of people:

- Giver: They prefer to give more than they get. They generously share their expertise, time and connections with the team so that they can benefit from them.
- Taker: They are interested in self-advancement, self-promotion and are always looking out for what others can offer them. They like to receive more than they give. They want to climb to the top by using others as ladders. They take credit for work done by the team.
- Matcher: They try to create an equitable balance between giving and taking.

Guess who makes it to the top of the corporate ladder?

You may be tempted to opt for the 'taker', since they will leverage all available resources to advance their career.

But Adam Grant's research picks givers as the winners, because they put into play two principles of behavioural science:

- Reciprocal principle: People who are beneficiaries of support from the givers tend to reciprocate by offering support to them.
- Likeability principle. It is natural for people to like the givers. When an opportunity arises, they spontaneously offer support and help to givers.

Humane leaders tend to be givers and the team members tend to give them a leg up till they reach the top rung of the organizational ladder.

By the way, people at the bottom are also givers. They also help others. But they do not know where to draw the line, end up investing all their precious resources in helping others and are left with little time for themselves. As a result, they find themselves languishing at the bottom of the organizational ladder.

Watermelon

You may be wondering if this strategy can deliver bountiful results in real life. Let me invite the late Manohar Parrikar, the former chief minister of Goa, to narrate an incident from his life.[265]

'I am from the village of Parra in Goa; hence we are called Parrikars. My village is famous for its watermelons. When I was a child, at the end of harvest season, a farmer would organize a watermelon-eating contest. All the kids would be invited to eat as many watermelons as we wanted. The farmer kept his best

watermelons for the contest. We were told not to bite into the seeds but to spit out the seeds into a bowl. He was collecting the seeds for his next crop. This way he got the best seeds which yielded even bigger watermelons the next year.

'After 6.5 years, I went to the market looking for watermelons. They were all gone. The ones that were there were so small.

'I went to see the farmer who hosted the watermelon-eating contest. His son had taken over. He was still hosting the contest but there was a difference. He realized that the larger watermelons would fetch more money in the market, so he sold the larger ones and kept the smaller ones for the contest. The next year, the watermelons were smaller, the year later even smaller. In watermelons the generation is one year. In seven years, Parra's best watermelons were finished.'

The earlier generation of farmers practised giving, and the village became renowned for juicy watermelons. When the younger generation stopped being givers, then the village lost its best watermelons.

Be a giver. It pays rich dividends, in life and in business.

11. Not Concerned with Who Gets the Credit

In 1953, Sir Edmund Hillary and Tenzing Norgay conquered Mount Everest.

'We agreed not to tell who stepped on the summit first. To a mountaineer, it's of no great consequence who sets foot first. Often, the one who puts more into the climb steps back and lets his partner stand on top first,' recalled Sir Edmund.

For decades, they stuck to their gentlemen's agreement. Finally, it was Tenzing who revealed in his autobiography *Tiger of the Snows* that Sir Edmund Hillary had, in fact, preceded him.[266]

Harry S. Truman hit the nail on the head when he said that it is amazing what you can accomplish if you do not care who gets credit.

Human leaders are never in a hurry to take credit. In fact, they take blame and give credit to the team.

12. Give Credit, Take Blame[267]

The 'people's President' A.P.J. Abdul Kalam shared a story from his life:

> The year was 1979. I was the project director. My mission was to put the satellite in the orbit. The countdown was going on, but the computer advised us to abort the mission. As the mission director, I decided to bypass the computer and launched the rocket. Disaster struck. Instead of putting the satellite in orbit, it went into the Bay of Bengal.
>
> ISRO chief Satish Dhawan held a press conference along with me and took the whole blame on himself. He said, 'Dear friends, we have failed today. I want to support my technologists, my scientists, my staff, so that next year they succeed.'
>
> Next year, on July 18, 1980, we successfully launched Rohini RS-1 into the orbit. Now Satish Dhawan asked me to conduct the press conference that day.
>
> I learned a very important lesson that day. When failure occurred, the leader of the organisation owned it. When success came, he gave it to his team.

Humane leaders take the lion's share of the blame when things go wrong but give or let the team take credit for success.

13. Supportive and Encouraging

Jack Welch,[268] the legendary CEO of General Electric, faced a moment of reckoning in the early part of his career. His actions lead to an explosion in the factory. Luckily, no one was injured. He was summoned by his superior. He expected to be fired. Instead, his boss was encouraging and engaged him in a calm conversation, asking him what he did wrong. What had he learnt?

This taught Welch that rather than beating somebody up when they are down, it's always better to be encouraging towards them.

Humane leaders remove the fear of failure from the hearts and minds of subordinates. They subscribe to the credo articulated by Soichiro Honda, founder of the Honda Motor Company, that success is 99 per cent failure. This approach creates an atmosphere in the company where people feel safe enough to experiment and fail.

Sourav Ganguly followed this strategy to transform Virender Sehwag into one of the most destructive batsmen the game of cricket has witnessed.

It started with Ganguly offering to let Sehwag open for India and removing the fear of failure. 'I will give you three to four innings as an opener. Even if you fail, you will continue to play. And before I drop you, I will again give you a chance in the middle (order),' he said. Devoid of fear, Sehwag batted in his natural style of not merely attacking bowlers, but assaulting them.[269]

When fear of failure is eliminated, people are motivated to:

a. Carry out experiments.
b. Make honest mistakes.
c. Attempt to learn from mistakes.
d. Freely express their points of view.

As a result, everybody benefits.

14. Be a Coach, Not a Leader

We were going on a family vacation. To ensure that I was not disturbed, I empowered the team to make decisions.

Much to my dismay, I still kept getting calls asking for decisions. Unknown to me, I had become an ATM for solving their problems. They would come to me with a problem, and I would instantly give them a solution. As a result, I had firmly established my position as a leader, but turned the rest of the team into followers.

Upon my return, I changed my strategy. I became a coach to them. Now, when my team members approached me with a problem, I would listen to them attentively and, instead of offering a solution, I would pose a question. When they answered it, the solution became evident.

Two benefits accrued to me when I transformed into a coach:

- People started gaining confidence in their abilities. Over time, they stopped coming to me with problems. In the process, they transformed into leaders.
- My time was freed up to focus on strategic issues.

As a result, the company grew, the careers of my team members flourished and so did mine.

By transforming into a humane leader, I had validated American author and political activist Ralph Nader's assertion by producing more leaders, not more followers.

15. Make People Feel Special

As president of J.K. Helene Curtis, I was returning from a business trip to Europe with a stopover in London. While waiting in the immigration line at Heathrow Airport, I received a message that my chairman had requested me to visit him.

I was taken aback. I was not mentally prepared to face him. Moreover, I was nursing a severe cold. But I did as I was told.

My chairman greeted me warmly. When he was informed that I would like to leave early since I was nursing a cold, he expressed concern and said, 'Have your dinner and then go to your hotel.'

I took a seat at the dining table. It was laden with sumptuous food. But I was on edge. Any moment, I was expecting him to question me about business. Instead, I heard him say, 'Serve yourself while I get you a paratha.' I quickly served myself. Moments later, he arrived with a hot paratha finely balanced on a ladle. Expertly, he served it to me on my plate and went back to make the next paratha for me.

I was in a trance. My chairman was making parathas and serving me. I was overwhelmed.

All along, he made polite conversation, but nothing related to business.

When I was ready to go to my hotel and had reached the front door, he said, 'Please wait.' I did as I was told.

Soon, he returned with a small paper pack. Handing it to me, he said, 'It has haldi in it. When you reach the hotel room, order a glass of hot milk. Put this haldi in it and have it. It will give you relief. If you are still not feeling well by tomorrow morning, let me know. I will send a doctor.'

'Yes, sir,' I said and started to move towards the waiting car.

'Do you have my number?' he asked.

'No, sir,' I said. He shared his number and said, 'Do not forget to call if you need any help.'

To paraphrase American poet Maya Angelou, humane leaders know that people will forget what you said, people will forget what you did, but people will never forget how you made them feel.

So true! More than a decade and a half has passed since that night. But I have never forgotten how special my chairman made me feel by his act of humanness.

16. Kind Not Clever

Let me invite Jeff Bezos to share a story with us:

> As a kid, I spent my summers with my grandparents on their ranch in Texas. Sometimes we would go on a trip. On one trip, I was about 10 years old, and my grandmother smoked throughout the trip. I hated the smell.
>
> I'd been hearing an ad campaign about smoking that every puff of a cigarette takes away two minutes

> off your life. I decided to do the math for my grandmother. I estimated the number of cigarettes per day, estimated the number of puffs per cigarette and so on. When I was satisfied that I'd come up with a reasonable number, I tapped my grandmother on the shoulder, and proudly proclaimed, 'At two minutes per puff, you've taken nine years off your life!'
>
> I expected to be applauded for my cleverness and arithmetic skills. Instead, my grandmother burst into tears. My grandfather gently and calmly said, 'Jeff, one day you'll understand that it's harder to be kind than clever.'[270]

Humanness demands that we refrain from indulging in acts of cleverness which make people feel small and miserable. Instead, we should treat them with kindness and make them come alive.

17. High on 'Decency Quotient'[271]

Successful business leaders have IQ and EQ, a combination of two familiar attributes, intellect and emotional intelligence.

But humane leaders have one additional attribute, DQ, the 'decency quotient'.

'DQ implies a person has not only empathy for employees and colleagues but also the genuine desire to care for them. It means wanting something positive for everyone in the workplace and ensuring everyone feels respected and valued. It is evident in daily interactions with others. It implies a focus on doing right by others.' Says Bill Boulding.[272]

You may be wondering if any business honcho values the DQ.

Ajay Banga, the former CEO of Mastercard, did. 'IQ is really important. EQ is important. What really matters to me is DQ. If you can bring your decency quotient to work every day, you will make the company a lot of fun for people—and people will enjoy being there and doing the right thing.'

Was I a Humane Leader?

A two-day all-India sales conference was held at our head office in Mumbai. Salespeople from all over India were in attendance. During the lunch break, I noticed that the area manager of Punjab and Haryana was looking preoccupied and worried. This was unlike him. By nature, he was gregarious. I called him and inquired if everything was fine.

He looked at me and said with a forced smile, 'Yes sir, everything is fine.'

But his voice lacked conviction. I asked him again if everything was fine. This time, he said, 'Sir, my son is unwell and I am worried.'

'Then why did you come?' I asked.

'Sir, my boss insisted that I come because this is a very important meeting,' he said.

I could empathize with him. If my son was unwell and I had to attend a company meeting, then I would be worried about my son too, and would silently hope to return quickly to his bedside.

I called his boss and told him that he should not have insisted that he attend this meeting. His boss agreed.

I turned my attention to the area manager and said, 'I want you to leave immediately for your home. The company will make your travel arrangements.'

My car dropped him to the airport. Although he was not eligible for air travel, I made an exception in this case. At the Delhi airport, a car was arranged to pick him up and take him home.

The same evening, he reached home. He phoned to thank me. His son was also recovering. Relief was palpable in his voice.

This gesture had not gone unnoticed. The rest of the sales team had witnessed the humane side of the company. Their attitude towards the company changed. No longer did they look upon it as a place they had to go to work, but as a place where they loved to go to work. They worked with a sense of ownership, believing that it was their company. Blockbuster results followed.

I Discovered Meaning in My Work

A few weeks later, I was on a market visit to a place that was the hometown of the area manager. After spending the entire day in the market, it was time to call it a day. The area manager looked at me and said, 'Sir, please have a cup of tea at my home.'

I agreed and we set off for his home. He made me comfortable in his drawing room and went inside to inform his wife to make tea for us.

I was alone in the drawing room. I noticed the curtain part and a lady wearing a white sari with a *ghoonghat* entered. I surmised that she must be his mother.

Without looking at me, she folded her hands and addressed me in Hindi: '*Main aapka dhanyavaad karna chahti hun. Aapke karan hamare bachche achche school jaa rahe hain. Hum sab surakshit anubhav karte hain ki koi hai jo hamara khyal karta hai* (I wish to thank you. Because of you, our children are going to a good school. We also feel assured that there is somebody looking after us).'

Upon saying this, she turned around and left the room.

A simple act of humanness helped me discover meaning in my job and life. I realized that through my work, I was touching the lives of the families of the people whom I had the pleasure of serving.

In this resides an important reason for practising humanness. To paraphrase American essayist and poet Ralph Waldo Emerson, it is one of the most beautiful compensations of this life that no man can sincerely try to be humane and help others without helping himself.

Advantage of Practising Humanness

When people are treated with humanness, they will be motivated to bring their complete selves—*mind, heart and body*—to work.

While working, they:

- Are made aware of their potential and guidance is provided to realize it.
- Are made to feel special and this motivates them to give their best on the job.
- Are treated as human beings.

- Bring their minds, hearts and bodies to work. It has the potential of unlocking the unlimited potential of people.
- Utilize their brains to think while doing their jobs.
- Work with passion by putting their hearts into the work.
- Start on a journey to transform themselves into leaders and coaches.

They think while working and work with passion, without getting fatigued. They also set foot on the path to becoming coaches and leaders.

Checklist for Transforming into a Humane Leader

Here is a synopsis of the dos and don'ts for being humane. If you agree with them, internalize and practise them.

- Dos
    - Lead with your heart.
    - Preach what you practise.
    - Self-penalize for mistakes made by others.
    - Be empathetic and compassionate. Demonstrate care.
    - Show appreciation and gratitude. But it should be sincere, authentic and genuine.
    - Help people realize their potential.
    - Be a giver.
    - Give credit. Take blame.
    - Shine the spotlight on your team.
    - Be supportive and encouraging.
    - Be caring and kind towards your people.

  - Be a coach, not merely a leader.
  - Make people feel special.
- Don'ts
  - Be a taker, nor a balancer.
  - Take credit and blame your team.
  - Grab the spotlight from your team members.
  - Throw your people under the bus when they commit honest mistakes.
  - Be a command-and-control leader.
  - Be clever.
  - Be power-hungry, egocentric or want to prove yourself right.
  - Indulge in self-promotion.

Postscript

In olden times, when a master carpet weaver noticed a mistake in weaving, he would not castigate the weaver, nor undo the mistake. Instead, he would make the mistake a part of the design.

In Japan, *kintsugi*[273] is a centuries-old art of mending broken pottery by repairing the cracks with gold powder. Instead of camouflaging the 'scars', it highlights them and makes them appear like a design.

Humane people embody qualities of the master weaver. They do not castigate people for committing mistakes, but convert them into opportunities for learning. Instead of camouflaging mistakes, they highlight them to derive wisdom from them.

Humanness in a Nutshell

Humanness

Fourth Industrial Revolution is upon us. It is leading to proliferation in 'thinking jobs'. This requires people be engaged and motivated at work. The traditional approach of motivating people by offering carrot and stick and financial incentives is proving to be ineffective. The new approach requires adoption of 'people first' policy which views people as 'human' who must treated with 'humanness'. This approach has the potential of unlocking the unlimited potential of people to give their best on the job.

Being Humane

1. Lead with your heart.
2. Preach what you practise.
3. Self-penalize for mistakes committed by others.
4. Kiss down.
5. Share the pain equitably.
6. Demonstrate care.
7. Express appreciation and gratitude.
8. Make people aware of their potential.
9. Be a 'giver'.
10. Do not worry about who gets the credit.
11. Give credit. Take blame.
12. Supportive and encouraging.
13. Be a coach, not a leader.
14. Make people feel special and wanted.
15. Be kind, not clever.
16. Score high on 'Decency Quotient'.

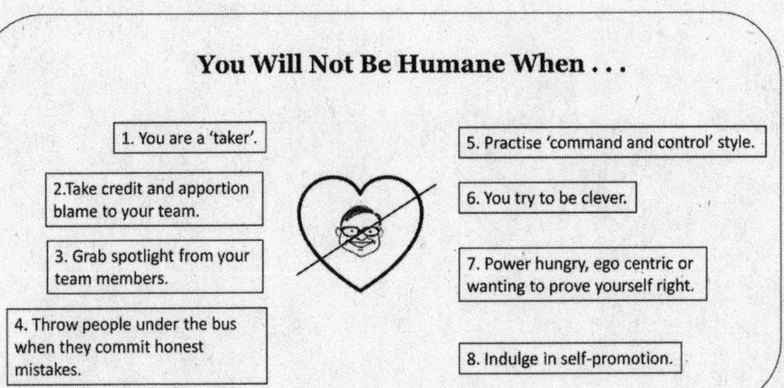

Advantage of Practising Humanness . . .

1. People are made aware of their potential and guidance is provided to realize it.

2.People are made to feel special, and this motivates them to give their best on the job.

3. It has the potential of unlocking unlimited potential of people.

4. Bring their mind, heart and body to work.

5. Utilize their 'brain' to 'think' while doing their jobs.

6. Work with 'passion' by putting their heart in the work.

7. Start on a journey to transform into a leader and coach.

Skill 10
Entrepreneurial Spirit

It is an intangible energy which inspires people to have aspirations greater than the resources at their disposal. When this spirit is alive, businesses keep their mojo and maintain their edge.

Mukesh Ambani[274] returned from Stanford University and joined Reliance Industries, the company founded by his late father, Dhirubhai Ambani.

'What is going to be my job?' he asked.

Dhirubhai Ambani reflected for a moment and said, 'If you are looking for a job, a role and responsibilities, then you are a manger. But if you are an entrepreneur, then you will figure out what to do.'

Mukesh Ambani figured out that he wanted to discover problems to solve.

Where did he learn the art of finding problems to solve?

'From my teacher at UDCT (since renamed Institute of Chemical Technology, Mumbai), who would say, "I am not going to give you a list of problems that you can work on. You find the problems. I will grade you on the quality of the problem that you find as well as the quality of the solutions."'

While attempting to solve problems, failure is par for the course. 'I have failed several times before succeeding. Learn from them but never give up,' says Ambani.

How can an entrepreneur keep their morale high when confronted with the spectre of failure?

'By being optimistic,' says Ambani. 'Look at a glass as half full. Never half empty.' Optimism is a state of mind characterized by hope and a belief that good things will happen in the future.

Also, the team is crucial to success. 'You cannot do anything without the right team. And it is important to align the team's passion to your own,' feels Ambani.

Entrepreneurial Spirit

Mukesh Ambani possesses entrepreneurial spirit.[275] It is a metaphor for a way of thinking and acting. It does not mean you have to be an actual entrepreneur who sets up a business, takes risks and enjoys the profits. You can be working as an employee in a company but could display an entrepreneurial spirit through your thoughts and actions. On the other hand, you could be a business owner and not display any of these traits.

Entrepreneurial spirit can be considered as an intangible energy which, as the late Professor C.K. Prahalad, educator and author, said, inspires people to have aspirations greater than the resources at their disposal. When this spirit is alive, businesses keep their mojo and maintain their edge.

Traits Personifying Entrepreneurial Spirit

People possessing entrepreneurial spirt tend to possess many of the traits mentioned below:

- Unique and differentiated mindset.
- Perpetually on the lookout for opportunities.
- Challenge status quo.
- Discover their calling at work.
- In a state of perpetual beta.
- Show bias for System 2 thinking.
- Are solution seekers.
- Change the rules of the game.
- Have aspirations greater than their resources.
- Spend resources wisely.
- Have a proclivity for experimentation.
- Cultivate and nurture positive thoughts.
- Practise compassion.
- Get their team to think and act like owners.

- Perfect the art of saying 'no'.
- Show resilience, display grit and do not overthink.
- Are anti-fragile.
- Have higher 'return on luck (ROL)'.

Let us unpack each of these traits so that you gain insight into them.

1. Mindset

People embodying entrepreneurial spirit display these types of mindsets:

- **Aviation Mindset**

The aviation industry views every failure—accidents or near misses, no matter how trivial—as an opportunity to make air travel safer. When they occur, the blame game is never allowed to raise its ugly head. Instead, experts descend on the accident site to identify the reasons that caused it. Once identified, these reasons are removed from the root. It does not mean that accidents do not occur again. But they will not be caused due to the previous reasons. In this way, air travel becomes progressively safer.

Entrepreneurial-spirited people tend to possess an aviation mindset.[276] They look upon failures as opportunities to learn and improve. When faced with failure, they do not push it under the proverbial carpet. Instead, they make a conscious effort to identify the causes behind it and take action to eliminate them from the root. It does not mean that they do not make mistakes in future. They do. But those are unlikely to be the same mistakes made in the past. In this way, they become progressively better.

Traditional mangers tend to push their failures under the carpet so that they go undiscovered. In the process, they lose opportunities to learn. Worse, they continue to make the same mistakes again and again.

- **Olympian Mindset**

Olympians possess an innate desire to improve. This motivates them to practise every day and actively seek feedback from their coaches, which they incorporate into the next round of practice. By religiously following this process, they improve with every practice session, every day.

Entrepreneurial-spirited people, like Olympians, have an innate desire to improve. They seek feedback from their team by posing open-ended questions to them and to themselves, and act upon the answers they receive. Here are a few sample questions:

- How can we improve?
- How can we do this task better?
- Can you tell me what is wrong with my thinking?
- I think I can do better. Let me try again.

This is in sharp contrast to a traditional manager, who refrains from seeking feedback fearing that it may show them in a bad light or that it may be unpalatable.

- **Uber Map (Adaptable) Mindset**

When I am travelling in an Uber and the driver takes a wrong turn, the map quickly reconfigures and shows a revised route to the destination.

Entrepreneurial-spirited people do not lament their bad luck upon encountering bumps and hurdles. Like the Uber map, they adjust their plan and continue their journey.

Traditional managers curse their luck, the boss, the system or all of these upon encountering obstacles. But never themselves. They wait for solutions to be airdropped. As a result, they tend to stagnate.

- **Growth Mindset**

People with entrepreneurial spirit possess a growth mindset. They seek to learn at every opportunity and from everyone. They also have a belief that abilities can be developed through hard work and feedback, and that major challenges and setbacks provide an opportunity to learn.[277]

Traditional mangers tend to possess a fixed mindset, which gives them the mistaken belief that they are innately talented. They also harbour a feeling that they have all the answers. They whittle away their energies in trying to prove themselves right every time. Over time, they become irrelevant and eventually fade away.

- **Immigrant Mindset**

'I have an immigrant mentality, which is that the job can be taken away at any time, so make sure you earn it every day,' says Indra Nooyi.[278]

People possessing entrepreneurial spirt may not be immigrants, but they think like one.[279]

- Searching for opportunities in every direction and making the most of those that cross their path.

- Developing a unique ability to spot opportunities which are not noticed by others.
- Unleashing passion on seized opportunities.
- Adapting faster and reacting briskly to changes.
- Being on their toes all the time and acting with speed.

You may be wondering whether an immigrant mindset helps to build and run companies.

According to a study quoted in the *Harvard Business Review*, '40% of Fortune 500 companies operating in 2010 were founded by immigrants or their children—including some of the most well-known brands, from Apple and IBM to Disney and McDonalds. The companies mentioned in this study had combined revenues of $4.2 trillion—more than the GDP of most countries.'[280]

But traditional managers run away from opportunities because as Thomas Edison rightly pointed out that they come dressed in overalls and look like work. Then they lament that opportunities never come their way!

2. Look for Opportunities, Not Obstacles

Ricky Ponting is one of cricket's most prolific run-makers, and has scored over 13,000 runs in Test cricket and ODIs. Asked about his secret, he said, 'Every batsman surveys the field before taking strike, and notices the position of fielders and can see every fielder in their mind's eye. But in my head, I don't see the fielders. I only see the gaps!' He played in the 'gaps' between the fielders, which made him a prolific run-scorer.[281]

Entrepreneurial-spirited people, like Ponting, do not notice the obstacles standing in their path. Instead, they focus on finding gaps in the market to score wins.

In contrast, traditional managers notice the obstacles in their path and are paralysed into inaction.

3. Challenge Status Quo

Entrepreneurial-spirited people are unreasonable. They challenge status quo. They see things as they are and ask why and then reimagine them.

- Steve Jobs challenged the cell phone industry and introduced smartphones.
- Jeff Bezos challenged the retail industry by removing friction from the shopping process and made it frictionless and pleasurable.
- Reed Hastings challenged the entertainment industry and made it possible for us to be entertained anytime, anywhere, on a device of our choice and even while on the move.

George Bernard Shaw, an Irish playwright, captured their spirit accurately when he said the reasonable man adapts himself to the world; the unreasonable one persists in trying to adapt the world to himself. Therefore, all progress depends on the unreasonable man.

Traditional managers tend to follow tradition and the time-tested path of the industry. This ensures that they do not fail greatly. But as Robert Kennedy pointed out, neither do they achieve greatly, because only those who dare to fail greatly can achieve greatly.

4. Discover Their Calling at Work

What motivates the billionaire co-founders of Google, Larry Page and Sergey Brin, to come to work?

Many will attribute it to money.

'If we were motivated by money, we would have sold the company a long time ago and ended up on a beach,' says Larry Page.

Then where does the answer lie?

In the way they look upon their work. For them, it is not a job or a career, it is their calling.

What is the difference, you may ask?

Let me hand over the stage to Dr Amy Wrzesniewski, a Yale psychologist:

- A person who looks upon their work as a 'job' puts in daily effort so that they get a salary at the end of the month, and maybe a bonus at the end of the year. Instead of looking forward to coming to work every morning, such people look forward to the weekends and holidays!
- A person who looks upon their work as a 'career' puts in effort so that they make progress in their job and, in the process, climb the 'corporate ladder' of success, which leads to higher salary and professional recognition.
- A person who looks upon their work as their 'calling' ceases to work for money or for career advancements. Nor do they work to win other people's or societal approval. Nor to pursue somebody's dreams. They feel an emotional and personal connection with their work. They have purpose (read: calling), are enthusiastic and willing to work longer and harder to contribute. They pursue work as an end in itself.[282]

Both the co-founders find their calling in the Google mission, which is to organize the world's information and make it universally accessible and useful. This motivates them to come to work despite already being worth billions.

When people find their calling in their work, they get into a state of 'flow'.[283] In this state, their body and mind are stretched beyond their limits in a voluntary effort to achieve something difficult yet worthwhile. They find the work itself intrinsically rewarding.

Thomas Edison, one of the greatest inventors of all time, expressed it best when he said, 'I never did a day's work in my life. It was all fun.'

Traditional managers tend to look upon their work as a job or as a career. Their motivation to come to work is the salary and perks that the job offers them. They put in effort to earn increments, promotions and to advance their career.

5. Strive for Perfection[284]

While he was once building a fence, Paul Jobs, Steve Jobs's foster father, said, 'You got to make the back of the fence, that nobody will see, just as good-looking like the front of the fence. Even though nobody will see it, you will know, and that will show that you're dedicated to making something perfect.'

Later, Steve Jobs would share the lesson his father taught him using a chest of drawers for an analogy: when you're a carpenter making a beautiful chest of drawers, you're not going to use a piece of plywood on the back, even though it faces the wall, and nobody will ever see it.

You'll know it's there, so you're going to use a beautiful piece of wood on the back. For you to sleep well at night, the aesthetic, the quality, must be carried all the way through.

People endowed with entrepreneurial spirit strive to create a perfect product and refrain from taking shortcuts. Traditional managers tend to take shortcuts and, in the process, short-change themselves.

6. Always in a State of Perpetual Beta

Songs sung by the late Lata Mangeshkar, India's iconic singer, are flawless. But she disagreed on the above, saying, '*Achha hai . . . lekin aur bhi achha ho sakta hai* (It is fine. But I could have been better),' and added, 'An artiste should never be satisfied with what he or she does.'[285]

Leonardo da Vinci, arguably the world's most famous painter, also harboured similar feelings. According to folklore, his last words were, 'I have offended God and mankind, because my work did not reach the quality it could have.'

Elon Musk too is never satisfied with his creations. 'I'm always looking for what's wrong to make (Tesla) better. So, when I see the car, I see all the things that I think need to be fixed to make it better.'[286] In this way, Tesla keeps becoming better.

People with entrepreneurial spirit are never satisfied. No matter how well they have done their job, they believe there is still room for improvement.

Traditional managers tend to be satisfied with their effort. They seldom desire to improve the work they have completed. Therefore, they tend to hibernate in their job.

7. Bias for System 2 Thinking

Many students approach me to find out if they are endowed with an entrepreneurial spirit.

I pose three questions to them.

1. Assume poison is water. Now drink it.
2. How many legs does a dog have if you consider the tail a leg?[287]
3. Is there a difference between an accelerator and a brake?

Most students give the following response:

1. Yes, I will drink it.
2. Five.
3. They are different. One makes the car move fast while the other stops it.

But students possessing an entrepreneurial spirit offer different responses:

I. An assumption will not change poison into water. It will remain poison. Therefore, I will not drink it.
II. Four legs. Mere assumption does not make the tail a leg.
III. Both stop the car. The accelerator must be released and the brake must be pressed.

How did the students arrive at two different sets of response?

Psychologists have long believed that we rely on two modes of thinking: System 1 and System 2.

The first set of students relied on System 1, which is driven by instinct and prior learning. Students possessing an entrepreneurial bent of mind deployed System 2 thinking, which is a slow, deliberate, conscious, effortful, controlled mental process. It is also characterized by rational thinking.[288]

Traditional managers tend to be slaves of System 1 thinking. When faced with a problem, they jump to solutions relying on their past experiences. Therefore, they continue to perpetuate business practices which may have outlived their utility.

8. **Solution Seekers**

Dhirubhai Ambani launched the Vimal textile brand.[289] But wholesalers did not show interest in stocking it. Without their support, Vimal faced an uncertain future.

Dhirubhai decided to overcome this problem by bypassing the wholesalers and selling directly to retailers at attractive terms. Soon, Vimal was available at retail stores. He did not stop here. As a next step, he opened company-owned Vimal showrooms and stared franchising them. As a result, hundreds of Vimal stores sprung up across the country, which only stocked and sold the Vimal range of fabrics.

To ensure heavy footfall in the stores, he let loose an aggressive 'Only Vimal' campaign in the mass media.

Soon, 'Only Vimal' became a household brand name.

Dhirubhai Ambani displayed entrepreneurial spirt by moving heaven and earth to find a solution to a problem he faced. It got him to achieve his goal.

Traditional managers tend to be problem identifiers. They always have a bagful of reasons why something cannot be done. As a result, they are not able to achieve their goal.

9. Change the Rules of the Game

Till 1996, the Sri Lankan cricket team were regarded as minions of cricket. That year, they won the ICC Cricket World Cup. They achieved this remarkable feat by changing the rules of the game. Here is how they did it:

- Firepower at both ends: Normally, batsmen blasted the bowlers in the last overs. But Sri Lanka decided to have fireworks at both ends. They opened with explosive openers, who were given the goal of scoring 100 to 120 runs in the first fifteen overs. This took the opposition by surprise.
- Fitness: Every player's fitness diet was designed. The fitter they became, the more energy they had, which improved their batting, fielding and bowling.
- Feilding: Due to improvement in fitness, the standards of fielding went up. The players dove and saved runs—after all, a run saved is a run scored!
- Quick singles: Athletics who specialized in the 100-metre dash were drafted to teach the players the stance to take which would help them to take off at the slightest opportunity for taking every precious single.
- Run out from the deep: They were trained by expert throwers in the art of throwing from a distance and hitting the stumps.

Akin to the Sri Lankan cricketers, people with entrepreneurial spirit change the rules of the game. This enables them to pole vault over the competition and lead the field.

Traditional managers tend follow the rules of the industry in which they operate. The become predictable and defeat-able.

10. Spend Money Wisely to Keep the Burn Rate Low

In 2001, Eric Schmidt was hired as chief executive to run Google. He was allocated a small office with a makeshift desk made by resting a door on stands. The door was the tabletop!

'I have retained the door to remind myself of what it takes to be successful,' reminisces Eric Schmidt.[290] It also embodies entrepreneurial spirit.

People possessing entrepreneurial spirit tend to be frugal when it comes to splurging money on:

- Creating fancy overheads.
- Hiring people before the business is ready for them.
- Spending money before earning it.
- Offering liberal perks to attract talent.
- Buying sales by offering deep discounts and attractive offers.

They keep the burn rate low.

Elon Musk

Elon Musk also spent money wisely. Hear it from him:[291] 'We rented an office for $400 or $500 a month. It was a tiny little office in Palo Alto. It was cheaper than an apartment. Even cheaper than a garage. And then we bought futons that converted into a couch, which was a meeting area during the day. We would sleep there at night and shower at the YMCA, which was just a few blocks away. This meant an extremely low burn rate. When you are first starting out, you really need to make your burn rate ridiculously tiny. Don't spend more than you are sure you have.'

Jack Ma

Jack Ma,[292] when he started Alibaba, kept the burn rate low. He recollects, 'We had very little money and every dollar we spent very carefully. The office was opened in my apartment. We expanded after we raised money from Goldman Sachs in 1999 and then Softbank Corporation in 2000.'

Entrepreneurial-spirited people tend to spend money sagaciously and keep the burn rate low. On the other hand, traditional managers tend to spend money, believing that the party will never end. They are in for a rude surprise. 'Eventually the party ends, and many business "emperors" are found to have no clothes,' says Warren Buffet.[293]

11. Bias for Experimentation

Jeff Bezos desires that entrepreneurial spirit be all-pervasive at Amazon. This requires people to engage in experimentation. Many of them fail. But Amazon displays high tolerance for failure.

'I believe we are the best place in the world to fail (we have plenty of practice!), as failure and invention are inseparable twins. To invent you must experiment, and if you know in advance that it's going to work, it's not an experiment,' says Bezos,[294] and concludes by saying, 'Outsized returns often come from betting against conventional wisdom.'

Take the game of cricket. When a batsman swings and it connects, the maximum he can get is six runs! However, in business, when a swing is attempted (read: experimentation is undertaken) and it succeeds, it can fetch 1,000 runs (read: outsized rewards). That's the difference between cricket and business.

Over the years, Amazon has had failures, prominent among them being Fire Phone, which resulted in a $170-million loss in unsold devices.

'If the size of your failures isn't growing, you're not going to be inventing at a size that can actually move the needle,' Bezos wrote in the company's 2019 letter to shareholders.[295]

Traditional managers are averse to experimentation. Neither do they engage in it, nor do they encourage others to engage in it. If a team member engages and fails, they are thrown under the bus to serve as a reminder for others not to engage in it. Else, a similar fate awaits them.

12. Aspiration Greater Than Resources

Right after World War II, Masaru Ibuka and Akio Morita started a company, later named Sony, with an initial capital of about $500. At that time, Japan was known for producing poor-quality products. Although they had meagre resources at their command, that did not prevent them from aspiring to change the image of Japan in the eyes of the world and make it known for quality. By the 1990s, both Japan and Sony had well and truly succeeded in becoming known for producing high-quality products.[296]

Jack Ma

In 1999, Jack Ma invited eighteen people to his apartment and spoke to them for two hours about his vision of building an e-commerce ecosystem that allows consumers and businesses to conduct all aspects of business online, create 1 million jobs and make it the largest Internet market in the world. Everyone put their money on the table, which totalled $60,000, and Alibaba was born.[297]

The amount was insignificant when compared to the aspiration Jack Ma harboured. But it did not prevent him from holding it. Years later, his dream was realized not partially, but wholly and completely.

Elon Musk

Elon Musk aspires to make humans a multi-planet species. But the resources under his command were meagre. This did not seem to dampen his spirits. Instead, he looked upon it as an opportunity to innovate.

Until the 1980s, rockets launched into space never returned. Each launch cost $61 million. But Elon Musk's SpaceX developed 'reusable' rockets whose launch cost is between $5 million and $7 million.[298] The steep drop in cost helps Musk pursue his aspiration.

People imbued with an entrepreneurial spirit will have aspirations greater than the resources at their command. But they use ingenuity to bridge the gap, whereas traditional managers' aspiration magically matches or is less than the available resources.

13. Nurture Positive Thoughts

In 2015, Sheryl Sandburg, COO of Facebook, was traumatized after the sudden death of her husband. She was filled with pernicious thoughts and was unable to get over her grief. This made it difficult for her to get back into her work routine. Her friend Adam Grant, the renowned psychologist, shocked her by saying that she should be grateful for the situation she found herself in, because things could be worse. She was taken aback by his insensitive remark and exclaimed, 'Are you kidding? How could things be worse?'

'He could have had that cardiac arrhythmia while driving your children,' retorted Grant.

Hearing this, she felt better. She was able to appreciate that her kids were alive and healthy.[299] This made her accept the loss by consoling herself that things could have been worse.

The strategy Adam Grant used to make Sheryl Sandburg feel better despite going through the worst time in her life can be illustrated through the diagram:

Event ----- Thoughts ----- Emotions[300]

Sheryl Sandburg had no control over the event—the untimely demise of her husband. It had already occurred. But she could control her thoughts. A nudge from her friend Grant made her realize how fortunate she still was that no harm had befallen her children. This filled her with positive thoughts, which resulted in her experiencing a burst of positive emotions. She felt better and started to act with positive intent.

Rahul Dravid[301]

Rahul Dravid batted at number three while playing for India. He faced the new ball many times, which must have put pressure on him.

This made Sourav Ganguly ask him how he dealt with pressure.

'I do not look upon Test match or One Day as a pressure but as an opportunity,' he replied.

Rahul Dravid had intuitively followed the above model. He looked upon this 'event' as an 'opportunity', which filled him with positive thoughts. In this state of mind, he would have been filled with confidence (read: positive emotion). When he batted with confidence, he scored runs for India so consistently that he earned the moniker of 'the Wall'.

On the other hand, if he had viewed the same event as pressure, then he would have been filled with negative thoughts of impending doom. This would have filled him with fear, a negative emotion. If he had played fearfully, he would have turned in a poor performance with every outing and lost his place in the side.

Thomas Edison

Finally, let us get Thomas Edison into the debate. He faced failures (read: events), not once but 10,000 times. But he thought that he had not failed 10,000 times, but found 10,000 ways it would not work.[302] These positive thoughts filled him with positive emotions of hope and inspiration and must have motivated him to continue to work till he achieved success.

People imbued with an entrepreneurial spirit intuitively know that events are not in their control, but how they think about them is! They make a conscious effort to perceive the event as positive. This gives rise to positive thoughts, which in turn gives birth to positive emotions (read: confidence). When actions are carried out with confidence, victory follows.

Traditional managers, when faced with challenging events, are overwhelmed with negative thoughts. This automatically triggers negative emotions, which paralyses them into inaction. They end up failing.

14. Practise Compassion

A Tesla factory was reporting a higher than usual accident rate. Elon Musk decided to act.[303] He issued instructions that every accident should be reported directly to him because 'I would like to meet every injured person as soon as they are well, so that I can understand from them exactly what we need to do to make it better. I will then go down to the production line and perform the same task that they perform. This is what all managers at Tesla should do as a matter of course. At Tesla, we lead from the front line, not from some safe and comfortable ivory tower.'

The entrepreneurial-spirited display compassion towards their people and strive to protect their interests even more valiantly than their own. They demonstrate their intentions through actions, not mere words. This makes them earn the trust and goodwill of their team. When that happens, the engagement, productivity and performance of the team soars.

Traditional managers tend to issue orders from the comfort of their office. They display scant compassion towards their team. As a result, they are unable to win their goodwill and trust.

15. Align the Team to Think and Act like Owners

When team members think and act like owners, they become fully invested in the business. They then work with their heart and go beyond the call of duty.

Here are ways by which people with an entrepreneurial spirit instil a sense of ownership in their team:

- **Job Crafting**

They empower their team to redesign a part of their job. It is noticed that 'job crafters' tend to be more motivated and display a greater sense of ownership. It results in greater engagement and in thriving at work.[304]

- **Reduce Controls**

Mary Barra, the current CEO of General Motors, decided to reduce several pages detailing its complex dress code policy to just two words: dress appropriately!

Her reasoning, 'If employees can't handle "dress appropriately", then how can they be trusted to handle bigger business decisions?'

She again had two words of advice for her 1,55,000 employees on the future of work: work appropriately. This empowers employees to have the flexibility to work from anywhere so that they can make the greatest contribution in helping GM achieves its goals.

People imbued with an entrepreneurial spirit loosen their control and let the team take appropriate decisions.

- **Empower the Team to Take Decisions**

Nordstrom, the chain of luxury department stores renowned for its customer service, is reputed to have the shortest employee handbook to guide their behaviour. Here is their entire rulebook. Rule #1: Use best judgement in all situations. There will be no additional rules.

Reed Hastings of Netflix has also empowered his team to take decisions which are in the best interests of Netflix.

- **Educate the Team on What Is Expected from Them but Not on How to Do It**

Entrepreneurial-spirited people educate their team about what is expected from them but refrain from telling them how to do it. Let them use their judgement to take decisions which are in the best interests of the company.

You may be wondering if team members will misuse the trust and power reposed in them. Some will. To address this challenge, people with entrepreneurial spirit tend to follow the Russian saying that translates to 'trust but verify.' This means they trust their team members, but also put in place a system to identify those misusing it. They come down heavily, decisively and swiftly on these black sheep.

Here is an example: at Wipro, a senior person was caught padding the expense statement. He was immediately asked to leave, despite his stellar professional performance.

Now for the good news. Empirical evidence indicates that the number of employees likely to misuse trust and power do not exceed 5 per cent of the workforce. Now, should you plan a system that will favour 95 per cent of your employees who are trustworthy or focus on the 5 per cent who may not be? You decide.

Traditional managers tend to focus on the 5 per cent of people who strive to game the system. Elaborate bureaucratic systems and processes are put in place to checkmate them. This convoluted system may check the minority from gaming the system, but it also demotivates the majority. As a result, the performance of the company suffers.

16. Learn the Art of Saying 'No'

'The difference between successful people and really successful people is that really successful people say "no" to almost everything,'[305] says Warren Buffet.

Entrepreneurial-spirited people perfect the art of saying no. This frees up their time to focus on what is truly important.

Traditional managers fear saying no because they feel that it might lead to conflict. This results in them investing their time in non-value-creating activities. As a result, they are perpetually pressed for time.

17. Show Grit

Walt Disney started his own cartoon business, Laugh-O-Gram Studios. It failed. He then created Oswald the Lucky Rabbit. Misfortune stuck again. He lost the legal rights to it. But he did not play the victim card. Instead, he looked upon it as a learning opportunity to become stronger and bounce back higher. Filled with these positive thoughts, he created Mickey Mouse and waltzed his way to success and global recognition. Mickey Mouse has worldwide brand awareness of 97 per cent—higher than Santa Claus—and generates billions of dollars in annual revenues for Disney. It has become the most famous fictional character in the world.

Walt Disney showed grit,[306] which entails working to overcome challenges and maintaining effort and interest over time despite failures, adversities and plateaus in progress.

Entrepreneurial-spirited people are like Walt Disney. They tend to be gritty. They believe in Nietzsche's advice—what does not kill them, makes them stronger. This motivates them to keep persevering over a long time despite facing failures and setbacks.

Traditional managers, when confronted with challenges and misfortune, throw in the towel. In the process withers away the opportunity to learn from the mistake and bounce back.

18. Display Resilience

In 1989, the Test match series between India and Pakistan was underway. In the fourth Test match, India were struggling to save the match. It was a green top and Waqar Yunus and Wasim Akram were showering the batsman with bouncers, yorkers and in-swingers.

Navjot Singh Sidhu was keeping one end intact. A wicket fell and a sixteen-year-old Sachin Tendulkar walked to the crease to make his debut in Test cricket.

Waqar bowled a bouncer which hit Sachin on his nose, and he started to bleed profusely. Sidhu rushed towards Sachin and asked him, '*Khelega* (Will you continue playing)?' With determination in his voice, he said, '*Mai khelega* (I will play),' and hit Waqar's next delivery for a four. He made fifty-seven runs and, along with Sidhu, ensured that India drew the match.

Sachin Tendulkar displayed resilience[307] by adapting well in the face of adversity, trauma and threats.

People with entrepreneurial spirit often get a bloody nose. At such moments, they display resilience.

Traditional managers do not display resilience when dealt a body blow. They tend to give up, not realizing that in the middle of adversity lies success.

19. Do Not Overthink

Aerodynamic principles say that a bumblebee cannot fly. Its wingspan is too short to support its massive body in flight. But a bumblebee doesn't know. It never took a physics class. So, it flies.[308]

Entrepreneurial-spirited people are like the bumblebee. Therefore, they succeed.

20. Anti-Fragile

Nearly 1500 years ago, the Romans built the walls of piers, breakwaters and harbours. They are still standing. These walls were built by mixing volcanic ash, lime (calcium oxide), sea water and lumps of volcanic rocks. Each time the sea water hit the wall, it reacted with the volcanic material, creating new minerals that made the bonding, and hence the wall, stronger.[309]

Ironically, the wall built to keep the sea water at bay benefitted from the shock of the sea water striking it. Each strike made it stronger and anti-fragile. Anti-fragile does mean merely withstanding a shock, but improving and becoming stronger because of it.

Entrepreneurial-spirited people tend to be anti-fragile. Adversity has the opposite effect on them. It makes them stronger.

Traditional managers tend to be fragile. They come apart when faced with adversity.

21. Higher Return on Luck[310]

Many people consider Bill Gates lucky. After all, he grew up in an upper middle-class American family, attended a secondary school with access to computing and knew how to program in Basic.

But he was not the only person lucky to have such advantages. There were thousands of others who were also lucky to have similar advantages. Therefore, the difference between Gates and similarly advantaged people is not luck but return on luck. Gates worked with ferocious intensity to get an outsized return on his luck. And this is the important difference. Luck, good and bad, happens to everyone. But people like Gates recognize luck, seize it and get a high 'return on luck' (ROL).

Getting a high ROL requires throwing oneself at the luck event with ferocious intensity, disrupting life and not letting up. Bill Gates did exactly that. He kept pushing, driving, working and sustained that effort for more than two decades. That's not luck—that's return on luck.

Like Gates, people bestowed with entrepreneurial spirit do not get more good luck, less bad luck or a bigger slice of luck. But they make more of the luck than others by getting a higher ROL.

The Mann Deshi Mahila Sahakari Bank[311]

A poor woman, working as welder and living with her family on the footpaths, wanted to save Rs 10 every day so that she could buy a plastic sheet to protect her home from the rain. She approached a bank to open a savings bank account. But the bank manager refused, saying the amount was too small and not worth his time.

She approached Chetna Sinha, a social activist, and shared her plight. Sinha was appalled that a poor woman, who was not asking for a loan but a safe place to keep her savings, could not open a bank account. She resolved to set up a bank for such women. She approached the Reserve Bank of India (RBI) to get a bank license. But the RBI refused, stating that a bank licence could not be issued to bank promotors who were illiterate.

Chetna Sinha was in tears as she narrated the reasons to these women. They told her to stop crying and start a programme which could help them read and write.

A literacy programme was started, and these poor women, after doing back-breaking work the whole day, came at night to learn to read and write.

Five months later, a team comprising Chetna Sinha and fifteen women from the literacy programme went to the RBI to again seek the bank licence. They told the bank officer that they were earlier denied the bank licence because they were illiterate. But where they were growing up, there were no schools in the vicinity. So they were not responsible for their illiteracy. They now challenged the bank officer to give them a principal amount for calculation of interest. If they were unable to calculate it, then the bank licence should be denied. But they put a condition: get other bank officers to also calculate the interest, but without using a calculator, and let him see who calculated faster.

Needless to say, the bank licence was issued to the women and the Mann Deshi Mahila Sahakari Bank was started. It is the first cooperative bank for women in rural India.[312]

These poor women came from impoverished backgrounds and could not be deemed to be born lucky. But they threw themselves at the luck event that came their way and did not let disappointments and rejections stop them. Instead, they found a solution to every obstacle that came their way and they kept on pushing themselves till they succeeded. That's not getting lucky. That's getting a high return on luck.

People bestowed with entrepreneurial spirit prepare for luck events by following Abraham Lincoln's advice, 'I will prepare and someday my chance (read: luck) will come.' And when it comes, I will not be found wanting. Concurrently, they also prepare themselves for bad luck events by building reserves (e.g., cash on the balance sheet) and running lean operations in good times.[313]

Traditional managers keep waiting to get lucky. When luck finally comes their way, they are inadequately prepared to get a good ROL. More importantly, when bad luck strikes, they are so inadequately prepared for it that they go under.

A Few More Traits That Entrepreneurial-Spirited People Have

Entrepreneurial-spirited[314] people possess many of these desirable traits:

- They are comfortable even if they do not have all the answers.
- They are at ease in seeking help.
- They display the traits of a marathon runner, not of a sprinter. This makes them patient, and display perseverance, grit and resilience.
- They are self-driven. Every day, they show up with the same enthusiasm which they had shown when they were starting out.
- They do not feel threatened or uncomfortable when challenged.

- They proactively challenge tradition, question assumptions defy prevailing norms and status quo.
- They focus on things they can control and do not let the uncontrollable worry them.
- They are always on the lookout for opportunities.
- They tend to be anti-fragile. Adversity has the opposite effect on them. It makes them stronger.
- They focus not on getting lucky, but on getting a better return on luck when luck strikes.

Why Is Possessing an Entrepreneurial Spirit Critical?

We live in a VUCA world, where volatility, uncertainty, complexity and ambiguity are par for the course. Entrepreneurial-spirited people are comfortable working in such conditions and are best poised to triumph in such circumstances.

Postscript

In the 1950s, Sir Edmund Hillary, the first man to step on Mount Everest, was once on a reconnaissance expedition to the Mount Everest region. He looked towards the mighty mountain and said, 'I will come again and conquer you because as a mountain you can't grow, but as a human I can.'[315]

Three years later, Sir Edmund Hillary and Tenzing Norgay conquered Mount Everest.

Entrepreneurial-spirited people look at intractable problems and say, I will come at you again and again till I conquer you. They do!

Entrepreneurial Spirit in a Nutshell

Entrepreneurial Spirit

It is an intangible energy which inspires people to have aspirations greater than the resources at their disposal. When this spirit is alive, businesses keep their mojo and maintain their edge.

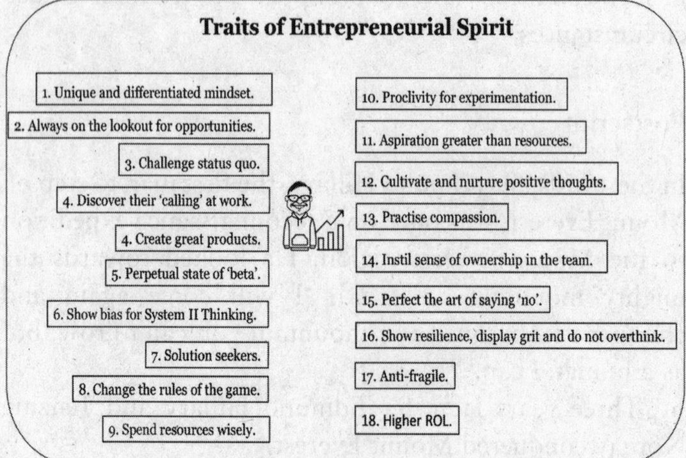

Advantages of Acquiring Entrepreneurial Spirit

1. Comfortable even if you do not have all the answers.

2. At ease while asking for help.

3. Possess 'traits of a marathon runner, not of a sprinter.

4. Self-driven.

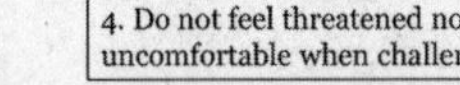

4. Do not feel threatened nor uncomfortable when challenged.

5. Proactively challenge tradition, question assumptions and defy norms and status quo.

6. Focus on things they can control.

Notes

1 James Manyika, Susan Lund, Michael Chui, Jacques Bughin, Jonathan Woetzel, Parul Batra, Ryan Ko, Saurabh Sanghvi, 'Jobs lost, jobs gained: What the future of work will mean for jobs, skills and wages', McKinsey Global Institute, 28 November 2017, https://www.mckinsey.com/featured-insights/future-of-work/jobs-lost-jobs-gained-what-the-future-of-work-will-mean-for-jobs-skills-and-wages
2 Amanda Russo, 'Recession and Automation Changes or Future of Work, But There are Jobs coming, Report Says', World Economic Forum, 20 October 2020, https://www.weforum.org/press/2020/10/recession-and-automation-changes-our-future-of-work-but-there-are-jobs-coming-report-says-52c5162fce/
3 Klaus Schwab, 'The Fourth Industrial Revolution: what it means, how to respond', World Economic Forum, 14 January 2016, https://www.weforum.org/agenda/2016/01/the-fourth-industrial-revolution-what-it-means-and-how-to-respond/
4 Scott D. Anthony, 'Innovation Is a Discipline, Not a Cliché', *Harvard Business Review*, 30 May 2012, https://hbr.org/2012/05/four-innovation-

misconceptions#:~:text=As%20The%20Little%20Black%20Book,that%20idea%20to%20achieve%20results

5 'How to use the data to tell compelling and meaningful stories?', Brainfeed Higher Education Plus, accessed on 23 May 2022, https://highereducationplus.com/how-to-use-the-data-to-tell-compelling-and-meaningful-stories/

6 'Why human creativity is not computable', Mind Matters News, 20 March 2021, https://mindmatters.ai/2021/03/why-human-creativity-is-not-computable/

7 'Charles Arthur, Nokia's chief executive to staff: We are standing on a burning platform', *Guardian*, 9 February 2011, https://www.theguardian.com/technology/blog/2011/feb/09/nokia-burning-platform-memo-elop

8 Noah's Ark, Kids' Korner, https://www.biblewise.com/kids/read/young/noahs-ark2.php

9 Lauren Atkins, 'Picture a Year from Now: Begin Today', Medium.com, 14 August 2018, https://medium.com/@info_67796/a-year-from-now-you-will-wish-you-had-started-today-karen-lamb-5b79d5f9b80b

10 Richard Branson, 'How to come up with more brilliant ideas', Richard Branson's Blog, December 2020, https://www.virgin.com/branson-family/richard-branson-blog/how-to-come-up-with-more-brilliant-ideas

11 Adam Brandenburger, 'Strategy Needs Creativity', *Harvard Business Review*, March–April 2019, https://hbr.org/2019/03/strategy-needs-creativity

12 'What Henry Ford learned from a slaughterhouse', 17 December 2010, http://www.mstaires.com/what-

henry-ford-learned-from-a-slaughter-house/#:~:text=History%20tells%20us%20that's%20when,idea%20of%20the%20assembly%20line.&text=The%20saw%20the%20carcasses%20hung,%22dis%2Dassembly%22%20line.

13 Kaylie Duffy, 'Today in Engineering History: Ford Launches Moving Assembly Line', Design World, 7 October 2015, https://www.designworldonline.com/today-in-engineering-history-ford-launches-moving-assembly-line/#:~:text=The%20new%20system%20dramatically%20reduced,%24850%20to%20less%20than%20%24300.

14 David Aaker, 'The Genius Bar – Branding the Innovation', *Harvard Business Review*, 2 January 2012, https://hbr.org/2012/01/the-genius-bar-branding-the-in

15 'Red Bull: The Real Story Behind the Can', YouTube, https://www.youtube.com/watch?v=Ri0XXjmiviM

16 'Brand Value of Red Bull Worldwide from 2016 to 2021', Statista, https://www.statista.com/statistics/1225791/red-bull-brand-value/

17 'Mohandas "Mahatma" Gandhi', BBC, 25 August 2009, https://www.bbc.co.uk/religion/religions/hinduism/people/gandhi_1.shtml#:~:text=Born%20in%201869%20in%20Porbandar,by%20Jainism%20in%20his%20youth.

18 'Ahimsa', BBC, 11 September 2009, https://www.bbc.co.uk/religion/religions/jainism/living/ahimsa_1.shtml

19 Erin Blakemore, 'Barbie's Secret Sister Was a Sexy German Novelty Doll', History, https://www.history.com/news/barbie-inspiration-bild-lilli

20 Eliana Dockterman, 'Barbie's Got a New Body', *TIME*, https://time.com/barbie-new-body-cover-story/
21 Adam Brandenburger, 'Strategy Needs Creativity', *Harvard Business Review*, March–April 2019, https://hbr.org/2019/03/strategy-needs-creativity
22 Mihir Dalal, 'Strong beer overpowers milder version in the Indian market', *Mint*, 21 March 2013. https://www.livemint.com/Industry/p3WoGTQ54DJeGs2JfwDbSM/Strong-beer-overpowers-milder-version-in-the-Indian-market.html
23 Brittany Matter, 'Stan Lee on What Made Spider-Man So Special', Marvel Comics, 13 November 2018, https://www.marvel.com/articles/comics/stan-lee-on-what-made-spider-man-so-special
24 Elizabeth Weise, 'Bezos: "Star Trek" was inspiration for Amazon Echo', *USA Today*, 18 May 2016,
25 Kate Ravilious, 'Isaac Newton: Who He Was, Why Apples Are Falling', *National Geographic*, 12 March 2020, https://www.nationalgeographic.org/article/isaac-newton-who-he-was-why-apples-are-falling/
26 Alok Jha, 'Newton's Universal Law of Gravitation', Guardian, 13 October 2013, https://www.theguardian.com/science/2013/oct/13/newtons-universal-law-of-gravitation
27 'Microwave Oven', Wikipedia, https://en.wikipedia.org/wiki/Microwave_oven#:~:text=In%201945%2C%20the%20heating%20effect,he%20had%20in%20his%20pocket.
28 'The Innovator. Jack Dorsey', CBS News, 17 March 2013, https://www.usatoday.com/story/tech/2016/05/18/jeff-bezos-amazon-transformers-

washington-post/84548082/https://www.youtube.com/watch?v=eKHoTOYTFH8&%3Bt=7s

29 'Buoyancy', Encylopedia.com, updated 27 February 2021, https://www.encyclopedia.com/science-and-technology/physics/physics/buoyancy

30 Taylor Locke, 'At age 30, Jeff Bezos thought this would be his one big regret in life', CNBC Make It, 18 January 2020, https://www.cnbc.com/2020/01/17/at-age-30-jeff-bezos-thought-this-would-be-his-one-big-regret-in-life.html

31 Thomas Roulet and Ben Laker, 'Your Career Needs a Little Luck. Here's How to Cultivate It', *Harvard Business Review*, 19 January 2022, https://hbr.org/2022/01/your-career-needs-a-little-luck-heres-how-to-cultivate-it?utm_campaign=hbr&utm_medium=social&utm_ource=facebook&fbclid=IwAR0Gwb7jQdZPMc5PBCEwRVjv1Vh1waAIIrRkkGEslJN0flbfCShmyiH6G3U

32 Edward de Bono, *How to Have Creative Ideas*, Vermillion, 2007.

33 'Invention of Velcro Brand Hook and Loop', Hook and Loop, https://www.hookandloop.com/invention-velcro-brand/

34 Adam Brandenburger, 'To Change the Way You Think, Change the Way You See', *Harvard Business Review*, 16 April 2019, https://hbr.org/2019/04/to-change-the-way-you-think-change-the-way-you-see

35 Rebecca Shambaugh, 'How to Unlock Your Team's Creativity', *Harvard Business Review*, 31 January 2019, https://hbr.org/2019/01/how-to-unlock-your-teams-creativity

36 Alto Nivel, 'Steve Jobs and Albert Einstein Applied the Concept of "No Time" to Boost Their Creativity. What Does It Entail?' *Entrepreneur India*, 25 May 2021, https://www.entrepreneur.com/article/366785
37 Sarthak Dogra, 'Apple CEO Tim Cook explains why he starts his day before 4 am', *India Today*, 23 August 2021, https://www.indiatoday.in/technology/news/story/apple-ceo-tim-cook-explains-why-he-starts-his-day-before-4-am-1844293-2021-08-23
38 Annie McKee, 'How to Free Your Innate Creativity', *Harvard Business Review*, 11 December 2015, https://hbr.org/2015/12/how-to-free-your-innate-creativity
39 Carmine Gallo, 'The 7 Innovations Secrets of Steve Jobs', Forbes, 2 May 2014, https://www.forbes.com/sites/carminegallo/2014/05/02/the-7-innovation-secrets-of-steve-jobs/?sh=78b03859751c
40 Adam Brandenburger, 'Strategy Needs Creativity', *Harvard Business Review*, March–April 2019, https://hbr.org/2019/03/strategy-needs-creativity
41 Neil Patel, '12 lessons You Can Learn from Amazon Gounder and CEO Jeff Bezos', https://neilpatel.com/blog/lessons-from-jeff-bezos/
42 Annie McKee, 'How to Free Your Innate Creativity', *Harvard Business Review*, 11 December 2015, https://hbr.org/2015/12/how-to-free-your-innate-creativity
43 Adam Brandenburger, 'To Change the Way You Think, Change the Way You See', *Harvard Business Review*, 16 April 2019, https://hbr.org/2019/04/to-change-the-way-you-think-change-the-way-you-see

44 Adam Grant, *Originals: How Non-Conformists Change the World*, Penguin Random House, 2017.

45 Lucinda Shen, 'Warby Parker raises $245 million for a valuation of a $3 billion valuation', *Fortune*, 27 August 2020, https://fortune.com/2020/08/27/warby-parker-3-billion-dollar-valuation-245-million-funding/

46 'Peter Mukerjea pens a memory, says it's not intended to open a can of worms', *Indian Express*, 20 March 2021.

47 Mayo Oshin, 'Pablo Picasso on the Myth of Overnight Success', Thrive Global, 20 February 2019, https://thriveglobal.com/stories/pablo-picasso-myth-overnight-success/

48 Adam Grant, *Originals: How Non-Conformists Change the World*, Penguin Random House, 2007.

49 Roberto Verganti and Don Norman, 'Why Criticism Is Good for Creativity', *Harvard Business Review*, 16 July 2019, https://hbr.org/2019/07/why-criticism-is-good-for-creativity

50 Kaylie Duffy, 'Today in Engineering History: Ford Launches Moving Assembly Line', Design World, 7 October 2015, https://www.designworldonline.com/today-in-engineering-history-ford-launches-moving-assembly-line/#:~:text=The%20new%20system%20dramatically%20reduced,%24850%20to%20less%20than%20%24300

51 Jeff Bezos, '2020 Letter to Shareholders', Amazon, 15 April 2021, https://www-aboutamazon-com.cdn.ampproject.org/c/s/www.aboutamazon.com/news/company-news/2020-letter-to-shareholders?_amp=true

52 Carmine Gallo, 'The 7 Innovations Secretes of Steve Jobs', *Forbes*, 2 May 2014, https://www.forbes.com/sites/carminegallo/2014/05/02/the-7-innovation-secrets-of-steve-jobs/?sh=78b03859751c
53 Vijay Govindarajan, 'Innovation is Not Creativity', *Harvard Business Review*, 3 August 2010, https://hbr.org/2010/08/innovation-is-not-creativity?autocomplete=true
54 Vijay Govindarajan and Srikanth Srinivas, 'The Innovation Mindset in Action: 3M Corporation', 6 August 2013, https://hbr.org/2013/08/the-innovation-mindset-in-acti-3
55 Carol Kinsey Goman, '5 Tips for Sparking Innovation', *Forbes*, 29 May 2012, https://www.forbes.com/sites/carolkinseygoman/2012/05/29/5-tips-for-sparking-innovation/#2128a2b91bc1
56 Vijay Govindarajan, 'Innovation is Not Creativity', *Harvard Business Review*, 3 August 2010, https://hbr.org/2010/08/innovation-is-not-creativity?autocomplete=true
57 Roger Schwarz, 'What the Research Tells Us about Team Creativity and Innovation', *Harvard Business Review*, 15 December 2015, https://hbr.org/2015/12/what-the-research-tells-us-about-team-creativity-and-innovation
58 'Revaluating Incremental Innovation', *Harvard Business Review*, September–October 2018, https://hbr.org/2018/09/reevaluating-incremental-innovation
59 Ava Seave, 'Fast Followers Not First Movers Are The Real Winners', *Forbes*, 14 October 2014,

https://www.forbes.com/sites/avaseave/2014/10/14/fast-followers-not-first-movers-are-the-real-winners/#ba4ecb1314cc

60 Joel Lee, '7 Search Engines That Rocked before Google Even Existed', MUO, 30 November 2015, https://www.makeuseof.com/tag/7-search-engines-that-rocked-before-google-even-existed/

61 Evan Tarver, '3 Social Media Networks before Facebook', Investopedia, 3 April 2020, https://www.investopedia.com/articles/markets/081315/3-social-media-networks-facebook.asp

62 Jim Collins, 'Best Beats First', Jim Collins.com, August 2000, https://www.jimcollins.com/article_topics/articles/best-beats-first.html

63 Vinod Mahanta, 'How GE got out of the GE way to create the Nano of ECGs', *Economic Times*, 11 March 2011, https://economictimes.indiatimes.com/how-ge-got-out-of-the-ge-way-to-create-the-nano-of-ecgs/articleshow/7673404.cms

64 Vijay Govindarajan, 'A Reverse-Innovation Playbook', *Harvard Business Review*, April 2012, https://hbr.org/2012/04/a-reverse-innovation-playbook

65 Afaf, 'Crowdsourcing the Boeing 787', Digital Innovation and Transformation, 20 March 2017, https://digital.hbs.edu/platform-digit/submission/crowdsourcing-the-boeing-787/

66 'The Immunity Charm: Making Immunization A Tradition', McCann Health, https://www.mccannhealth.com/case-studies/the-immunity-charm-making-immunization-a-tradition/

67 Navi Radjou and Jaideep Prabhu, 'Frugal Innovation: A New Business Paradigm', Knowledge, INSEAD, https://knowledge.insead.edu/innovation/frugal-innovation-a-new-business-paradigm-2375

68 Drew Boyd, 'Inside the Box: The Subtraction Technique–When Less becomes More', *Industry Week*, 15 October 2013, https://www.industryweek.com/innovation/article/21961428/inside-the-box-the-subtraction-technique-when-less-becomes-more

69 Frederick E. Allen, 'The Zen at the Heart of Steve Jobs' Genius', *Forbes*, 20 March 2012, https://www.forbes.com/sites/frederickallen/2012/03/20/the-zen-at-the-heart-of-steve-jobs-genius/?sh=4e36e4b8198c

70 'Steve Jobs and Zen Design', Zero Abundance, https://www.interactiongreen.com/jobs-zen/

71 Carmine Gallo, 'How Google's 11-Word Pitch Wowed Investors and Changed the World', Inc.com, 29 October 2018, https://www.inc.com/carmine-gallo/how-googles-11-word-pitch-wowed-investors-changed-world.html

72 Katherine Ellen Foley, 'Viagra's famous surprising origin story is actually a pretty common way to find new drugs', Quartz, 17 September 2017, https://qz.com/1070732/viagras-famously-surprising-origin-story-is-actually-a-pretty-common-way-to-find-new-drugs/

73 Leigh Ann Anderson, 'Viagra: How a Little Blue Pill Changed the World', Drug.com, 24 February 2020, https://www.drugs.com/slideshow/viagra-little-blue-pill-1043#:~:text=The%20sildenafil%20compound%20was%20originally,inducing%20erections%20than%20treating%20angina.

74 Sarah Jane Gilbert, 'The Accident Innovator', Working Knowledge, Harvard Business School, 5 July 2006, https://hbswk.hbs.edu/item/the-accidental-innovator

75 Airbnb Luxe, Luxury Retreats, 'Every home is a destination', Airbnb, https://www.airbnb.co.in/luxury

76 Jonathan Ponciano, 'Airbnb Skyrockets 120% In IPO Valuation Blows Past $100 Billion–More Than Marriott, Hilton and Hyatt', *Forbes*, 10 December 2020, https://www.forbes.com/sites/jonathanponciano/2020/12/10/airbnb-ipo-shares-valuation-billion-more-than-marriott-hilton-hyatt/?sh=32777b3020ef

77 Christian Hopp, David Antons, Jermain Kaminski and Torsten Oliver Salge, 'What 40 Years of Research Reveals about the Difference between Disruptive and Radical Innovation', *Harvard Business Review*, 9 April 2018, https://hbr.org/2018/04/what-40-years-of-research-reveals-about-the-difference-between-disruptive-and-radical-innovation

78 Christian Hopp, David Antons, Jermain Kaminski and Torsten Oliver Salge, 'What 40 Years of Research Reveals about the Difference between Disruptive and Radical Innovation,' *Harvard Business Review*, 9 April 2018, https://hbr.org/2018/04/what-40-years-of-research-reveals-about-the-difference-between-disruptive-and-radical-innovation; Guy Kawasaki, 'The Art of Innovation', Bizagi Catalyst, 31 January 2019, https://www.youtube.com/watch?v=VkGaHbKAp0I

79 Oliver Wyman, 'Supporting The Circular Economy Transition', Marsh & McLennan, https://www.oliverwyman.com/content/dam/oliver-wyman/v2/publications/2017/sep/CircularEconomy_print.pdf
80 Alex Thornton, 'These 11 companies are leading the way to a circular economy', World Economic Forum, 26 February 2019, https://www.weforum.org/agenda/2019/02/companies-leading-way-to-circular-economy/
81 'Johnnie Walker whisky to be sold in paper bottles', BBC News, 13 July 2020, https://www.bbc.com/news/business-53392949?fbclid=IwAR3c16J5zA54SMDJp9kEF_u6RQfnehy3Te4-iVTMSlHeHWPUCkvdRZ7iTgc
82 Rajesh Srivastava, *The New Rules of Business*, Penguin Random House India, 2019.
83 Sunil Gupta, *Driving Digital Strategy*, Harvard Business Review Press, 2018.
84 IBM Simon, Wikipedia, https://en.wikipedia.org/wiki/IBM_Simon
85 Anton Troianovski, 'Nokia's Bad Call on Smartphones', *Wall Street Journal*, 18 July 2012, https://www.wsj.com/articles/SB10001424052702304388004577531002591315494
86 'Recycling an Apple product is as easy as it is good for the planet', Apple.com, https://www.apple.com/in/recycling/
87 Natalie, 'Amazon Studios: Crowdsourcing Content and Feedback, Digital Innovation and Transformation', Digital Initiative, 20 March 2017, https://digital.hbs.edu/platform-digit/submission/

amazon-studios-crowdsourcing-content-and-feedback/

88 'Recycling', Amazon, https://sustainability.aboutamazon.com/environment/circular-economy/recycling

89 Catherine Clifford, 'Jeff Bezos to exec after product totally flopped: You can't, for one minute, feel bad', CNBC, 22 May 2020, https://www.cnbc.com/2020/05/22/jeff-bezos-why-you-cant-feel-bad-about-failure.html

90 Scott D. Anthony, Paul Cobban, Tahul Nair and Natalie Painchaud, 'Breaking Down Barriers to Innovation', *Harvard Business Review*, November–December 2019, https://hbr.org/2019/11/breaking-down-the-barriers-to-innovation

91 Scott Horton, 'Mill – Progress through Contact with the Unknown', *Harper's Magazine*, 17 March 2009, https://harpers.org/2009/05/mill-progress-through-contact-with-the-unknown/

92 Richard Farson and Ralph Keyes, 'The Failure Tolerant Leader', *Harvard Business Review*, August 2002, https://hbr.org/2002/08/the-failure-tolerant-leader

93 L.D. DeSimone, George N. Hatsopoulos, William F. O'Brien, Bill Harris and Charles P. Holt, 'How Can Big Companies Keep the Entrepreneurial Spirit Alive', *Harvard Business Review*, November–December 1995, https://hbr.org/1995/11/how-can-big-companies-keep-the-entrepreneurial-spirit-alive

94 Bill Murphy Jr, 'Google Says It Still Uses the "20-Percent Rule," and You Should Totally Copy

It', Inc.com, 1 November 2020, https://www.inc.com/bill-murphy-jr/google-says-it-still-uses-20-percent-rule-you-should-totally-copy-it.html

95 Adam Robinson, 'Want to Boost Your Bottom Line? Encourage Your Employees to Work on Side Projects', Inc.com, 12 March 2018, https://www.inc.com/adam-robinson/google-employees-dedicate-20-percent-of-their-time-to-side-projects-heres-how-it-works.html

96 Betty Liu, 'Elon Musk: I Listen to Negative Feedback', LinkedIn, 10 December 2013, https://www.linkedin.com/pulse/20131210010653-123941699-elon-musk-i-listen-to-negative-feedback/

97 Scott D. Anthony, Paul Cobban, Rahul Nair and Natalie Painhaud, 'Breaking Down the Barriers to Innovation', *Harvard Business Review*, November–December 2019, https://hbr.org/2019/11/breaking-down-the-barriers-to-innovation

98 Nathaniel Meyersohn, 'Walmart made changes to greeter jobs at stores. Workers with disabilities got squeezed', CNN Business, 1 March 2019, https://edition.cnn.com/2019/02/26/business/walmart-greeters/index.html

99 Dale Hartley, 'The Cobra Effect: No Loophole Goes Unexploited', *Psychology Today*, 14 October 2020, https://www.psychologytoday.com/us/blog/machiavellians-gulling-the-rubes/202010/the-cobra-effect-no-loophole-goes-unexploited#:~:text=The%20Cobra%20Effect%20refers%20to,collect%20rewards%20for%20their%20capture.

100 Sarah Todd, 'The Steve Jobs speech that made Silicon Valley obsessed with pirates', Quartz, 22 October 2019, https://qz.com/1719898/steve-jobs-speech-that-made-silicon-valley-obsessed-with-pirates/

101 Ron Johnson, 'What I Learned Building the Apple Store', *Harvard Business Review*, 21 November 2011, https://hbr.org/2011/11/what-i-learned-building-the-ap

102 Tim Rajarin, 'How Apple's iPhone Changed These 5 Major Industries', *Time*, 26 June 2017, https://time.com/4832599/iphone-anniversary-industry-change/

103 Adam Brandenburger, 'Strategy Needs Creativity', *Harvard Business Review*, March–April 2019, https://hbr.org/2019/03/strategy-needs-creativity

104 Robert Burgelman, Robert Siegel, Henry Lippincott, 'PayPal in 2015: Reshaping the Financial Services Landscape', *Harvard Business Review*, 12 November 2015, https://store.hbr.org/product/paypal-in-2015-reshaping-the-financial-services-landscape/E572

105 Emily Bary, 'PayPal valued at over $300 billion for the first time', Market Watch, 4 February 2021, https://www.marketwatch.com/story/paypal-valued-at-over-300-billion-for-the-first-time-11612463466

106 Sergei Klebnikov, 'Tesla Is Now the World's Most Valuable Car Company with a $208 Billion Valuation', *Forbes*, 1 July 2020, https://www.forbes.com/sites/sergeiklebnikov/2020/07/01/tesla-is-

now-the-worlds-most-valuable-car-company-with-a-valuation-of-208-billion/?sh=16b2784d5334

107 David Dawkins, 'Elon Musk's SpaceX Gets Bullish $100 Billion Valuation from Morgan Stanley, Double What Investors Said It Was Worth in August', *Forbes*, 23 October 2020, https://www.forbes.com/sites/daviddawkins/2020/10/23/elon-musks-spacex-gets-bullish-100-billion-valuation-from-morgan-stanley-double-what-investors-said-it-was-worth-in-august/?sh=44c283fe6e79

108 Matt Plummer, 'A Short Guide to Building Your Team's Critical Thinking Skills', *Harvard Business Review*, 11 October 2019, https://hbr.org/2019/10/a-short-guide-to-building-your-teams-critical-thinking-skills

109 Thomas H. Davenport, 'Robert S. McNamara's Good Brain – And Bad Judgement', *Harvard Business Review*, 7 July 2009, https://hbr.org/2009/07/robert-s-mcnamaras-good-brain

110 Rahul Venkat, 'From Phogat sisters to Sakshi Malik: The rise of India's top women wrestlers', Olympic Channel, 30 August 2020, https://www.olympicchannel.com/en/stories/features/detail/indian-best-women-wrestling-geeta-babita-vinesh-phogat-sakshi-malik/

111 Bill Taylor, 'What Breaking the 4-Minute Mile Taught Us about the Limits of Conventional Thinking', *Harvard Business Review*, 9 March 2018, https://hbr.org/2018/03/what-breaking-the-4-minute-mile-taught-us-about-the-limits-of-conventional-thinking

112 Ibid.
113 Alan Iny and Luc Brabandere, 'Apple's new iPhone 5C and 5S: The Results of Creativity or Innovation', *Harvard Business Review*, 10 September 2013, https://hbr.org/2013/09/apples-new-iphone-5c-and-5s-th
114 Eric S. Hintz, 'The Fosbury Flop – A Game-Changing Technique', Lemelson Centre for the Study of Invention and Innovation, 8 April 2021, https://invention.si.edu/fosbury-flop-game-changing-technique
115 Kendra Cherry, 'What Is Cognitive Bias?', Very Well Mind, 19 July 2020, https://www.verywellmind.com/what-is-a-cognitive-bias-2794963
116 Alicia Nortje, 'Cognitive Biases Defined: 7 Examples and Resources', Positive Psychology.com, 13 November 2020, https://positivepsychology.com/cognitive-biases/
117 Don A. Moore, 'Overconfidence', *Psychology Today*, 22 January 2018, https://www.psychologytoday.com/intl/blog/perfectly-confident/201801/overconfidence
118 *Psychology Today*, https://www.psychologytoday.com/us/basics/dunning-kruger-effect
119 Jack B. Soll, Katherine L. Milkman and John W. Payne, 'Outsmart Your Own Biases', *Harvard Business Review*, May 2015, https://hbr.org/2015/05/outsmart-your-own-biases
120 Edwin Shaw, 'How to Make Friends with Your Reptilian Brain', IAHE.com, 31 January 2017,

https://www.iahe.com/docs/articles/how-to-make-friends-with-your-reptilian-brain.pdf

121 'J.K. Rowling, British Author', Britannica, https://www.britannica.com/biography/J-K-Rowling

122 Tom Popomaronis, 'Billionaire Warren Buffett has a "simple" test for making touch decisions – here's how it works', CNBC Make It, 11 May 2019, https://www.cnbc.com/2019/05/10/billionaire-warren-buffett-use-this-simple-test-when-making-tough-decisions.html

123 Jill Suttie, 'Why Thinking Like a Scientist Is Good for You', *Greater Good Magazine*, accessed on 20 May 2022, https://greatergood.berkeley.edu/article/item/why_thinking_like_a_scientist_is_good_for_you

124 Jessica Stillman, 'This Is the Number 1 Sign of High Intelligence, According to Jeff Bezos', Inc.com, 25 September 2018, https://www.inc.com/jessica-stillman/this-is-number-1-sign-of-high-intelligence-according-to-jeff-bezos.html

125 Julia Galef, 'Why "scout mindset" is crucial to good judgement', TEDx Talks, 5 April 2016, https://www.youtube.com/watch?v=3MYEtQ5Zdn8

126 'You Just Chip Away Everything That Doesn't Look Like David', Quote Investigator, https://quoteinvestigator.com/2014/06/22/chip-away/

127 Ina Fried, 'Microsoft CEO focused on "new demand" caused by coronavirus', Axios, 22 March 2020, https://www.axios.com/microsoft-coronavirus-satya-nadella-938dc807-39f9-4246-94ff-9a103303901a.html

128 Warren Berger, *A More Beautiful Question*, Bloomsbury, 2004.

129 Art Markman, 'How You Define the Problem Determines Whether You Solve It', *Harvard Business Review*, 8 June 2017, https://hbr.org/2017/06/how-you-define-the-problem-determines-whether-you-solve-it?utm_medium=social&utm_campaign=hbr&utm_source=linkedin&tpcc=orgsocial_edit

130 Ibid.

131 Alison Wood Brooks and Leslie K. John, 'The Surprising Power of Questions', *Harvard Business Review*, May–June 2018, https://hbr.org/2018/05/the-surprising-power-of-questions

132 Jeanne Liedtka, 'Why Design Thinking Works?', *Harvard Business Review*, September–October 2018, https://hbr.org/2018/09/why-design-thinking-works

133 Warren Berger, *A More Beautiful Question*.

134 Alan H. Palmer, 'Stop Asking "Why" and Start Asking "How"', *Harvard Business Review*, 18 October 2021, https://hbr.org/2021/10/stop-asking-why-and-start-asking-how?utm_medium=social&utm_campaign=hbr&utm_source=twitter&tpcc=orgsocial_edit

135 Warren Berger, *A More Beautiful Question*.

136 Alison Wood Brooks and Leslie K. John, 'The Surprising Power of Questions', *Harvard Business Review*, May–June 2018, https://hbr.org/2018/05/the-surprising-power-of-questions

137 John Hagel, John Seely Brown, Andrew de Maar and Maggie Wooli, 'Frame a powerful question',

Deloitte Insights, 31 January 2018, https://www2.deloitte.com/us/en/insights/topics/talent/business-performance-improvement/framing-powerful-questions.html

138 'Why do we have to wait for the picture', A More Beautiful Question, accessed on 20 May 2022, https://amorebeautifulquestion.com/why-do-we-have-to-wait-for-the-picture/

139 'Edwin Land's daughter Wanted a Selfie, So He Invented Polaroid', History Daily, 11 February 2019, https://historydaily.org/edwin-lands-daughter-wanted-a-selfie-so-he-invented-polaroid

140 Uber Blog, 'So, what is Uber all about? Fun facts about the Uber story', 16 January 2020, https://www.uber.com/en-PK/blog/facts-about-uber/

141 Thomas F. Rosenbaum, 'How Zoom Supported the New Virtual Society and Then Adapted to the World It Created', Breakthrough, the Caltech Campaign, https://breakthrough.caltech.edu/zoom-eric-yuan/

142 Warren Berger, *A More Beautiful Question*.

143 Nagesh Belludi, 'Looking at Problems from an Outsider's Perspective', Right Attitude, 28 March 2017, https://www.rightattitudes.com/2017/03/28/outsider-perspective/

144 Adam Brandenburger and Barry Nalebuff, 'Inside Intel', *Harvard Business Review*, https://hbr.org/1996/11/inside-intel

145 Ibid.

146 Eric Schmidt, Jonathan Rosenberg and Alan Eagle, *Trillion Dollar Coach: The Leadership Handbook*

of Silicon Valley's Bill Campbell, John Murray, 2020.

147 Catherine Clifford, 'Former Apple CEO John Scully: What I learned from Steve Jobs', CNBC Make It, 29 May 2018, https://www.cnbc.com/2018/05/29/what-ex-apple-pepsi-ceo-john-sculley-learned-from-steve-jobs.html#:~:text=John%20Sculley%20and%20Apple%20co,Jobs%20after%20Thanksgiving%20in%201982.&text=On%20April%2011%2C%201983%2C%20Sculley%20joined%20Apple%20as%20the%20CEO.

148 Gregory Ferenstein, 'Uber CEO Spells Out His Endgame, In 2 Quotes', *Forbes*, 16 September 2015, https://www.forbes.com/sites/gregoryferenstein/2015/09/16/uber-ceo-spells-out-his-endgame-in-2-quotes/#36ddbe177bec

149 Kit Eaton, 'Tim Cook, Apple CEO, Auburn University Commencement Speech 2010', Fast Company, 26 August 2011, https://www.fastcompany.com/1776338/tim-cook-apple-ceo-auburn-university-commencement-speech-2010

150 Jason Fell, 'How Steve Jobs Saved Apple', Entrepreneur, 27 October 2011, https://www.entrepreneur.com/article/220604

151 Thomas Koulopoulos, '5 Unforgettable Leadership Lessons from "Manager of the Century" Jack Welch', Inc.com, https://www.inc.com/thomas-koulopoulos/jack-welch-ceo-general-electric-business-leadership-management-lessons.html

152 Claudio Fernandez-Araoz, 'Jack Welch's Approach to Leadership', *Harvard Business Review*, 3

March 2020, https://hbr.org/2020/03/jack-welchs-approach-to-leadership

153 Greg Bustin, 'The Legacy of Peter Drucker', Executive Leadership Blog, 3 November 2010, https://bustin.com/executive-leadership-blog/legacy-peter-drucker/#:~:text=Drucker%20posed%20two%20questions%20to,going%20to%20do%20about%20it%3F%E2%80%9D

154 Thomas Koulopoulos, '5 Unforgettable Leadership Lessons from "Manager of the Century" Jack Welch', Inc.com, https://www.inc.com/thomas-koulopoulos/jack-welch-ceo-general-electric-business-leadership-management-lessons.html

155 Arun Maira, 'JRD Tata–The Democratic Capitalist', *Hindu Business Line*, 23 May 2020, https://www.thehindubusinessline.com/opinion/jrd-tata-the-democratic-capitalist/article31652225.ece

156 Helen Tupper and Sarah Ellis, 'Make Learning a Part of Your Daily Routine', *Harvard Business Review*, 4 November 2021, https://hbr.org/2021/11/make-learning-a-part-of-your-daily-routine?autocomplete=tru

157 Ibid.

158 Sudipta Sarangi, *The Economics of Small Things*, Penguin Random House India, 2020.

159 Tina Seelig, 'The $5 Challenge', *Psychology Today*, 5 August 2009, https://www.psychologytoday.com/us/blog/creativityrulz/200908/the-5-challenge

160 Ibid.

161 Jennifer Magnolfi, 'Why Apple's New HQ Is Nothing Like the Rest of Silicon Valley', *Harvard*

Business Review, 26 June 2017, https://hbr.org/2017/06/why-apples-new-hq-is-nothing-like-the-rest-of-silicon-valley

162 Lucinda Shen, 'Here Are the Fortune 500's 10 Most Valuable Companies by Lucinda Shen', *Fortune*, 21 May 2018, https://fortune.com/2018/05/21/fortune-500-most-valuable-companies-2018/

163 'Toyota Parts Fuels a Baby Incubator', Toyota Parts Only, 28 November 2018, http://toyotapartsonly.com/toyota-parts-fuel-a-baby-incubator/

164 'The Socrates Questioning Technique', Intel Teach Program, https://www.intel.com/content/dam/www/program/education/us/en/documents/project-design/strategies/dep-question-socratic.pdf

165 ALU Editors, 'Understanding the Socratic Method of Teaching', Abraham Lincoln University, 10 February 2020, https://www.alu.edu/alublog/understanding-the-socratic-method-of-teaching/

166 '6 Top Classic Examples of Lateral Thinking', Magichoth, accessed on 20 May 2022, https://magichoth.com/6-top-classic-examples-of-lateral-thinking/

167 '5 Whys: The Ultimate Root Cause Analysis Tool', Kanbanize, https://kanbanize.com/lean-management/improvement/5-whys-analysis-tool

168 Julia Kirby and Thomas A. Stewart, 'The Institutional Yes', *Harvard Business Review*, October 2007, https://hbr.org/2007/10/the-institutional-yes

169 Thomas Wedell-Wedellsborg, 'Are You Solving the Right Problem?', *Harvard Business Review*,

January–February 2017 issue, https://hbr.org/2017/01/are-you-solving-the-right-problems

170 Ibid.

171 Carmine Gallo, 'Jeff Bezos Requires Amazon's Leaders to Perform This Powerful Ritual Before Launching Anything', Inc.com, 28 June 2019, https://www.inc.com/carmine-gallo/jeff-bezos-requires-amazons-leaders-to-perform-this-powerful-ritual-before-launching-anything.html

172 Dave Bailey, 'Why You Need to Follow the Steve Jobs Method and "Work Backwards"', Inc.com, 13 July 2017, https://www.inc.com/dave-bailey/why-you-need-to-follow-the-steve-jobs-method-and-w.html

173 Marc Emmer, '95 Percent of New Products Fail. Here Are 6 Steps to Make Sure Yours Don't', Inc.com, https://www.inc.com/marc-emmer/95-percent-of-new-products-fail-here-are-6-steps-to-make-sure-yours-dont.html

174 Steve Blank, 'Why the Lean Start-Up Changes Everything', *Harvard Business Review*, May 2013, https://hbr.org/2013/05/why-the-lean-start-up-changes-everything

175 Ibid.

176 Giovanni Gavettti and Jan W. Rivkin, 'How Strategists Really Think: Tapping the Power of Analogy', *Harvard Business Review*, April 2005, https://hbr.org/2005/04/how-strategists-really-think-tapping-the-power-of-analogy

177 'Mental Models, First Principles: The Building Blocks of True Knowledge', FS, accessed on 22 May 2022, https://fs.blog/2018/04/first-principles/
178 'Innomind: The First Principles Method Explained by Elon Musk', YouTube, 4 December 2013, https://www.youtube.com/watch?v=NV3sBlRgzTI
179 Arun Maria, *The Learning Factory: How the Leaders of Tata Became Nation Builders*, Penguin Random House India, 2020.
180 Gary Klein, 'Performing a Project Premortem', *Harvard Business Review*, September 2007, https://hbr.org/2007/09/performing-a-project-premortem
181 'When data gives the wrong solution', Trevor Bragdon, 7 September 2017, https://www.trevorbragdon.com/when-data-gives-the-wrong-solution/
182 'What is Design Thinking?', Ideo, https://www.ideou.com/blogs/inspiration/what-is-design-thinking
183 'Simplify Your Life', PillPack by Amazon Pharmacy, accessed on 20 May 2022, https://www.pillpack.com/how-it-works
184 Charles Conn and Robert Mclean, 'Six problem-solving mindsets for very uncertain times', McKinsey Quarterly, September 2020, https://www.mckinsey.com/business-functions/strategy-and-corporate-finance/our-insights/six-problem-solving-mindsets-for-very-uncertain-times
185 Ibid.
186 Ibid.
187 Ibid.

188 Ibid.
189 Ibid.
190 Ibid.
191 Ibid.
192 John S. Hammond, Ralph L. Keeney and Howard Raiffla, 'The Hidden Traps in Decision Making', *Harvard Business Review*, September–October 1998, https://hbr.org/1998/09/the-hidden-traps-in-decision-making-2
193 Scott Barry Kaufman and Jerome L. Singer, 'The Creativity of Dual Process "System 1" Thinking', *Scientific American*, 17 January 2012, https://blogs.scientificamerican.com/guest-blog/the-creativity-of-dual-process-system-1-thinking/
194 'Understanding The Psychology of Willful Blindness', Joanne Reed, 2 August 2019, https://authorjoannereed.net/understanding-the-psychology-of-willful-blindness/
195 'Why are we satisfied by "good enough"?', Decision Lab, https://thedecisionlab.com/biases/bounded-rationality/
196 Chunka Mui, 'Big Decision? Consider It Both Drunk and Sober', *Forbes*, 22 March 2016, https://www.forbes.com/sites/chunkamui/2016/03/22/wine-and-sleep-make-for-better-decisions/?sh=70ab17e424b1
197 Carol Dweck, 'What Having a "Growth Mindset" Actually Means', *Harvard Business Review*, 13 January 2016, https://hbr.org/2016/01/what-having-a-growth-mindset-actually-means

198 WorkLab, 'Want to Improve Your Performance? Start with Mindset', Microsoft, https://www.microsoft.com/en-us/worklab/athletes-improve-their-mindset

199 John Rampton, 'The 5-Hour Rule Used by Bill Gates, Jack Ma and Elon Musk', *Entrepreneur*, 15 February 2019, https://www.entrepreneur.com/article/317602#:~:text=The%20five%2Dhour%20rule%20was,this%20across%20their%20entire%20career.

200 'Continuous Improvement: How It Works and How to Master It', James Clear, https://jamesclear.com/continuous-improvement

201 Bradley R. Staats, *Never Stop Learning*, Harvard Business Review Press, 2018.

202 Ibid.

203 'The Buffett Formula: Going to Bed Smarter Than When You Woke Up', FS, https://fs.blog/2013/05/the-buffett-formula/

204 'Yellow and Red Cards in Football', Football Stadiums, https://www.football-stadiums.co.uk/articles/yellow-and-red-cards/

205 'The Benefits of Self-Study (And How Your Child Can Use It)', Grade Power, https://gradepowerlearning.com/what-is-self-study/

206 Niraj Chokshi, 'The Trappist monk whose calligraphy inspired Steve Jobs–and influenced Apple's designs', *Washington Post*, 8 March 2016, https://www.washingtonpost.com/news/arts-and-entertainment/wp/2016/03/08/the-trappist-monk-whose-calligraphy-inspired-steve-jobs-and-influenced-apples-designs/

207 '"You've got to find what you love," Jobs says', Stanford News, 14 June 2015, https://news.stanford.edu/2005/06/14/jobs-061505/

208 Ibid.

209 Kai Sato, 'Why the 5 People Around You Are Crucial to Your Success', *Entrepreneur*, 9 May 2014, https://www.entrepreneur.com/article/233444

210 Liz Burton, 'What is Unconscious Bias in Recruitment?', HUB, 18 December 2017, https://www.highspeedtraining.co.uk/hub/types-of-unconscious-bias/

211 Jessica Stillman, 'Humility Is an Undersung Leadership Skill. Adam Grant Says These 2 Interview Questions Screen for It', Inc.com, 13 September 2021, https://www.inc.com/jessica-stillman/adam-grant-leadership-hiring-humility-job-interviews.html

212 Stephen J. Dubner, 'How to Succeed by Being Authentic', Freakonomics, 4 November 2020, https://freakonomics.com/podcast/john-mackey/

213 Paul Arnold, 'Summary of Bounce–The Science of Success by Matthew Syed', Ignition Blog, 2 February 2012, https://slooowdown.wordpress.com/2012/02/05/summary-of-summarised-by-paul-arnold-trainer-facilitator-paul_arnoldme-com/

214 David Perell, 'How to 10 Your Learning Skills', YouTube, 5 November 2021, https://www.youtube.com/watch?v=_DxmiWL5c28

215 Gary Drevitch (reviewer), 'What's the Curse of Knowledge, and How Can You Break It?',

Psychology Today, 28 April 2021, https://www.psychologytoday.com/us/blog/i-hear-you/202104/whats-the-curse-knowledge-and-how-can-you-break-it

216 Bailey Reiners, '12 Unconscious Bias Examples and How to Avoid Them in the Workplace', Builtin, updated 1 September 2020, https://builtin.com/diversity-inclusion/unconscious-bias-examples

217 Peter Bregman, 'If You Want to Get Better at Something, Ask Yourself These Two Questions', *Harvard Business Review*, 8 November 2018, https://hbr.org/2018/11/if-you-want-to-get-better-at-something-ask-yourself-these-two-questions

218 'The Buffett Formula: Going to Bed Smarter Than When You Woke Up', FS, https://fs.blog/2013/05/the-buffett-formula/

219 Robert McKee, Robert McKee Quotes, AZ Quotes, https://www.azquotes.com/author/22237-Robert_McKee

220 Maria Popova, 'Significant Objects: How Stories Confer Value Upon the Vacant', Brain Pickings, https://www.brainpickings.org/2012/08/06/significant-objects-book/

221 James L. McGaugh, 'Making Lasting Memories: Remembering the Significant', PubMed Central, 18 June 2013, https://www.ncbi.nlm.nih.gov/pmc/articles/PMC3690616/#:~:text=The%20adrenal%20stress%20hormones%20epinephrine,mediating%20these%20stress%20hormone%20influences

222 Philip Verghis, 'Direct the Rider, Motivate the Elephant, and Shape the Path', HDI, 29 July 2016, https://www.thinkhdi.com/library/supportworld/2016/direct-the-rider-motivate-the-elephant-shape-the-path.aspx#:~:text=Psychologists%20have%20long%20told%20us,rational%20side%20is%20the%20rider.

223 Harrison Monarth, 'The Irresistible Power of Storytelling as a Strategic Business Tool', *Harvard Business Review*, 11 March 2014, https://hbr.org/2014/03/the-irresistible-power-of-storytelling-as-a-strategic-business-tool

224 Lea Winerman, 'The Mind's Mirror', American Psychological Association, October 2005, https://www.apa.org/monitor/oct05/mirror

225 Patricia Inacio, 'Dopamine Neurons Participate in Forming New Long-term Memories, Study Shows', Parkinson's News Today, 9 May 2018, https://parkinsonsnewstoday.com/2018/05/09/dopamine-neurons-participate-forming-new-memories-study-shows/#:~:text=Nerve%20cells%20that%20produce%20dopamine,are%20considered%20long%2Dterm%20memories.

226 Allison Shapira and David Horsager, 'To Win over an Audience Focus on Building Trust', *Harvard Business Review*, 9 Mach 2022, https://hbr.org/2022/03/to-win-over-an-audience-focus-on-building-trust?utm_campaign=hbr&utm_medium=social&utm_source=facebook&fbclid=IwAR3CleLvLyAMf2wMNk2--Z-5BWmnsYIIarR9k1oaeWC3ZngALlCXpDOlUqI

227 Patricia Inacio, 'Dopamine Neurons Participate in Forming New Long-term Memories, Study Shows', Parkinson's News Today.

228 Michael Brenner, 'How the Significant Objects Social Experiment Proved the Economic Value of Storytelling', *Entrepreneur*, 11 January 2016, https://www.entrepreneur.com/article/253947

229 James L. McGaugh, 'Making Lasting memories: Remembering the significant', PubMed Central, 18 June 2013, https://www.ncbi.nlm.nih.gov/pmc/articles/PMC3690616/#:~:text=The%20adrenal%20stress%20hormones%20epinephrine,mediating%20these%20stress%20hormone%20influences.

230 Kate Harrison, 'A Good Presentation Is about Data and Story', *Forbes*, 20 January 2015, https://www.forbes.com/sites/kateharrison/2015/01/20/a-good-presentation-is-about-data-and-story/?sh=6e19ab30450f

231 Daniel Newman, 'Why Visual Content Will Explode in 2015', *Forbes*, 23 December 2014, https://www.forbes.com/sites/danielnewman/2014/12/23/why-visual-content-will-explode-in-2015/?sh=15e0d2e21cb5

232 Kate Miller-Wilson, 'What Is the Cartier Trinity Ring?' Love to Know, https://engagementrings.lovetoknow.com/cartier-trinity-ring

233 Nestle Cocoa Plan Progress report 2009, https://www.nestlecocoaplan.com/themes/custom/cocoa/dist/assets/nestle-cocoa-plan-annual-report-final.pdf

234 Nestle Cocoa Plan, https://www.nestlecocoaplan.com/page/8

235 Laura Pappalardo, 'The Curious Anecdote on the Nose of Michelangelo's David', It's Tuscany, 7 January 2019, https://www.itstuscany.com/en/the-curious-anecdote-on-the-nose-of-michelangelos-david/

236 NDTV, 'Rishi Kapoor Recounts Memories Working with His Father Raj Kapoor', YouTube, 15 February 2018, https://www.youtube.com/watch?v=WBN9f5U-Z-8

237 'But You Did That in Thirty Seconds. "No, It had taken me Forty Years To DO That"', Quote Investigator, https://quoteinvestigator.com/2018/01/14/time-art/

238 Mayo Oshin, 'Pablo Picasso on the Myth of Overnight Success', Thrive Global, 20 February 2019, https://thriveglobal.com/stories/pablo-picasso-myth-overnight-success/

239 The Startup Show, 'MS Dhoni explains how he stays cool during hard situations', YouTube, 26 June 2021, https://www.youtube.com/watch?v=SojpUrYH61s

240 Sam Grobart, 'How Samsung Became the World's No.1 Smartphone Maker', Bloomberg, 29 March 2013, https://www.bloomberg.com/news/articles/2013-03-28/how-samsung-became-the-worlds-no-dot-1-smartphone-maker

241 Janine Kurnoff and Lee Lazarus, 'The Key to Landing Your Next Job? Storytelling', *Harvard Business Review*, 13 May 2021, https://hbr.

org/2021/05/the-key-to-landing-your-next-job-storytelling?utm_campaign=ascend&utm_source=facebook&utm_medium=social&fbclid=IwAR1SYTe5U0c3BV2jOM6Ucc2ncuQr1cu4GXxAPZHUMHciMRvnp6lYPJ-F-j8

242 Harrison Monarth, 'The Irresistible Power of Storytelling as a Strategic Business Tool', *Harvard Business Review*, 11 March 2014, https://hbr.org/2014/03/the-irresistible-power-of-storytelling-as-a-strategic-business-tool

243 Carmine Gallo, 'How Google's 11-word Pitch Wowed Investors and Changed the World', Inc.com, 29 October 2018, https://www.inc.com/carmine-gallo/how-googles-11-word-pitch-wowed-investors-changed-world.html

244 Ben Laker and Charmi Patel, 'Strengthen Your ability to Influence People', *Harvard Business Review*, 28 August 2020, https://hbr.org/2020/08/strengthen-your-ability-to-influence-people?ab=at_articlepage_recommendedarticles_bottom1x1

245 Ibid.

246 Rebecca Knight, 'How to Increase Your Influence at Work', *Harvard Business Review*, 16 February 2018, https://hbr.org/2018/02/how-to-increase-your-influence-at-work

247 Amy J.C. Cuddy, Matthew Kohut and John Neffinger, 'Connect, Then Lead', *Harvard Business Review*, July–August 2013, https://hbr.org/2013/07/connect-then-lead

248 'Philip Chetwode, 1st Baron Chetwode', Wikipedia, https://en.wikipedia.org/wiki/Philip_Chetwode,_1st_Baron_Chetwode#:~:text=The%20honour%2C%20welfare%20and%20comfort,passing%20out%20from%20the%20Academy.

249 David Gelles, 'The C.E.O. Who Promised There Would Be No Layoff', New York Times, 6 November 2020, https://www.nytimes.com/2020/11/06/business/corner-office-ajay-banga-mastercard.html#:~:text=Who%20Promised%20There%20Would%20Be%20No%20Layoffs,-Credit...&text=When%20the%20pandemic%20hit%2C%20Mastercard's,destruction%20wrought%20by%20the%20virus.

250 Art Markman, 'Influence People by Leveraging the Brain's Laziness', Harvard Business Review, 29 May 2015, https://hbr.org/2015/05/influence-people-by-leveraging-the-brains-laziness

251 Ravi Shastri, The Players in My Life, Harper Collins Publishers, 2021.

252 Paolo Gallo and Vaitka Hlupic, 'Humane leadership must be the Fourth Industrial Revolution's real innovation', World Economic Forum, https://www.weforum.org/agenda/2019/05/humane-leadership-is-the-4irs-big-management-innovation/

253 Klaus Schwab, 'The Fourth Industrial Revolution: What It Means, How to Respond', World Economic Forum, 14 January 2016, https://www.weforum.org/agenda/2016/01/the-fourth-industrial-revolution-what-it-means-and-how-to-respond/

254 Zach Ferres, 'The Human Element: Your Most Important Business Resource', Entrepreneur, 11 May 2015, https://www.entrepreneur.com/article/245848#:~:text=No%20matter%20what%20business%20you,to%20attain%20success%20in%20business.

255 Paolo Gallo and Vaitka Hlupic, 'A Humane Leadership Must Be the Fourth Industrial Revolution's Real Innovation', World Economic Forum, https://www.weforum.org/agenda/2019/05/humane-leadership-is-the-4irs-big-management-innovation/

256 'Leadership Insights – Dr Shashank Shah, Leadership Decisions at the Tata Group', YouTube, 19 April 2020, https://www.youtube.com/watch?v=W54UDhQvxpM

257 Harvey Mackay, 'Harvey Mackey: 4 Stories with Great Management Lessons', *Business Journal*, 23 February 2014, https://www.bizjournals.com/bizjournals/how-to/growth-strategies/2014/02/great-stories-great-management-lessons.html#:~:text=%22Why%2C%20Madam%2C%22%20replied,stories%20that%20teach%20a%20lesson.

258 Ellen Fried, 'An Extraordinary President and His Remarkable Cabinet', National Archives, Spring 2006, https://www.archives.gov/publications/prologue/2006/spring/interview.html

259 Ramchandra Guha, 'Gandhi's last (and greatest) fast', *Hindustan Times*, 8 September 2018, https://www.hindustantimes.com/india-

news/gandhi-s-last-and-greatest-fast/story-wpf0NL3LgsWUegv7uVTopL.html

260 'When MS Dhoni suggested a Rs 10,000 fine, no one ever came late again for team', *India Today*, 15 May 2019, https://www.indiatoday.in/sports/cricket/story/ms-dhoni-indian-cricket-team-captain-fine-rs-10-000-late-comers-1525529-2019-05-15

261 Laura Montini, 'The Positive Power of Your Team's Darkest Days', Inc.com, 14 March 2014, https://www.inc.com/laura-montini/how-you-can-actually-boost-morale-in-your-companys-darkest-days.html

262 Marguerite Ward, 'Why Pepsico CEO Indra Nooyi writes letters to her employees' parents', CNBC Make It, 1 February 2017, https://www.cnbc.com/2017/02/01/why-pepsico-ceo-indra-nooyi-writes-letters-to-her-employees-parents.html

263 Ibid.

264 PTI, 'Indian Premier League 2020—We have not played to our potential this season: MS Dhoni', *The Hindu*, 24 October 2020, https://www.thehindu.com/sport/cricket/we-have-not-played-to-our-potential-this-season-csk-captain-dhoni/article32933794.ece

265 'A story of watermelons', Founding Fuel, https://www.foundingfuel.com/article/wfh-daily-184-a-story-of-watermelons/

266 'Everest 1953, First Footsteps – Sir Edmund Hillary and Tenzing Norgay', *National Geographic*, 4 March 2003, https://www.nationalgeographic.com/adventure/article/sir-edmund-hillary-tenzing-

norgay-1953#:~:text=Sir%20Edmund%20Hillary%20and%20Tenzing%20Norgay%20%2D%201953%20Everest&text=Edmund%20Hillary%20(left)%20and%20Sherpa,atop%20the%20world's%20highest%20mountain.

267 'Chandrayaan-2: What Dr. Abdul Kalam said on failure after ISRO's SLV-3 mission crashed', *Indian Express*, 7 September 2019, https://indianexpress.com/article/india/chandrayaan-2-dr-abdul-kalam-on-failure-after-isro-slv-3-mission-crash-5974097/

268 'How Blowing Up A Factory Changed Jack Welch', Leadership Freak, 13 October 2011, https://leadershipfreak.blog/2011/10/13/how-blowing-up-a-factory-changed-jack-welch/

269 'How Sourav Ganguly convinced Virender Sehwag to open – Delhi batsman shares inspirational story', *Hindustan Times*, 29 October 2019, https://www.hindustantimes.com/cricket/how-sourav-ganguly-convinced-virender-sehwag-to-open-delhi-batsman-shares-inspirational-story/story-Ix6XtWTTai6dbZ6EDz1ohJ.html

270 Jeff Bezos, 'What matters more than your talents', TED Talks, https://www.ted.com/talks/jeff_bezos_what_matters_more_than_your_talents

271 Bill Boulding, 'For Leaders, Decency Is Just as Important as Intelligence', *Harvard Business Review*, 16 July 2019, https://hbr.org/2019/07/for-leaders-decency-is-just-as-important-as-intelligence

272 Ibid.

273 Tiffany Ayuda, 'How the Japanese art of Kintsugi can help you deal with stressful situations', Better

by Today, NBC News, 26 April 2018, https://www.nbcnews.com/better/health/how-japanese-art-technique-kintsugi-can-help-you-be-more-ncna866471

274 Masoom Gupta, 'Entrepreneurs, take heed! Here are Mukesh Ambani's 5 career lessons', *Economic Times*, 27 February 2017, https://economictimes.indiatimes.com/magazines/panache/entrepreneurs-take-heed-here-are-mukesh-ambanis-5-career-lessons/articleshow/57321703.cms

275 Gary Klien, 'Mindsets', Psychology Today, 1 May 2016, https://www.psychologytoday.com/us/blog/seeing-what-others-dont/201605/mindsets#:~:text=A%20mindset%20is%20a%20belief,and%20what%20we%20should%20do.&text=The%20Stanford%20University%20psychologist%20Carol,where%20our%20abilities%20come%20from.

276 Matthew Syed, *Black Box Thinking: Marginal Gains and the Secrets of High Performance*, John Murray, 2016.

277 Thomas H. Lee and Angela L. Duckworth, 'Organizational Grit', *Harvard Business Review*, September–October 2018, https://hbr.org/2018/09/organizational-grit

278 'What Does Immigrant Mentality Mean?', IMMI Group, https://www.immigroup.com/news/what-does-immigrant-mentality-mean

279 Glenn Llopis, 'Adopt an Immigrant Mindset to Advance Your Career', *Harvard Business Review*,

23 August 2012, https://hbr.org/2012/08/adopt-an-immigrant-mindset-to

280 Ibid.

281 'Ricky Ponting', ESPN Cricinfo, https://www.espncricinfo.com/player/ricky-ponting-7133

282 Melody Wilding, 'Do You have a Job, Career or a Calling? The Difference Matters', *Forbes*, 23 April 2018, https://www.forbes.com/sites/melodywilding/2018/04/23/do-you-have-a-job-career-or-calling-the-difference-matters/?sh=426bdb59632a

283 Mike Oppland, '8 Ways To Create Flow According to Mihaly Csikszentmihalyi', PositivePsychology.com, 15 February 2021, https://positivepsychology.com/mihaly-csikszentmihalyi-father-of-flow/

284 Jane Burnett, 'What Steve Jobs learned building fences with his father that changed the course of history', Ladders, 11 May 2018, https://www.theladders.com/career-advice/this-is-what-steve-jobs-learned-building-fences-with-his-dad-that-changed-the-course-of-human-history

285 Subhash Jha, 'I couldn't bear to hear myself: Lata Mangeshkar', Quint, 28 September 2016, https://www.thequint.com/entertainment/lata-mangeshkar-best-and-worst-of-her-glorious-life-exclusive-birthday-interview-kishore-kumar-amitabh-bachchan

286 Max Farx, 'Elon Musk on Critical Thinking', YouTube, 21 August 2016, https://www.youtube.com/watch?v=qd4-GdU490M

287 Tom Popomaronis, 'Warren Buffett really loves this "favorite" riddle from Abraham Lincoln–and it makes perfect sense why', CNBC Make It, 25 February 2019, https://www.cnbc.com/2019/02/25/warren-buffett-loves-this-riddle-from-abraham-lincoln--heres-why.html

288 Astrid Groenewgen, 'Kahneman Fast and Slow Thinking Explained', Behavioural Design, 2022, https://suebehaviouraldesign.com/kahneman-fast-slow-thinking/

289 Prince Peter, 'Dhirubhai Ambani – The Reliance Epic; How one man built India's biggest entrepreneurial empire from scratch', Blazetrue, updated 20 October 2021, http://blazetrue.com/dhirubhai-ambani-reliance

290 Arjun Kharpal, 'Why Eric Schmidt has a 15-year-old door stored in his fancy Google office', CNBC, 16 June 2016, https://www.cnbc.com/2016/06/15/why-eric-schmidt-has-a-15-year-old-door-stored-in-his-fancy-google-office-u200e.html

291 'Entrepreneur Elon Musk: Why It's Important to Pinch Pennies on the Road to Riches', Knowledge at Wharton, 27 May 2009, https://knowledge.wharton.upenn.edu/article/entrepreneur-elon-musk-why-its-important-to-pinch-pennies-on-the-road-to-riches/

292 Rebecca Fannin, 'How I Did It: Jack Ma, Alibaba.com', Inc.com, 1 January 2008, https://www.inc.com/magazine/20080101/how-i-did-it-jack-ma-alibaba.html

293 Tinesh Bhasin, 'Warren Buffett's nuggets of wisdom for investors from his latest letter to shareholders', *Mint*, 1 March 2021, https://www.livemint.com/market/stock-market-news/buffetts-nuggets-of-wisdom-for-investors-from-his-latest-letter-to-shareholders-11614590970189.html

294 'A rare insight into Amazon's experimental culture', Conversion Rate Exerts, https://conversion-rate-experts.com/amazon/

295 Ben Gilbert, 'Amazon's Jeff Bezos highlights the importance of "wandering" and failing in his annual shareholder letter', *Business Insider India*, 11 April 2019, https://www.businessinsider.in/retail/amazons-jeff-bezos-highlights-the-importance-of-wandering-and-failing-big-in-his-annual-shareholder-letter/articleshow/68835600.cms

296 Roshan Thiran, 'Are you relentless in pursuing your dream? Akio Morita's vision enable Sony to soar', My Starjob, 5 October 2013, http://mystarjob.com/articles/story.aspx?file=/2013/10/5/mystarjob_careerguide/13652946&sec=mystarjob_careerguide

297 Rebecca Fannin, 'How I Did It: Jack Ma, Alibaba.com', Inc.com, 1 January 2008, https://www.inc.com/magazine/20080101/how-i-did-it-jack-ma-alibaba.html

298 Alex Knapp, 'Reusable Rockets Could Open Up Space to Everyone', *Forbes*, 29 February 2016, https://www.forbes.com/sites/

alexknapp/2016/02/10/reusable-rockets-could-open-up-space-to-everyone/?sh=1917168c64ff

299 Adi Ignatius, 'Above All, Acknowledge the Pain', *Harvard Business Review*, May-June 2017, https://hbr.org/2017/05/above-all-acknowledge-the-pain

300 Tal Ben-Shahar, *The Pursuit of Perfect: How to Stop Chasing Perfection and Start Living a Richer, Happier Life*, McGraw Hill Education, 2009.

301 Anubhav Jain, 'Rahul Dravid's life-changing advice to Sourav Ganguly', Sportskeeda, 22 December 2019, https://www.sportskeeda.com/cricket/rahul-dravid-life-changing-advice-to-sourav-ganguly

302 Erica R. Hendry, '7 Epic Fails Brought to You By the Genius Mind of Thomas Edison', Smithsonian, 20 November 2013, https://www.smithsonianmag.com/innovation/7-epic-fails-brought-to-you-by-the-genius-mind-of-thomas-edison-180947786/

303 Fred Lambert, 'Elon Musk says he will perform same tasks as Tesla workers getting injured in the factory', Electrck, 2 June 2017, https://electrek.co/2017/06/02/elon-musk-tesla-injury-factory/

304 Justin M. Berg, Jane E. Dutton, Amy Wrzeniewski, 'What is Job Crafting and Why Does It Matter', Michigan Ross School, For the Center for Positive Organizational Scholarship, 9 September 2007, https://positiveorgs.bus.umich.edu/wp-content/uploads/What-is-Job-Crafting-and-Why-Does-it-Matter1.pdf

305 Ruth Umoh, 'Saying "no", being spontaneous and other lessons learned from a $650000 lunch with Warren Buffet', CNBC Make It, 31 August 2018,

https://www.cnbc.com/2018/08/31/3-things-two-men-learned-from-their-650000-lunch-with-warren-buffett.html

306 APA Dictionary of Psychology, American Psychological Association, 2022, https://dictionary.apa.org/grit

307 'Building your resilience', American Psychology Association, 1 February 2020, https://www.apa.org/topics/resilience

308 Rebecca Sprague, 'Legends, Trailblazers Inspire NASA's Future', NASA, Education at Kennedy, 8 April 2010, https://www.nasa.gov/offices/education/centers/kennedy/home/msef.html

309 Nicola Davis, 'Why Roman concrete still stands strong while modern versions decay', *Guardian*, 4 July 2017, https://www.theguardian.com/science/2017/jul/04/why-roman-concrete-still-stands-strong-while-modern-version-decays

310 'Return on Luck', Jim Collins, https://wHowww.jimcollins.com/concepts/return-on-luck.html

311 TED, 'How women in rural India turned courage into capital – Chetna Gala Sinha', YouTube, 10 September 2018, https://www.youtube.com/watch?v=v5c3FE_qRnI&t=39s

312 Mann Deshi Bank, https://manndeshibank.com/about/our-story/

313 Morten T. Hansen, 'You Can Manage Luck. Here's How', *Harvard Business Review*, 4 November 2011, https://hbr.org/2011/11/three-ways-to-manage-good-or-b

314 Pooja Dhingra, 'Why Entrepreneurship Is So Hard', *Harvard Business Review*, 29 October 2020, https://hbr.org/2020/10/why-entrepreneurship-is-so-hard?utm_medium=social&utm_source=facebook&utm_campaign=ascend&fbclid=IwAR24kBLWOFIP_-t41RBHzqeVPLpy-jdQfnU9GcXPhyXF1EYG0Yo0FRJc4W4

315 George and Alexandra, 'The Mountain Isn't Going Anywhere', Edmund Hillary.com, https://www.edmundhillary.com/blogs/news/the-mountain-isnt-going-anywhere